Chicken Soup for the Soul.

Thanks Mom

Is Presented To:

_____

_____

_____

Date:

_____

Chicken Soup for the Soul

Thanks Mom

Chicken Soup for the Soul: Thanks Mom;
101 Stories of Gratitude, Love, and Good Times
by Jack Canfield, Mark Victor Hansen, Wendy Walker. Foreword by Joan Lunden.

Published by Chicken Soup for the Soul Publishing, LLC www.chickensoup.com

The publisher gratefully acknowledges the many publishers and individuals who
granted Chicken Soup for the Soul permission to reprint the cited material.

We thank 1-800-FLOWERS (1800flowers.com) for the photo on the front cover of
one of their beautiful arrangements, Elegant Wishes.

Cover photo courtesy of iStockPhoto.com/© Nancy Louie (nano).
Back cover photo courtesy of Annie Watson Photography, Greenwich, CT
Photo in foreword courtesy of Tom Eccerle.

Cover and Interior Design & Layout by Pneuma Books, LLC
For more info on Pneuma Books, visit www.pneumabooks.com

Distributed to the booktrade by Simon & Schuster. SAN: 200-2442

Publisher's Cataloging-in-Publication Data
(Prepared by The Donohue Group)

Chicken soup for the soul : thanks mom : 101 stories of gratitude, love, and
  good times / [compiled by] Jack Canfield, Mark Victor Hansen [and] Wendy
  Walker ; foreword by Joan Lunden.

    p. ; cm.

  ISBN: 978-1-935096-45-0

1. Mothers--Literary collections. 2. Mothers--Conduct of life--Literary collections.
3. Mother and child--Literary collections. 4. Mothers--Anecdotes. 5. Mothers--
Conduct of life--Anecdotes. 6. Mother and child--Anecdotes. I. Canfield, Jack,
1944- II. Hansen, Mark Victor. III. Walker, Wendy, 1967- IV. Lunden, Joan. V.
Title: Thanks mom

PN6071.M7 C45 2009
810.8/092052   2009943349

PRINTED IN THE UNITED STATES OF AMERICA
on acid∞free paper
17 16 15 14 13 12 11 10   02 03 04 05 06 07 08

Chicken Soup for the Soul®

Thanks Mom

101 Stories of Gratitude, Love, and Good Times

Jack Canfield
Mark Victor Hansen
Wendy Walker
Foreword by Joan Lunden

Chicken Soup for the Soul Publishing, LLC
Cos Cob, CT

Chicken Soup *for the* Soul

www.chickensoup.com

Contents

Foreword, *Joan Lunden* xiii

❶

~Following in Her Footsteps~

1. What My Mother Gave Me Before She Died,
   Brad Meltzer 1
2. Struggles Are Relative, *Desiree Diana Amadeo* 5
3. A Lasting Lesson, *Jim Dow* 8
4. My Inspiration, *Michelle Anglin* 12
5. Adolescent Awakening, *Tasha Mitchell* 16
6. Doing the Right Thing, *Steve Chapman* 18
7. A Letter to My Mother, *Gary B. Luerding* 20
8. The Simple Life, *Julie Bradford Brand* 23
9. My Mother, The Patriot, *Terrilynne Walker* 26
10. A Son's Admiration, *Aaron Felder* 28
11. Someone Who Cares, *Janelle In't Veldt* 31
12. Discount Shopping, *Keith Smith* 34

❷

~Mom Knows Best~

13. Little Trouper, *Penny Orloff* 41
14. Lip Drama, *Emily Osburne* 45
15. My Mother, My Teacher, *Jessica Gauthier* 49
16. The Pantsuit, *Harriet Cooper* 51

17. Thank You for Not Pushing, *Christy Barge* 54
18. The Chest, *Judy M. Miller*..56
19. Just in Case, *Ann O'Farrell* 58
20. You'll Always Be "Mom", *Rebecca Hill*................................60
21. Our Mother, *Sandra R. Bishop* 62
22. I've Got the Power, *Aditi Ashok* 65
23. Blooms of Wisdom, *Kathy Harris*..67
24. Is Anybody Dead?, *Corrina Lawson* 69

❸
~Making Sacrifices~

25. Seven Sticks, *Sandy M. Smith* 75
26. Believing in the Writer in Me, *John P. Buentello* 78
27. A Mother at Last, *Joyce A. Anthony* 81
28. My Mother, My Friend, *Elizabeth M. Hunt*............................83
29. First Anniversaries, *Kate E. Meadows*..................................86
30. Role Model, *Kiashaye Leonard* 89
31. Bright Lights, Big City, *Tom LaPointe* 91
32. A New Mom in Town, *Al Serradell*.......................................94
33. My Supermom, *Mary Laufer*...97
34. My Mom, My Hero, *Brandy Widner*....................................101
35. Surprise!, *Carolyn Mott Ford*..104
36. The Old Green Coat, *Kathy Smith Solarino* 106

❹
~Favorite Moments~

37. Cape Towns, *Saralee Perel*...111
38. Taking Time, *Teresa Hoy* 115
39. The Birthday, *Wayne Summers*..118
40. Our Evenings with Alex Trebek, *Maryanne Curran* 122
41. Dark Winter, *Lucas Youmans* 125
42. The Gift in the Plain Brown Wrapper, *Jennie Ivey*..............127
43. A Different Kind of Experience, *Christina Flaaen*................130

44. Duck and Cover, *Gemma Halliday* 132
45. Secret Stash, *Joanne Faries* 135
46. Walking with Mom, *Dallas Woodburn* 138

❺

~Mom to the Rescue~

47. Driving Me Home, *Wendy Walker* 145
48. Pretty Baby, *Diane Gardner* 149
49. Loving Hands, *Jennifer Quasha* 151
50. A Mother Takes On Big Tony, *Michael Jordan Segal* 154
51. From Mama to Mom, *Jane Dunn Wiatrek* 158
52. Fear, *Stephen D. Rogers* 161
53. To Keep Me from the Rain, *Joyce Stark* 163
54. With Ears Wide Open, *Carol Chiodo Fleischman* 165
55. The Day My Mother Took On the Principal,
    Barbara Mayer 168
56. Lifeline, *Kiran Kaur* 172
57. A Quest for Answers, *Stephanie Haefner* 175
58. Carrying Me Forward, *Aviva Drescher* 178

❻

~What Goes Around~

59. Chicken Soup from the Heart, *Annmarie B. Tait* 185
60. Mom's Jewel, *Ferida Wolff* 189
61. Just Like Mom, *Shannon Scott* 192
62. Finding Joy in a Time of Loss, *Megan Dupree* 194
63. Turning Into My Mother, *Karen Kullgren* 197
64. Tunnel Vision, *Norma Favor* 200
65. The Magic of the Mess, *Ronda Armstrong* 202
66. Dusting Off Memories, *Jenny R. George* 205
67. The Letter, *Kathy Marotta* 208
68. Lasting Impressions, *Janine Pickett* 210
69. Happy to Be You, *Saralee Perel* 212

❼
~One of a Kind~

70. How to Be Special, *Jeannie Mai* 217
71. My Blessing, *Linda Burks Lohman* 220
72. My Mother's Legacy, *H.M. Gruendler-Schierloh* 223
73. Mom's Many Hats, *Gail Wilkinson* 227
74. Fish Lips, *Terri L. Lacher* 229
75. Making Her Own Way, *Kara Townsend* 232
76. Beauty Never Fades, *Betsy S. Franz* 234
77. Mom's Heart, *Rachel Furey* 236
78. Somebody to Turn the Rope, *Elizabeth Atwater* 238
79. Spilt Milk, *Rebecca Lasley Thomas* 241

❽
~Gifts of the Heart~

80. Because You Were There, *Stephen Rusiniak* 247
81. The Quilt, *Hope Justice* 250
82. A Mother's Faith, *Mimi Greenwood Knight* 253
83. Nobody's Child But Mom's, *Ellen Fink* 256
84. The Blue Dress, *Jennifer Gilkison* 260
85. The Best Coloring Book Ever, *Rebecca Olker* 264
86. Fan Appreciation, *Doug Hirschhorn* 267
87. Silent Reassurance, *Kym Gordon Moore* 271
88. New Dresses, *Stacia Marie Erckenbrack* 274
89. A Ride Down Memory Lane, *Christopher Hartman* 276
90. The World's Best Care Packages, *Mark Damon Puckett* 280

❾
~My Mother's Legacy~

91. A Thousand and One Stories, A Million and One Words,
    Jacquelyn Mitchard 287

92. Hand-Me-Downs, *Shawnelle Eliasen* 291
93. A Poem in Her Pocket, *Michelle Dette Gannon* 294
94. Ode to Old Yeller, *Theresa Sanders* 296
95. But Wait, There's More, *Sheila Curran* 300
96. A Simple, Lasting Legacy, *Pamela Underhill Altendorf* 304
97. Retaining Memories, *Robert S. Nussbaum* 306
98. China, *Ray M. Wong* 309
99. Things My Mother Taught Me, *Kris Hale* 313
100. The Note, *Tom Phillips* 317
101. Why I Play, *Samuel Torres* 319

Meet Our Contributors 325
Meet Our Authors 343
About Joan Lunden 345
Thank You! 347
About Chicken Soup for the Soul 348

Bonus Story: How I Became an Author in the
Back of My Minivan, *Wendy Walker* 354

Foreword

You can be anything you want to be:
the word "impossible" isn't in our dictionary.
~Gladyce Blunden (Joan's mother)

For the first thirteen years of my life I lived an idyllic childhood in a small suburban community in Northern California. My mother was a stay-at-home mom to my brother and me, and my father was a prominent physician in the community. My parents had struggled to have children, and they finally adopted my brother Jeff as a newborn baby. They brought my brother home when he was just three days old. Mom's friends came to give her a shower; however she was in the bathroom sick to her stomach. Little did she know, she was pregnant with me! As soon as she stopped trying to have a baby, she must have become less stressed, and she got pregnant and carried me to term with no difficulties. So I was born less than eight months after my brother Jeff, and we were raised, essentially, as twins.

My dad was an avid private pilot, and we travelled a lot as a family in our plane. When I was thirteen years old, my father needed to fly to Southern California on a short business trip to speak at a medical convention. He had asked my mom, my brother and me to accompany him since it was a brand new plane. Mom said no, thinking we shouldn't miss school. She later changed her mind, picked us up and drove to the airfield (no cell phones in those days to call and say we were on our way). As fate would have it, just as we pulled up to the runway, my father's plane was lifting off the ground. We missed him by a moment. I stood and waved goodbye, totally unaware that this was the last time I would ever see my father. His plane crashed during a bad storm, in Malibu Canyon returning home.

I'll never forget the knock at the door in the middle of the night when the police officer came to tell us that my father's plane was missing and they feared the worst. My mom had been up all night waiting, worrying and was now weeping uncontrollably. Life can change in an instant, and that night would change our family forever. My mother became a widow at age forty, with two young teenagers. She had been active in the community but she was not a career woman; she had devoted herself to raising us. However now she had to take the lead in our family and had to support us as well. So while dealing with her grief, she also went back to school, got her license to sell residential real estate and joined the forces of working moms.

We were typical teenagers; we just wanted life to be the same. I was also a stridently independent young woman and challenged my mom every step of the way. When I grew up and became a working mom, and later a single working mom, I often thought of how I had challenged her and how tough I was on her. So this is not only a "Thanks Mom" but also a "Sorry Mom!"

Mom had always been ferociously protective of us; our home was surrounded by a big wall, perhaps modeled after homes in Mexico, where my parents often vacationed. My brother joked that we weren't allowed outside the big wall. But my mom actually worked very hard to make sure that we *were* exposed to a lot—museums, ballet, theater, circus, trips, and foreign countries. She wanted us to see the world, to "broaden our horizons"—those were her words.

My mom also made sure that she always talked about my dad, and how he had saved so many lives and taken care of so many families, so that my brother and I didn't lose his influence on what we should do with our lives.

My dad had been born in Australia, raised in China before coming to America where he became an oncologist, and spoke several languages. He was a world traveler, yet I think it was *my mom* who really made me the adventurer that I am. She would often tell me to "Hitch my wagon to a star." She wanted me to know no boundaries and to always reach for the stars. Mom constantly told me that I would do great things with my life. Those were positive affirmations that had a long-term effect. An important ingredient for success is self-confidence, and I got a huge dose from my mom every day.

While a parent might naturally want to keep children near and protect them, it's important to let children go and expose them to new things. When I was graduating from high school I had applied to several colleges. However my mom had other plans for me. Unbeknownst to me, Mom actually took my college essay and filled out an application for me to attend World Campus Afloat, a university aboard a ship that travelled around the world. She told me about her clever deed when I was accepted. That three-month experience changed me and my expectations of life dramatically. It was actually a very selfless act for a widowed mom. I had skipped grades in school so I was only sixteen when I set off for that college adventure round the world and she could have tried to keep me closer to home, but instead she made sure that I had an amazing growth experience.

My mom's influence on my brother and me was enormous. She always wanted us to have a positive attitude, to always try to do the best we could. My mom's friends had always called her Hap, which was short for Happy. And no wonder—she always saw the glass as half full, and taught me to approach each day with a smile. Mom tried to teach us to be fair, to care, to have integrity and to think big.

Perhaps the quality that I am most grateful to her for instilling in me is never holding a grudge. It's such a waste of precious time, a drain of energy, and frankly it solves nothing. My mom believed in kissing and making up, forgiving and forgetting. If we had a disagreement, Mom insisted that we talk about it, get it out, and then let it go, and it was never long before she would reappear with a smile on her face, as if it had never happened. I loved that. I consider that one of the greatest attributes I got from my mom.

When we see our mom exhibit strength, it makes us strong. When we see our mom "let things roll off her back" it teaches us patience and compassion. When we see our mom challenge herself and dare to try new things, it teaches us that we too can expect greater things of ourselves. Motherhood is one of the most important and challenging jobs in the world! The rewards are rich, but the demands can be overwhelming. Every day we do our best to take care of our home and our family and help make them happy, healthy and successful. It's been said many times that "kids don't come with instruction books." Most of us feel so unprepared when we become parents. However we all have actually spent many years preparing under the tutelage of our moms; we have learned by example and know much more than we think we do.

When I was little, my mom picked me up from school every day and took me to my dance lessons and piano lessons and singing lessons. When I look back on it, she truly was a taxi service. On weekends I had parades, shows and recitals. She was my stylist and my assistant. Yet when we would get home, it always smelled so good in the house. When I asked Mom how she did that, with all the running around she did for us, she said, "As soon as we'd get home I would run right in to the kitchen and put some onions into a pan with some butter and start cooking them, and that would make the whole house smell good." Those are the little things we remember.

I think being a mom used to be much easier in general, for it was more defined and the responsibilities and roles were not questioned. Today we don't know if we are supposed to stay at home and take care of kids, or hold down a job and help support the family, or both. And if we do both, how do we do that, and do both jobs well? Can we be as good as our mothers, who devoted themselves only to taking care of us? Today's mothers juggle many balls, struggle with overwhelming schedules so that their children can play every possible sport and take every special class, and yet always feel like we are not spending enough time... with our kids, on our jobs or volunteer activities, with our mates, supporting older parents, or maintaining our homes.

Now that we have it all, how do we do it all? I remember my early days on television, before working mothers were as common, when I brought my babies to work while I was breastfeeding. In those days I'd start *Good Morning America* as Joan Lunden and end the show as Dolly Parton! One particular morning I was interviewing a U.S. Senator about then President Ronald Reagan's "trickle down" economics. You may remember that economic theory, but what I remember about that interview is that all of a sudden I was experiencing inflation and "trickle down" firsthand. It was time for my baby Jamie to feed and my boobs knew it. I'll never forget frantically blow-drying my very wet silk blouse during commercial break.

Embarking on motherhood is the ultimate "on the job training," learning by trial and error, and that of course creates stress and frustration. The pressure is really on mothers to make it all work—the house, the meals, the kids. And for many women, they must do that in addition to holding down a job outside the home. That has left many women worn out, stressed out and unhappy. We all know that when Mom is happy, everyone else is happy. Studies now show us that happy moms mean happy kids. So it's important for moms to recognize how much they bring to the table, having learned from their own moms. It's important for moms to have support and help from their partners. It's important for moms to find ways to get breaks, and to ask for help. If we never talk to our husbands when we are overwhelmed, and we never ask for some equal distribution of duties in the household, then we will remain resentful and tired, and our families will just think we are crabby. It's important for moms to know that their children and husbands are grateful!

That is one of the reasons I am so excited about this terrific Chicken Soup for the Soul book for moms of all ages. I've always loved the Chicken Soup for the Soul series, and this book speaks to me in particular, as I am passionate about this subject—moms need to know they are appreciated, that they do make a difference, that their children really are listening and learning important life skills and attitudes from them. When you read these 101 stories, you will share in the personal stories from all types of children of all ages, expressing their love and admiration for their mothers. These children recognize how hard their mothers work and they value their mothers as role models, as leaders, and as the primary influences on their lives. And most importantly... these children, whether sixteen or sixty, love and respect their moms despite the fact that some of them can't clean, some of them can't cook, some of them weren't always there... yes, these moms are not "perfect," but they are perfect for *their* children!

It's OK to not be everything and be everywhere; you don't need to be "the perfect mom." If you can't be in the car pool line because you are at work, don't worry. My daughters may not remember seeing me every day in the car pool line, but they do remember me at every horse show, every recital, every teacher conference, everything that was important. And if you're the stay-at-home mom who rolls up her sleeves, while your daughter's friend has that "cool" mom who does something, anything, that you *don't* do, don't worry about that either. Your daughter really prefers you.

I think we all question whether we are good moms. Whether you are a stay-at-home mom or have a job outside the home, you always question if you've spent enough "quality time" with your children, read to them enough or taught them the right life lessons. No matter how organized you are, there are those days when you feel like you can't possibly cook another dinner or wash enough clothes for everyone to have a matching outfit. Motherhood is hard. I know at my house, with two sets of twins, it is loud, messy, and crazy hectic. Kim and Jack are five, and Max and Kate are six. And I still spend a lot of time and mental energy on my three grown daughters, Jamie, Lindsay, and Sarah, who are all in their twenties. After all these years and seven kids, every day I wonder if I'm doing it right.

Just remember, despite all the juggling, the tricky balancing act, and the just plain hard work, I decided to have a second round of children. In looking for a new mate I made sure I found a man who loved children and wanted a family. My husband Jeff is ten years younger than me and we have our four young children, so I am back at school sitting at little tables making gingerbread houses, I am buying and sorting clothes every six months for growing bodies, I am wiping noses and tears, and I am reading silly stories. I love the sound of little feet running down the hall in the morning, coming in to snuggle with Mommy and Daddy. I can't think of anything more fascinating than watching little children grow and learn and become people.

I'm often asked if it isn't exhausting "at my age." I remember having a party when the second set of twins was born. My type-A girlfriends, most of whom had high-powered jobs, walked in and said "Oh my gosh, I'm tired just looking at them all." But the French caterers who had come in earlier looked at the same scene and said, "Oh my, you will never grow old." Two sets of eyes looking at the same thing—the first set saw it as exhilarating, and the second set saw it as exhausting. My mom taught me to look at life with the first set of eyes, to *choose* to approach every situation with a smile and a positive attitude. She taught me to never set limits for myself and that nothing is impossible. I love every moment of my life as a mother of seven, a wife, a daughter, and a working woman, and I thank my mom every day for that positive attitude.

~Joan Lunden

Chapter 1

Thanks Mom

Following in Her Footsteps

What My Mother Gave Me Before She Died

God could not be everywhere, so he created mothers.
~Jewish Proverb

She's the kind of woman who would say, "Ucch, what a depressing funeral." And so the obvious thing to say is that I want to celebrate my mom. But what I really want to do is share my mom. Not the person who was here the past few months, but the woman who was here the past sixty-three years.

My mother fought to have me. She tried for three years to get pregnant. And I think that struggle always left her feeling thankful for what she had. It is, to this moment, the only rational way to explain the never-ending love she gave to me.

As I entered grade school, my father, who breathes baseball, signed me up for Little League. I lasted one year. But it wasn't until a few months ago that I finally found out just who saved me from year two. *Stewie, don't make him play if he doesn't want to play.* Even back then, she knew me. And for all of childhood, she nurtured me, growing my little artsy side and always making sure that I could find my own adventure. And she fed it with one of the greatest seeds of imagination: Television.

This will sound silly and trite, but in my mother's honor, I'm not apologizing for it. One of my clearest memories of childhood is sitting at the side of my mom's bed—the side that faced the TV—and watching show after show with her. To be clear, TV wasn't something that watched me—she didn't put it on just so she could go do something else. My mother watched with me. Or rather, I watched with her. Old movies like *Auntie Mame*, and modern classics like *Taxi*, *Soap*, *MASH* and, of course, our favorite for every Wednesday night, *Dynasty*. (Please, what else are you gonna do with a son who doesn't play baseball?) Some mothers and sons never find anything they can truly share. But my mom always treated me like an adult, always let me stay up late to watch the good stuff, and in those moments, she did one of the best things any parent can do: She shared what she loved with me.

When I was thirteen, my mom faced the worst tragedy of her life—the death of her father. My Poppy. Poppy would do anything for my mother, and when he died, I remember being at his funeral. My mom was screaming and yelling wildly because the funeral home had neglected to shave him and she wanted him to look just right. It was a ferocity she saved for people messing with her family—something I had never seen before and would never see again. And I know she put that one in me, too.

When I think of my mom—more than anything else—I think of the pure, immeasurable, almost crazy love she had for me. I remember the first time I gave her *The Tenth Justice*. It was my first published novel, my first time ever putting real work out for anyone to see. I was terrified when she said she'd finished it. And then she looked right at me and said, "Bradley, I know I'm your mother, but I have to be honest with you. This book... *is the greatest book of all time!*"

When someone was recounting the story to me a few days ago, he called my mother the queen of hyperbole. But as I think about it, he had it wrong. Hyperbole is a deliberate exaggeration. My mother never used hyperbole. My mother actually *believed* it. In her eyes, I really did write the greatest book of all time.

A few years ago, I went to the headquarters of Borders Books up in Ann Arbor. And when I was there the main buyer for Borders said to me, "Guess where your books sell more than anywhere else? Straight sales, not even per capita." So of course I said, "New York." That's eight million New Yorkers in one city.

"No."

"Washington, DC? I write about DC."

"No."

"Chicago, the flagship superstore?"

"No."

The number one place my books sell was the Boca Raton Borders, two miles from the furniture store where my mother worked. That means my mother *single-handedly* beat eight million New Yorkers. Messing with the power of a Jewish mother is one thing, but never ever mess with the power that was Teri Meltzer.

Of course, what made my mom *my mom* was the fact that that love—that love that burned in her brighter than fifty suns—was there even when times were bad. When *The First Counsel* was published, *USA Today* gave me a ruthless review. It was the kind of review that just felt like a public humiliation. The headline was: "Make First Your Last." But when my mother saw it, she said to me, "Don't worry. No one reads that paper anyway." It's the number one paper in the entire country!

And when the second novel had bombed and I was wracked with fear, I'll never forget my mom on the phone—she said to me, "I'd love you if you were a garbage man." And to this day, EVERY day that I sit down to write these books, I say those words to myself—"I'd love you if you were a garbage man." I don't care where she is—my mother is *always* there for me.

Let me be clear: All our strength, confidence, any success my sister and I have been blessed enough to receive, those were all watered and nurtured by the strength of the love that my mother showered on us. When I found out the last book had hit the top spot on the bestseller list, the first person I called was my mother. And of course my mom started crying hysterically. She was so proud. And when I heard her crying, I of course started crying. And in the midst of this tear-fest, I said to her, "Where are you now?" And through her sobs, she said to me, "I'm at Marshall's."

Of course she's at Marshall's, still trying to buy irregular socks for two dollars. It was my mother's greatest lesson: Never, ever, ever, ever change for anyone. And her second greatest lesson: That Marshall's just may be the greatest store on Earth.

In the end, my mother died the same way she lived. She laughed and smiled and enjoyed everything she could get from life, most of all, her grandchildren. They were the second great love of her life. When each of my children was born, my mother said to me, "Now you'll understand how I love you."

She was right. And it was the first time I got to see life through my mom's eyes.

I don't miss particular moments with my mother. I can always remember those moments. What I miss is my mother, and her reactions, and how she never hesitated to tell you whom she hated or what she thought, and most of all, how she loved me and my family with more love than one person should be able to muster.

She once said to me, "I'd saw off my own arm for you." Again, not an exaggeration. Just Teri Meltzer being Teri Meltzer.

That love my mom gave me is my strength. It never. Ever. Wavered. It's like the hum of an airplane engine—it's there and it never lets up and it never stops—and you get so used to it, it just becomes part of the ride. But you'd know the second it was gone. My mother's love for us never stopped.

It was a constant.

A foundation.

A law.

It is the pillar that has carried me everywhere and holds me up right now. Her love is a gift that she gave me. And it is the part of her that I hope I carry with me every time my child or grandchild shows me a picture they colored, every time I say thank you to the valet who parks my car, and damn well every time I drive past Marshall's.

I miss you, Mom. And I thank you. I thank you for teaching me how a parent is supposed to love their child. And I hope you know that, in that and so much else, you live on forever.

~Brad Meltzer

Struggles Are Relative

And mothers are their daughters' role model, their biological and emotional
road map, the arbiter of all their relationships.
~Victoria Secunda

t seems strange to think of Mom right now as I struggle up this hill near the end of a race. I mentally relive being six years old and sobbing in my big sister's arms, as Mom was loaded into an ambulance. The doctors had thought she had grown progressively weak due to the flu. But tests revealed an exacerbation of multiple sclerosis. Mom's vision, hearing and ambulation were gone that day and would be gone for months. That night changed my life forever.

My legs grow weary at this point in the race. But the thought of my mother's delight at every opportunity to walk supports me. My arms pump hard in efforts to propel my fatigued body forward. Mentally, I see her struggle just making it from one room to another. There is a curve in the next pass so I inhale deeply, ready to face the next obstacle that lies ahead. She faces obstacles with every breath she takes.

My breath becomes shallow, my calves tighten. She talks about "charley horses" and leg spasms from disuse. I gasp with air hunger. Mom often takes a startled breath when her blood oxygen level is low. I close my eyes, frantically trying to search the depths of my body for that last ounce of energy. She would find the energy. Somehow, somewhere, she would find the energy.

A quick glance at the top of the hill revives my hope. The finish line is so close. Another shallow breath comes. She would do this if she could. Then I hear her, somewhere in the distance. She's always there for me, no matter how she feels. Knowing that the next relay runner needs to run her portion of the 5K, I charge past the finish line. Mom is calling my name. Race completed, I turn about to cheer on the rest of the first heat as they conquer that same hill. Then I look about. At first she can only be heard, but suddenly I see her. There she is, as always, in her chair, cheering me on.

I am struck by the parallels between this race and the obstacles of life. Some obstacles are more difficult than others, but courage helps you face problems head on. Perseverance gets you through to the finish line. Mom taught me that, just by living. For a dozen years she has been living with multiple sclerosis. Our home is a gathering place of wheelchairs, electric scooters, Lofstrand crutches and colorful canes. For years, she lived exclusively from the wheelchair, being carted around by her three children and loving husband. As a registered nurse, she made good judgment calls on medications, physical therapy and procuring a meticulous medical staff. There is no cure for MS but many treatments. Through research, experience and faith, she does whatever she is capable of to keep her body healthy. Whereas twelve years ago she had periods of blindness, paralysis and hearing loss, today my mother can walk unaided for up to a half hour at a time.

Through MRIs she has discovered that although MS lesions are still present on her brain and spinal cord, their "signal" is less intense. A balance of mind, body and spirit seems to have "turned off" the erratic firings in her brain. She is enjoying her life and reminding me to enjoy mine, too. During middle and high school's typical teenage angst, I used my mother's example to approach life one day at a time and to maintain focus on what was important.

My mother taught me the joy of completing a task, no matter how trivial it may seem. She showed me that large goals are often achieved by many small tasks and a mighty grateful heart. Mom showed me individual success is great and the thrill of accomplishment in working for others is terrific. Teamwork means so much more when there is the pride of helping one another. My mom has shown me that so much more is learned by trial and error, little failures and mundane tasks than immediate, easy successes.

As a cross-country runner, I imagine my mother beside me at every race, struggling with every step, fatigued and weakened but never giving up. Together, we recognize the best way to conquer the challenge; we run it at full force and give it everything we have. The task may be difficult, but the success at the end makes the whole journey worthwhile. Together we are victors, not victims.

~Desiree Diana Amadeo

A Lasting Lesson

As long as the world shall last there will be wrongs, and if no man objected
and no man rebelled, those wrongs would last forever.
~Clarence Darrow

I t was vacation time—two years before lung cancer would take Dad and twelve years before Mom would succumb to a different form of the same disease. But that was all yet to be. For now, we were all together—and all excited.

Mom, Dad, my two sisters and I were going on a trip. Vacations were rare in our family. We had love, caring, togetherness, and all the other intangibles that make a family name worth bearing. What we didn't have was money. We didn't have a car; meals in restaurants were an extremely rare treat. But at the age of six, I spent little time pondering such matters. My sisters, aged nine and eleven at the time, and I had food, good clothes to wear, and a safe and comfortable place to live. We also had the very best of parents.

It was a time of happy anticipation. My mother's parents had moved down to Florida and we were invited to visit. And while I was most excited about the train ride, I would leave that trip having learned a profound lesson from my mother that would stay with me forever.

It often took years before we grasped the meaning of Mom's lessons. Many times we didn't realize that a lesson had been taught—not until we experienced more of life, not until we had our own families, our own crises, our own sorrows. The irony of this whole manner of teaching and learning is that I don't think she ever realized what valuable training she was passing on to us.

She taught mostly by example, by living her life in a way that was unwavering in its commitment to the values she held to be true and important. We learned about honesty, respect for others, the importance of education; we learned how to face disaster with resolve and hope, when to be afraid, and when to be fearless. All this we learned by watching this simple, yet special, woman live her life.

The trip down to Florida was just as exciting as any six-year-old could hope for — gleaming railway cars, cities, farms, and open fields flashing past the window; sleeping in plush, reclining seats, our heads resting on fluffy, oversized pillows; listening to the sound of the conductor bellowing out the names of the various stops. These are all wonderful remembrances, but it was one incident that will always stand out. This "incident" is not something that made headlines, or caused any uproar of any kind. Indeed, it is unlikely that anyone beside my sisters and I recall what transpired. It is, however, something that eventually shaped many of my opinions regarding bias, hate, foolishness — and Mom.

It was a hot day in Florida, and we were reluctantly off on some mission with Mom. I don't remember where it was that we were going, but I do remember Dad had cleverly managed to avoid being dragged along. Not having a car, we headed for the nearest bus stop and waited for our ride to appear. When the bus pulled up, the driver yanked on a lever and the doors fluttered open. We pushed ahead of Mom, jumped up the couple of steps that led to where the driver sat, and immediately checked to see if our favorite seats were free. They were. While our mother dropped coins in the fare box, we made a dash for the back of the bus.

We reached the rear seat, which in those days was a bench-like design that spanned the width of the bus. This perch was desirable for two reasons: the rear window and the bounce. By facing backward and kneeling on the seat you could make faces at the people in the cars that followed. The bounce was the result of the primitive shock absorber system in use at the time. If the bus hit a good size bump in the road or a big enough pothole, the resulting jolt would cause the whole bus to bounce. This sensation was felt most strongly in the back. A really good hit could launch you a few inches above the seat, sometimes as much as a foot on those rare occasions when a poorly maintained bus met a sizeable imperfection in the road.

The back seat was empty that day and we ran to stake out our spots. Mom took a seat in the row in front of us. The driver pulled the door closed, but instead of speeding away from the stop, he got up and made his way down the aisle, much to the annoyance of my sisters and myself; we were anxious for the fun to begin. He stopped in front of our little group and, incredibly, informed us that we would have to move to the front of the bus. My mother responded that we would sit wherever her children wanted to sit; we were perfectly fine where we were, and not about to move.

Judging from Mom's northern accent, the driver apparently deduced that we were "foreigners." He explained that the back of the bus was where "colored folks" sat. White people sat in the front. My mother refused to move. The driver said he wouldn't move the bus until she did. She still refused. It wasn't until the driver threatened to bring in the police that she finally gave in.

To this day, I am convinced that if not for the presence of her children on that bus, she would have held her ground. Indeed, several years later, I would see her stand up to some New York City cops she felt were acting improperly, refusing to back down even after they threatened to arrest her.

Certainly, at the age of six, I had absolutely no idea of the roots of the coming civil rights struggles that would begin to right so many wrongs. For my part, I was just angry at these people in Florida who had somehow managed to usurp the best seats on the bus for their own use.

My reaction may seem ironic now, but it contains within it a very valuable lesson. I learned that by limiting the rights and freedoms of others, we are all impacted. Although such segregation can no longer be legislated, we still suffer the effects of the mindset that created it. Thanks, Mom, for this gift of understanding.

~Jim Dow

My Inspiration

When it is dark enough, you can see the stars.
~Ralph Waldo Emerson

When I wake up at seven, I head downstairs to find my mom sitting in her usual spot on the couch with the television tuned to the same station it has been every other morning for as long as I can remember—QVC. My mom, usually enthralled in some new outfit from Sport Savvy or an exquisite piece of Diamonique jewelry, listens intently to the detailed descriptions of the item being displayed, determining whether or not she should make yet another purchase.

"Is that something I would wear?" she asks me.

"I don't know... I guess," I say, with a disgusted tone in my voice.

"Michelle, don't get annoyed with me."

"I know. I'm sorry."

I sometimes forget that my mom cannot see. My mom is legally blind, and has been for my entire life. She was born with a disorder called retinitis pigmentosa, a disorder that has impaired her vision since the day she was born. Often forgetting that she lacks sight, I become easily frustrated when she asks me simple questions. It isn't until the hateful words come spilling out of my mouth that I realize what I've just said, wishing I could take it back.

I know the lack of understanding I so often display is a result of the deep resentment I carry within. Not resentment toward my mom, but resentment toward God. I resent him for depriving my mom of her sight. However, this tragedy has only made my mother stronger than any woman I know, and her strength is one of the many reasons I love her and admire her so dearly.

I tease my mom all the time about her "QVC addiction." Every day (literally) a new package arrives at our doorstep, unmistakable with its bright yellow and red QVC wrapping; the UPS man must know the route to our house by heart. My mom will be wearing a new ensemble or using a fancy gadget in the kitchen, and before she tells me where she bought it, I just say, "Let me guess, QVC?" Still, I have realized that QVC is my mom's way of "going shopping." Where she has to depend on others to take her to a mall, QVC brings the mall to her.

My dad, my sister and I do as much for my mom as we can, when we can. However, her constant dependency on the three of us can be challenging. I have always served as my mother's eyes, doing for her what she could not do for herself. When I was younger, I would assist her with the small things, such as sorting laundry or reading recipes when she cooked. As I grew older, the tasks grew larger. Life became easier for my mom when I turned sixteen and could drive. I happily offered to do the grocery shopping and any other errands my mom could never do when my dad was at work.

I would be lying if I said having a blind mother didn't make my life somewhat different from my friends. I didn't have a mom who could take me to the mall, or a mom who let me play hooky from school one day just so she could take me to lunch. I don't think about it often, but at times I do realize that my mom has never actually seen me. When shopping for prom dresses in high school, I often had to hide the tears forming in my eyes as I looked around the dress boutique and saw other high school girls with their moms. "You look gorgeous!" and "Oh, how stunning!" I would hear throughout the shop. I wished I could hear those words from my mom. She would always feel the dresses I tried on, running her hands over the intricate patterns of gems and sequins. "I wish I could see how pretty you look right now," she would say. I think about my wedding day and how my mother will not see me walking down the aisle in a gorgeous white dress, or how she will never see her grandchildren.

But growing up, she attended every soccer game, cheering me on from the sidelines. She sat contentedly through every dance recital, taking pride that I, her daughter, was up on that stage, even though she couldn't see me. My mom has always been my biggest fan, and still supports me in all of my endeavors, having faith that I can pursue all of my dreams.

My mother's life, with this physical challenge, has been anything but negative. She may be physically different from most people around her, but what really makes her different is her refusal to dwell on her blindness with regret. Instead, she sees her disability as a challenge given to her by God, one that compels her to live a normal, productive life. In my twenty-two years, she has never allowed her setbacks to bring her spirits down. My mom values what she does have in her life, rather than the one thing she is lacking—her vision.

My mom is my heroine, and although this is rather clichéd, she is the wind beneath my wings. She had bestowed a great deal of knowledge upon me over the years, but one piece of wisdom I carry with me to this day is her belief in the value of life. I remember coming home after an extensive day of hard work when I was in high school. In distress, I cried out, "Why are things always so stressful and complicated? I hate my life!" Overhearing my rage, my mother firmly replied, "Michelle, I choose to look more closely at what I am satisfied with in my life, rather than at the things I'm unhappy with."

Whenever I face a difficult obstacle in life, I think of my mother's wise words.

August Wilson once said:

Confront the dark parts of yourself, and work to banish them with illumination and forgiveness. Your willingness to wrestle with your demons will cause your angels to sing. Use the pain as fuel, as a reminder of your strength.

My mother's fuel is blindness. It has empowered her to become the woman she is today.

~Michelle Anglin

Adolescent Awakening

We often take for granted the very things that most deserve our gratitude.
~Cynthia Ozick

Growing up, I wanted to be just like my mom. She was kind and compassionate. People always seemed to feel comfortable in her presence. For years, she was a volunteer in our community. I loved going to the local nursing home with her to help while she taught the residents a ceramic class. Their eyes lit up when Mama walked through the door. The ladies, their lips stained crimson, would gossip and snicker as they painted their pottery. I looked forward to those days. Until I hit my pre-teen years. Suddenly, I was too caught up in my adolescent world to worry about helping others. On one particular summer day, when I was twelve, Mama came into my room and told me to get up, get dressed and meet her at the car.

I had planned to spend the day at the lake with friends. Why did she have to ruin everything? Eventually, I made my way outside. The sun was stifling. I imagined the cool, crisp lake water relieving my sweltering skin. Irritated, I climbed into the car and slammed the door shut. We sat in silence. I was too upset to make conversation.

"Tasha, would you like to know where we are going?" Mama asked calmly.

"I guess," I muttered under my breath.

"Sweetheart, we are going to volunteer at a children's shelter today. I have been there before and I think it would benefit you to visit," she explained.

I felt a knot slowly form in my stomach. How was I supposed to help there?

When we reached the shelter, I was rather surprised. It was a spacious white Victorian home. As we approached the large front porch, I noticed a porch swing and several rocking chairs. Wind chimes played a soothing tune while hanging ferns welcomed us. Maybe this wasn't going to be so bad.

Mama rang the doorbell. As we stood waiting, my hands began to sweat. I wasn't sure if it was the summer heat or the anticipation of what I was about to encounter. Moments later, the heavy oak door flew open and we were greeted by a plump woman with fiery red hair and sapphire eyes. She led us to the front room where all of the children were playing. Toys were spread out across the floor. I noticed a baby whose body was scarred with iron marks. I was told it was because she wouldn't stop crying. I cringed at the thought. The majority of the children had noticeable physical scars such as dark bruises, deep scratches and blistering burns. Others hid their emotional wounds.

As I took in my surroundings, I felt a gentle tug on my shirt. I looked down to see a little girl with brown eyes looking up at me.

"Hi. I'm Ashley. You wanna play dolls with me?" she asked, her cherub face beaming.

I looked over at Mama for reinforcement. She smiled and nodded.

I turned back toward the young girl and whispered, "Sure. I would love to play dolls."

Her tiny hand reached up and grabbed mine, as if to comfort me. And we walked toward the dollhouse.

My mom taught me a valuable lesson that summer. I returned to the shelter with her several times. During those visits, some of the children shared their troubled pasts with me in great detail and I learned to be grateful for all that I had. Today, as I strive to instill values and morals in my own child, I reflect back to that experience. It was a profound time in my young life that I will never forget.

~Tasha Mitchell

Doing the Right Thing

You don't raise heroes, you raise sons. And if you treat them like sons, they'll
turn out to be heroes, even if it's just in your own eyes.
~Walter M. Schirra, Sr.

I have come to realize that while we are growing up, some of the lessons we need to learn the most are often the ones that we don't appreciate until later in life. Let me share with you one such lesson that I learned.

When I was seventeen, I found a watch while walking down the hallway of my high school. The watch was expensive looking, set with gold and pearls. As I picked it up, greed suddenly came over me, and instead of taking the watch and turning it into the office like I should have, I decided to keep it.

When I got home from school, I found my mother cooking dinner in the kitchen. Thinking that she would be impressed, I proudly held out my prize for her to see. Mom, however, was far from impressed. Instead, she was angry that I had kept the watch instead of turning it in. Mom then ordered me to drive straight back to the school and take the watch to someone at the office. I started to argue, but after taking a good look at the expression on Mom's face, I realized that would get me nowhere. There was nothing left for me to do but obey.

I have to admit, I was rather angry with Mom for making me give up the watch. I felt that it was justly mine since I was the one who had found it. Yes, I knew she was right, but greed had compelled me to keep the watch, and now pride wouldn't allow me to admit that I had done something wrong. But time passed, and I forgot all about the watch until four years later.

While I was attending college, I had managed to get a job at a Walmart pushing carts off the parking lot. One morning, I found a checkbook that had been left in a shopping cart. Immediately, I took it to the customer service desk and gave it to the employee there so that the customer who had lost it could pick it up.

Later, as I was outside pushing carts, a man came up to me and told me that his wife had left their checkbook in a shopping cart the night before; he wanted to know if it had been found. When he told me his name, I realized that he was the owner of the checkbook I had found. I explained to him that I'd found his checkbook that morning, and that he could go inside and claim it at the service desk.

The look on the man's face was a combination of gratitude and relief. He pulled out his wallet and offered me some cash, but I refused. I was proud of myself, prouder than I had been in a long time, and I wasn't about to let something like money spoil that.

As I watched the man go to pick up his checkbook, my thoughts went back to the day when Mom had made me return the watch. Suddenly, the lesson she'd taught me that day came into focus.

Mom wasn't trying to be mean when she made me give back the watch. She wanted to make sure that her son would always be honest, and never take what didn't belong to him. Because of her, I did the right thing when I found that checkbook. Because of her, I had been rewarded with a feeling of self-worth that no amount of money could buy.

Thanks, Mom, for teaching me to do the right thing.

~Steve Chapman

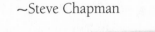

A Letter to My Mother

Perseverance is the hard work you do after you get tired of doing the hard work you already did.
~Newt Gingrich

Dear Mom,

How does a son say thank you when his mother has been gone well over twenty years? I wonder, now that I'm in the twilight of my life, if you ever knew how much I appreciated all that you gave me even though many times I simply said, "Thanks Mom." Those words sound so trite and shallow given the circumstances.

Growing up I thought nothing of the fact that you had only one arm and one leg, for you made everything look so easy. Missing those limbs seemed normal to me. As a small boy, I thought it was no big deal when you tied my shoes. I didn't have an inkling of what it must have taken for you to learn that skill.

Nor did I give much thought to you as a little girl of three, being swept under a trolley car, those steel wheels severing your left leg. Or the horrible moment when the motorman panicked and put the car in reverse, backing over your left arm and taking it off below the elbow. I couldn't comprehend the agony your mom and dad must have felt seeing you lying torn and broken in your hospital bed.

Later on, of course, I did appreciate all that you'd gone through. I cried when my grandmother told me the story of your uncle taking you swimming a year after your accident. You couldn't wait to get to the public pool, but your enthusiasm was dashed when many of the adult bathers stared and the children pointed at you. And you were mortified when your uncle picked you up in his arms and said to the onlookers, "Have a good look!" You were too young to realize that he was trying to protect you, yet for a long time, you were so embarrassed that you wouldn't go anywhere, not even answer the doorbell, without first strapping on your prosthetic arm.

Neither could I appreciate the joy they must have felt one visiting day as they approached the amputee ward and heard your voice singing loudly, "When It's Apple Blossom Time in Normandy." Right then they must have known you were a fighter, that your sunny disposition would infuse your entire life and shine on those fortunate enough to know you.

Of course, being just a kid, I didn't relate to the little girl who danced professionally with her sisters on the stage of the Curran Theater. I didn't see you as the accomplished musician who, at the age of sixteen, became a member of the San Francisco all girl symphony orchestra. Nor did I see the teenager who learned to drive a stick shift on the hilly streets of San Francisco.

Thank you for teaching me how to live life by your example. You taught me that nothing is impossible if you want it badly enough and go after it hard enough. I'm reading your sentiments now as I look at the article and photo in the *San Francisco Examiner*. It quotes a sixteen-year-old girl holding her trumpet in her right hand while smiling at the camera and speaking those words. Words I've remembered and put to use as I've gone through life. Words I've tried to instill in my own children.

As a child, I had a rebellious nature. You may not know it, but Grandma always said I took after you in that respect. She told me when you were a little girl you'd come in with blood dried stiff on your pants from falling down as you tried to roller skate wearing your artificial leg. But you never cried for fear those skates would be taken away. Instead you gritted your teeth as she bathed the abrasions on your knees. Then you'd go right back out, put those skates on, and try again. Nothing was going to stop you!

On your twelfth birthday, when Grandpa gave you your first trumpet, you had no way of knowing that you would instill in your son an intense love of music and of the piano. You always told me that if only the motorman hadn't put that streetcar in reverse, you would have been a pianist. But you didn't tell me until I was in my teens and had been taking lessons for four years. I guess you didn't want to influence me in any way. But once I decided I wanted to learn to play, you wouldn't let me quit when I got discouraged. Instead, you sat on a chair next to me correcting my mistakes in rhythm and phrasing and, most times, making it seem fun. But quitting wasn't an option. You never quit anything in your life and weren't about to allow your son to do so. You told me that being able to play piano would always be something I'd be able to fall back on when times were tough. I relied on that talent many times in my life in those early years when money was tight. The piano even played a part in courting my wife. For that, Mom, I thank you once again.

You might not have realized it, but when things I tried to accomplish seemed very difficult, I always thought of the myriad hardships you turned into triumphs. The times when I complained of those difficulties, I felt foolish.

When I joined the Army Special Forces, the training was rigorous and exhausting and many times I was tempted to quit. But then I'd recall the photo of that sixteen-year-old girl holding her trumpet and remember what you told that reporter so many years ago. "Nothing is impossible if you want it bad enough and go after it hard enough."

Mom, I fervently hope, for the time God granted us together, you realized how much you meant to me, how grateful I am for your guidance, and how much I love you for being my mother.

Thank you from the bottom of my heart.

Your son.

~Gary B. Luerding

The Simple Life

Children need love, especially when they do not deserve it.
~Harold Hulbert

My mother has always lived by a few simple rules: Go to church every Sunday, help people in need, don't worry about things you can't change, and bake an apple pie whenever you need to feel better. These simple rules have allowed her to live a very simple and contented life, and in doing so, she set an example for her children to follow.

Of course, I had broken all of these rules by the time I set off for college.

It was September, and I should have been ecstatic as I stood on my college campus saying goodbye to my parents. The other kids in my class were smiling and waving their parents off so they could embark on their new independent lives. I, on the other hand, was quietly crying, holding on for dear life, petrified of the approaching moment when my parents would get into their car and leave. I had never been away from home without family. I was one of five children, and although I wanted to escape from our small and crowded house, I never wanted to be far away from my mom. So I stood there frozen, not ready. I felt like an idiot, but that did not make the tears stop falling. My mom tried to reassure me to no avail. "We'll come back to get you next weekend and you can come home for a visit!"

I held on to that promise like a lifeline.

My homesickness made my freshman year in college difficult,

and I comforted myself by plunging into my academics. I spent all of my time studying, including weekends when everyone else attended parties and made new friends. I had always been a good student, in fact a perfectionist when it came to my grades. I would not settle for anything but an A, and when I got a 4.0 my first semester, a friend said to me, "That's great, but you can only go down from there!" Suddenly, I was more driven than ever.

My mom was worried about my social life. She was happy that I got good grades but had always told me there was more to life. What about faith? What about helping others? What about all the worry? She encouraged me to go to church. She believed that weekly attendance was the answer to my pathetic social situation. If I could meet even a couple of nice Lutherans, everything would be better.

During Easter break, I decided to stay on campus to work on a term paper and some other projects that would put me ahead when classes started up again. This seemed like a good idea at the time, and besides, it would save my mom the incredibly long drive. She kept asking me if I was sure I would be okay, alone on a holiday when most everyone would be gone. I assured her I would be fine and keep very busy with my schoolwork. And I was fine—until everyone actually left and the campus was quiet and deserted. Then the holiday came. I could not believe I was alone.

I can still picture this vividly in my mind. I was on the phone with my mom, crying because I could not hold it together for one more minute. The weekend was almost over, so it was too late to make a different decision. I was feeling sorry for myself, and counting the hours until friends arrived back on campus. The dining service was closed, so I had to eat packaged food that I bought at the mini-mart, the only place that was walking distance from campus. I was literally stuck there because I did not have a car. My mom didn't hesitate on the other end of the phone. She emphatically said, "Make a dinner reservation at the nicest restaurant in town. I am driving up to take you out to dinner!" That was absolutely crazy, but exactly what she did. Three hours later, we enjoyed a delicious holiday meal together. Then she got back in her car and drove home.

I have never forgotten that amazing act of love and selflessness. She would have been perfectly justified to use this as a lesson. Next time I would surely make a better decision. But my mom could not bear to see me suffer. There would be time for lessons later.

Sometimes, I find myself being critical of my mother's simple ways. It is difficult with three kids and a busy schedule to go to church every Sunday. And while I admire my mom's ability to help anyone in need, I complain that I do not have as much time as I wish to follow her example. I worry about everything else (some things never change), though I wish I did not. I sense my mom questioning my priorities and my faith—in God and myself—though she never judges me. She remains centered. She sees things with clarity. She has strength of purpose. She is the same woman who drove all the way to get to me on that April night so many years ago. Her simple rules have served her well, and though I don't follow them as much as I should, they are there like a beacon, calling for me to follow. And someday, I just might.

For now, I think I am going to bake an apple pie.

~Julie Bradford Brand

My Mother, The Patriot

He loves his country best who strives to make it best.
~Robert G. Ingersoll

Rain, wind, cold sleet on my face... I will never forget standing there, chilled to the bone in my slicker and boots, handing out fliers to weary voters entering the red school doors that I passed through on a daily basis. Today these doors represented change and American principles.

Next to me, also being beaten by the weather, was my mother. Looking up at her, I saw her friendly smile as she was meeting, greeting and conversing with our neighbors and residents of the local community. As the rain ran down her face, dripping from her eyelashes, she never stopped working, promoting and talking political issues that her favored candidates represented. I didn't understand any of the conversations; I just knew they were important, and that the whole process was patriotic.

Surrounding us were the local politicians extending handshakes to the hopeful people who wanted better for the community. Among them stood the principal of my school, who was running for an office of some distinction to improve educational policies. I also saw the neighborhood attorney, the local storeowner, the insurance man who visited our house to sell his policies to my dad; even our local doctor was there. There were also friends of my father, husbands of my mother's friends, men with hopes to better their lives, and the rest of us living in a neighborhood that was falling apart and facing ruin from economic changes. I was young, the only child there, but I loved being part of making change and doing something that would make a difference.

Now an adult, as I handed out fliers this past presidential election, I reflected on why I was standing in the rain in my slicker and boots once again. The image of my mother—a daughter of immigrants, a child abandoned by her mother and later orphaned by her father, a victim of the depression, a mother so loyal to America that she made her children stand and salute when the President addressed the nation on TV, and a citizen who totally appreciated living in America—came to mind. The image of my mother, a stay-at-home mom trying to keep America strong in the only way she knew how, trying to protect her children, her home, and her community, flashed by. Why, I was just like her! She instilled patriotism in me at a young age, by setting an example, by showing love for her country and by working for what she thought was right.

Thank you, Mom, for giving me this passion, this drive, this enthusiasm, this willingness to do whatever I can to maintain the values that my country represents. Thank you for passing on to me the appreciation of being born in America, and the determination to do whatever I can to help preserve freedom for my children and my grandchildren. Thank you for making me a patriot, too.

~Terrilynne Walker

10

A Son's Admiration

There are two lasting bequests we can give our children. One is roots.
The other is wings.
~Hodding Carter, Jr.

I admire my mother for committing herself to a career as a nurse and, subsequently, a nurse practitioner. It is the perfect expression of her caring nature and her passion for service and healing. Through her work, she set an extraordinary example for her three children.

On a more practical level, I am grateful for the convenience that her career choice provided for my brother and me as we figuratively and literally stumbled through our childhoods. More often than not, my mother happened to be employed by the hospital where my brother or I were deposited when we required medical attention for something stupid/brave/athletic that one or both of us had done. Our sister has always approached life with a certain dignity and reserve that was absent from her brothers. She herself is a distinguished healthcare professional due, in large part, to my mother's influence, and she never made use of the one-stop-shopping ER visits afforded so frequently to my brother and me.

My brother (fearless athlete until college) and I (aspiring concert pianist until college) calculated that we accumulated 105 stitches, six broken bones, four pairs of crutches, and innumerable sprains and strains as minors. This was spread across at least fifteen visits to the emergency room. Of course, most of those visits happened when both my mother and father were at work. My mother needed only to walk calmly to the emergency room to meet her ailing son — convenient for the whole family.

Though my brother can boast five sets of stitches in his face alone, I hold the record in that department. When I was ten years old, I fell through a rusted iron grate and was badly cut. I was taken to the hospital where my mother was working at the time. I was really frightened. It was a nasty, gory cut requiring fifty-seven stitches to close.

Through it all, my mother maintained her calm, nurturing way, reassuring me through a long day of needles and stitches that I would be fine, that she loved me. I still have an impressive train-track of a scar, and memories of that day that are oddly positive. It is not just the rosy glow of youth that colors those memories; it is a clear picture of my mother holding my hand and making me feel better.

A decade or so later, when my mother was working as a homecare hospice nurse, we were invited to Christmas Eve dinner at the home of one of my mother's patients. He had been living with multiple myeloma for a long time, and my mother gave him chemotherapy treatments at his home. By virtue of being my mother's son, I was welcomed as family into the home of a man living with a terminal illness on Christmas Eve. That alone would have been extraordinary, but what really stands out in my memory is the joy that permeated the entire evening, and the way that our host family seemed to love and be loved by my mother. At that moment, her quiet strength seemed boundless.

I have always struggled with understanding how my mother does the work she does, especially when we were growing up. She and my father managed to coordinate their demanding careers, the education and activities of their children, and my mother's own education as a nurse. It is not that her work doesn't affect her; it certainly does. I remember her coming home tired, angry, sad, energized, happy — sometimes all at once. Now she works as a nurse practitioner in palliative care, focusing on pain and symptom management, often treating people at the end of their lives.

My mother's mantra is "hope." She has studied it, written about it, and she lives it. She sees the pain in her patients' eyes, but she also sees the potential for healing (whether physical, spiritual, or both), and the extraordinary and unique value of the journey of each human being she encounters. My mother allows herself to be touched by each life that she, in turn, touches. She draws her quiet strength and resolve from that process. That is how she is able to approach her work, and her entire life, with what seems to be limitless compassion, boundless hope.

My sister, brother and I all followed in my mother's footsteps and chose careers in healthcare. My sister is an advance practice nurse, and my brother is an administrator in community health, as was I for close to ten years. Two years ago, at the age of thirty-two, I returned to music, my first love, and am now the Executive Director of a community music school in Brooklyn, New York. I love my job. It is the source of incredible joy in my life, and, I hope, in the lives of the thousands of students that the school reaches.

Still, there are times when I face a task (or a multitude of tasks) and I think, "I have no idea how I am going to approach this." I never doubt, however, that I will figure it out, whatever "it" might happen to be. At the end of the day, I might go home tired, angry, sad, energized, happy—sometimes all at once, like my mother, but also like my mother (in fact thanks to my mother), I draw my own quiet strength from my work and from those around me.

I thank my mother for instilling in me so much hope, so much quiet strength, and so much love.

~Aaron Felder

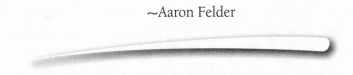

11

Someone Who Cares

Unselfish and noble actions are the most radiant pages in the
biography of souls.
~David Thomas

t was somewhere between spring and summer; just enough sunshine to be warm, but not so much that it was blistering hot.

My mom and I drove through the countryside—windows open, long hair whipping around in the breeze.

We were a long way from home, but it didn't matter. It was nice to just enjoy each other's company on the long drive. I was only eight or nine at the time, but this journey from Grandma's house by the lake back to our own house in the suburban city wasn't foreign to me.

A pot of flowers sat in the back seat, long ago forgotten by me, even though their heavenly scent filled the car as best as it could amidst the air blowing in through the windows. They didn't matter to me—they were just something someone had given to my mom.

Suddenly, in the middle of nowhere, my mom pulled over.

"What are you doing?" I asked, fearing that the car had broken down and we'd be stuck there, so far from home.

But that wasn't the case.

My mom hopped out of the car, grabbing the flowers from the back seat.

"I'll just be a minute," she called back through the open windows.

As she walked away, I noticed the humble little building hidden by a hedge just beyond the ditch. My eyes quickly scanned the edge of the road before settling on a little sign, proclaiming that it was a nursing home.

I looked back to the building, utterly confused, as my mom reappeared—empty-handed. She climbed back into the car and we drove away, without a word.

After a mile or two, I spoke.

"Do you know someone there, Mom?"

She absentmindedly shook her head no, checking her rearview mirrors.

"Then what'd you do with the flowers?"

She smiled slightly. "I gave them to the receptionist."

"Oh," I thought for a moment. "You gave the receptionist flowers?"

She laughed at my confusion. "No, I gave them to the receptionist to give to someone she thought really needed them, who hasn't gotten any in a while."

I sat in silence for a moment, thinking about this, before I spoke again.

"Did you leave your name?"

She answered instantly, "No. The receptionist asked, but I just told her 'someone who cares.'"

This time, I spoke quickly. "But why?" It had never occurred to me that people could purposefully give gifts without putting their name on them. "How will they thank you?"

My mother smiled again, speaking as though it was the most obvious answer in the world. "Because leaving flowers there for someone who will appreciate them more than we will makes me feel good. Knowing that those flowers will make someone smile is enough of a thank you for me."

My mom was oblivious to my amazement, as I stared at her in awe for quite a while longer.

For her, it was a simple act that she had done without even thinking.

But for me, it was a memory and lesson that would last for the rest of my life; the greatest gifts not only come from the heart, but are given without any expectations.

~Janelle In't Veldt

Discount Shopping

An ounce of mother is worth a pound of clergy.
~Spanish Proverb

The Belfast, Maine of my youth was not the coastal tourist village that it is today. At the time, Belfast was still a blue-collar town where Maplewood and Penobscot Poultry (a chicken processing company) and the shoe factory were the big-time employers. McDonald's had yet to move into town.

Before the supermarket existed, there was Cottle's, an independently-owned food market where my dad worked. And Cottle's is where my mother would do her once-a-week shopping. Because we lived a few miles inland from Belfast, we'd usually combine the grocery trip with a visit to see my grandmother. Of course, Grammie Stairs ALWAYS had cookies ready for the grandkids.

On one particular shopping day at Cottle's, I stood behind my mother as she was unloading the grocery cart and checking her items out at the register. The candy displays on either side of me were full of Life Savers, peanut butter cups, Clark Bars, Tootsie Rolls, Sugar Babies—you name it!

"Can I get some candy?" I asked.

My mother rarely veered from her list so I wasn't surprised with her response. "No."

This much I knew for certain. "No" always meant "No." There was no sense in me asking a second time. But I really, really wanted that candy!

I reached for a Sugar Baby package. My mother didn't notice. So I figured she probably wouldn't notice if I ever so coyly stuffed them into my pocket. We continued checking out and walked with the bag boy to the car where he loaded the bags into the car's trunk. No one detected my action—not my mother, not the cashier, not the bag boy—no one! I did it! Wow! My very first shoplifting experience! A five-finger discount! How exciting! How easy! How rewarding! Got my candy and didn't need one penny to get it!

I sat in the back seat as my mother drove across the bridge to where my grandmother lived. Slowly, so as not to make any unnecessary crinkling noise, I opened my prize and carefully slipped a Sugar Baby in my mouth. No one piece of candy ever tasted so good! She might have said, "No," but I'd said, "Yes," and look who'd won!

When we pulled into my grandmother's driveway, I knew I was in the clear. Miles and minutes separated me from Cottle's. As I prepared to open my car door, I confidently slipped a few more Sugar Babies into my mouth. They would tide me over until I got to Grammie Stairs' cookie jar inside.

Big mistake. "Keith, what have you got in your mouth?" I looked up at the rearview mirror and could see the reflection of my mother's eyes staring intently back at me. "I asked you a question! What have you got in your mouth?"

Though I'd recently become skilled in the art of shoplifting, I hadn't quite mastered the art of giving false testimony. "Uhhh... just some Sugar Babies."

"Sugar Babies? Where did you get the money to buy them?" Why was she asking such a foolish question? She knew I hadn't purchased them. It was no big deal. Nobody even saw me take them. It was one little package of Sugar Babies. Let's just go into Grammie's! "I... uh... didn't really buy them."

"That's what I thought!" And then, rather than just going into Grammie's house and giving me a good scolding, she began backing out of my grandmother's driveway. Evidently, the same God who spoke the Ten Commandments to Moses and the Israelites at the base of Mount Sinai (number eight being "Thou Shalt Not Steal"), inspired my mother that day with, "Thou Shalt Not Raise a Thieving Son." And it was obvious from her lowered eyebrows, clenched teeth, and pursed lips that Commandment number five ranked high in her book, too: "Honor... your mother, so that your days may be long in the land...."

As she drove away from my grandmother's house and then back across the bridge, I knew exactly where we were headed. To Cottle's! This was so stupid! We're talking twenty-five cents here! A return trip all the way back there was a ridiculous waste of gas and time, if you asked me. Why was she turning this into such an emotional drama? What was she trying to prove?

I didn't have long to find out.

My mother pulled into Cottle's parking lot, cast one more glare my way, and marched me into the store. She proceeded to hunt down Mr. Proulx, the store manager! Why would she want to bother an important man like Mr. Proulx about me needing to pay for some candy that any cashier could more easily just take care of?

Once she located him and got his full attention, she said, in a voice that could be heard from three aisles away, "Tell Mr. Proulx what you did!"

I knew Mr. Proulx. I liked Mr. Proulx. But on this day Mr. Proulx was taking all of his cues from my mother. There was no room for doubt... I was on trial and Mr. Proulx was judge and jury! Through tears, I admitted what I had done and apologized. My mother put a quarter in my hand to give to him. Mr. Proulx listened and accepted my apology along with the twenty-five cents. He then issued a stern warning, explaining what the consequences would be if there was ever a repeat performance. Snuffling, embarrassed, ashamed, I totally understood the significance of my actions and what they might lead to if not nipped in the bud: Sugar Babies today, grand theft auto tomorrow.

My mother seemed satisfied that I'd learned my lesson as she chose to take me home rather than drop me off at the Waldo County jail for a night or two of reflection with my fellow criminals.

To this day, often while in a checkout lane near a candy rack, I think back to the lesson I learned from my mother. Thanks, Mom, for keeping me from a life of crime.

~Keith Smith

Thanks Mom

Chapter 2

Mom Knows Best

Little Trouper

Supposing you have tried and failed again and again.
You may have a fresh start any moment you choose,
for this thing we call "failure" is not the falling down, but the staying down.
~Mary Pickford

"I can't do this anymore, Mom."

"Yes, you can."

"I'm twenty-eight years old." I started to cry. "I've been at this forever. I just want to come home."

"No," she said. "This was your dream."

"Please, Mom, please tell me to come home."

"No."

By the age of twenty-eight, my mother had already been married for six years and had four children.

Before settling down, her dad had wanted his only child to become a doctor, but she dreamed of being a dancer and was having a rough time in pre-med. She left college to drive trucks for the Army in World War II.

She headed west from Ohio to Los Angeles to stay with her grandparents, work in her uncle's store near the Army base, and wait in Schwab's to be discovered, as Lana Turner is thought to have been. She took ballet lessons four nights a week, and on weekends she poured punch and coffee at the USO club. And she danced. All the soldiers wanted to dance with my graceful, beautiful mother.

She had one audition, for Earl Carroll's *Vanities*. The audition notice specified "Showgirls, minimum height 5'7". Mom was barely five feet tall, but she knew she couldn't miss. She looked like Barbara Stanwyck, and danced like Rita Hayworth. She spent three weeks' salary on a new outfit, had her nails done in a swanky salon and worked for hours on her hair and make-up. She got off the bus in Hollywood, and glided into the dance studio right on time.

"Too short. Thank you, next!"

Years later, when she told me that story, I could see that the wound had still not healed. "They wouldn't even let me dance...." She had never gone on another audition. Not ever.

My earliest memory is of watching a Fred Astaire and Ginger Rogers movie on TV with my mother. I was still learning to feed and dress myself when I knew I would squander my life on Busby Berkeley's vision of heaven. Nothing would stop me. Like Ruby Keeler in *42nd Street*, I was a little trouper. I would never give up. Not ever. No sacrifice was too great if, at the end of everything, I could be up there under the lights when the curtain opened.

At twenty-three, I left Los Angeles and moved to New York City to attend Juilliard. A bathtub squatted against the wall of my one-room apartment at the top of a five-floor walk-up near the East River. A steam radiator hissed in the corner. The toilet gurgled in the closet under a cracked tank, which dripped orange-brown water stains down the peeling wall. Under the century-old roof, the ceiling leaked filthy rainwater all over most of my belongings whenever the precipitation lasted more than an hour.

The area had once been a charming district called German Town. A large number of pre-war Germans had stayed in the neighborhood for reasons of poverty and rent control. Their big activity each day was getting indoors before the twilight onslaught of marauding youths.

I learned not to wear a watch or carry a purse. I learned to drape something ratty from the secondhand store over my better clothes. I learned to strike a careless pose and whistle a happy tune. Gradually, my middle-class reticence dropped away and, though only five-foot-three, I began to have confidence in my ability to defend myself. And confidence is a good thing to have, if you're an actor. Showbiz is not for the faint-hearted.

Sometimes I played hooky and braved cattle-call auditions for touring shows.

"Best eight bars, we're running late. Thank you. Next!"

"The face is okay, but God! That hair..."

"The voice is okay, but God! Who dressed her?"

"Too short, thank you. Too tall, thank you. Next! Too plump, too thin, too young, too old, thank you, next. Next. NEXT!!"

But I was a little trouper. Nothing would stop me. I would hang in there and give it all I had. I decided if nothing had come of it by the time I was thirty-five, I would do something else.

Years passed. One evening, it all came crashing down. It had rained all day, and the roof was leaking pretty badly. I had placed pots and pans around the room to catch the water, and draped a tarp over my bed.

I was rehearsing in front of the full-length mirror for yet another humiliating audition for yet another stupendous part I wasn't going to get. Dirty rainwater dripped on my head. All of a sudden, I couldn't kid myself any more—it was hopeless. I knew now that Busby Berkeley's heaven was a cruel hoax. The childhood fantasy that had been my lifejacket slowly deflated and I sank, drowning in years of accumulated rejection.

I had promised myself I would hang in there until I was thirty-five. I was only twenty-eight. I had seven more years of this.

I dialed my parents' house.

"I can't do this anymore, Mom."

"Yes, you can."

"Please, Mom, please tell me to come home."

There was a long moment of silence.

"No," she said. And she hung up.

I ran a tubful of hot water, lit some candles in a memorial to the career that would never be, and took a look in the mirror at the face that would never play the Palace. A trick of light from the burning tapers, and a silent movie seemed to flicker....

I strutted my stuff in ostrich feathers and shimmering sequins....

Broadway audiences fell at my feet, conquered by the magnetism of my personality and the gossamer gown....

As I blazed up the Great White Way, Fred Astaire materialized, and we danced in each other's arms....

Music up. Curtain. Thunderous applause.

This was New York City, the Promised Land where a little trouper like me could make it on sheer guts and raw talent! I had promised myself I would hang in there and, by God, I would!

Six more months passed while I took acting classes and singing lessons, and went on audition after audition. And by the time I was twenty-nine, I was singing principal soprano roles at New York City Opera, and playing leads off-Broadway.

When I made my Broadway debut, my mother sat next to my dad, eighth row center. I stopped the show with my big song. Over the cheers, I could hear her screaming, "Bravo!! Bravo!!" In my dressing room afterwards, she said the words she had been waiting thirty years to say.

"To try, and fail, is to know that at least you tried. To fail to try is to never know what might have been. Never give up on your dream. Not ever."

In the decades since, from time to time I have been tempted by disappointment or heartbreak to throw in the towel. Then my mother's words lift me up, face me toward the horizon, and give me the courage to keep putting one foot in front of the other for as long as it takes. Or forever.

~Penny Orloff

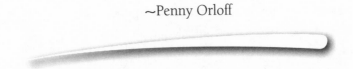

Lip Drama

Mother — that was the bank where we deposited all our hurts and worries.
~T. DeWitt Talmage

"Emily, I heard that Adam is going to kiss you today," Brittany whispered in my ear as we walked into Mrs. Cox's math class.

"What? Are you sure? We have only been going together for a week."

She leaned in as the bell was ringing. "He told Ashton that he was going to kiss you when he walks you to the bus this afternoon."

Mrs. Cox started the lesson, but I did not learn anything for the rest of the day. My mind was off to the races. Today? Is it too soon? Did he mean a real kiss? Maybe it was just a rumor.

Apparently not. By fifth period, the entire seventh grade seemed to be in on the secret. Notes were flying onto my desk from people I barely knew. I heard murmurs as I walked to my locker, and it felt like even the principal glared at me with a raised eyebrow. It was as if the morning news announced to the whole world that today was the day of Emily McClanahan's first kiss. All the high school and middle school kids hung out by the buses. It was the place to be. Everyone would be watching.

That seemed like a lot of pressure. So, I panicked. When the last bell rang for the day, I did the only thing I could think to do. I hid in the bathroom.

Even now, twenty years later, I can still hear Adam outside the bathroom asking, "Have you seen Emily? Did she check out today?" I stayed in the stall with my feet propped on the door until I was sure that no one was outside.

Lying in bed that night, I stared at the ceiling and thought about our magical moment. "Tomorrow is the day. I am going to have my first real kiss. Maybe I should practice with a teddy bear or on my arm. No, that's lame. I am sure that it'll be okay. People have been kissing since the beginning of time. How hard can it be? Plus, Adam is experienced. I think he has kissed two or three other girls. He will know what to do."

The next day, at 3:05, Adam faithfully met me at my locker. A small crowd formed behind us as we walked down the stairs and outside, through the basketball courts and down to the first line of buses. When we came to bus number twelve, I stopped like I always did. Usually, I just gave him a quick hug. But not this time. This time, I just looked at him and waited.

He leaned in and I closed my eyes. I braced myself for the magic. But it wasn't magical at all. It felt more like being kissed by a Golden Retriever.

The worst part was still to come, though. Adam took a few steps and joined his buddies, who were anxiously awaiting his comment. He looked at them and snickered, "She didn't even do it right." The entire crowd erupted in laughter. Humiliated, I ran onto the bus as fast as my feet would carry me.

By the time the bus pulled away, I was hysterical. I did not even try to hide my tears from my brother. He kept asking what was wrong, but I ignored him. As soon as we got home, he threw his book bag on the floor and reported to Mom. "Something is wrong with Emily. Talk to her! She said that she is going to jump off the roof."

I had already decided that I would not tell her. Mom and I talked about everything, but I knew that she would not understand this. This was the worst day of my life.

Mom saw my red face, though. She knew something had happened. "Em, is everything okay?"

"It's fine. Your son is a lunatic. Nothing is wrong with me. I am going outside to get some sun."

"Okay, then. I think I'll hang out with you."

Oh, nice try. Did she think I would cave just because she was sitting next to me? I would be a rock. I would never let her know what happened. I planned to take this miserable secret to my grave.

"So, tell me about school, hon."

"I am not talking about it, Mom. We can't talk about everything, you know."

"All right. You don't have to talk about why you are upset. Just tell me about something else. Did you do well on your test today?"

The tears started flowing. "Yes."

"Do you have a lot of homework?"

More sobbing now. "Not really."

She hugged me. "I'm here. Talk to me if you feel like it. If not, I'm just here."

"Adam kissed me... by the bus."

"Well, it must not have been a very good kiss if he made you cry. Maybe he needs to work on his technique."

"Mom!" She always knew how to make me laugh when I felt like crying.

"Actually, I'm the one who did not know what I was doing. He told his friends that I did it wrong!"

I don't remember every single word my mom said that afternoon in the backyard. I know that she laughed with me. She listened. She didn't ground me for kissing a boy at school. She never judged or told me that I had done anything wrong. She was just there.

Our conversation on the back porch that day was interrupted by a phone call from Adam. The catastrophe was over. It just worked itself out. I did not jump off the roof. But I decided that I was not ready for public displays of affection at school. Somehow Mom made me think that was my idea.

Middle school was full of drama and Mom took it in stride. I can remember countless days and nights when she just came in my room and talked until I confessed what was really happening in my life.

She never demanded it. She just cared enough to stay with me until the truth came out. I always felt better after Mom knew.

Thanks, Mom, for being there during the drama that defined my middle school years. Your presence was an anchor I could latch on to when the world was going up and down so quickly that everything looked blurry. You have always been my solid ground.

~Emily Osburne

My Mother, My Teacher

No one in the world can take the place of your mother.
Right or wrong, from her viewpoint you are always right.
She may scold you for little things, but never for the big ones.
~Harry Truman

My mother is a teacher, a fabulous teacher. I know this because I've observed her in her classroom when she is teaching her students. She is passionate not only about teaching middle school students the German language, but also about her love of the language itself and the German culture. She has tirelessly taught grades six through nine for more than twenty-six years, and she has been my teacher for almost thirty.

Back in kindergarten, when they asked us what we wanted to be when we grew up, I answered that I wanted to be a teacher. I saw how my mom could positively affect her students and colleagues, and how she would come home exhausted at the end of the school day, yet still be exhilarated for the next. Of course, as a precocious kindergartner, these complex thoughts weren't exactly what I was thinking when I answered the question. But somewhere inside I always knew that my mom loved being a teacher almost as much as she loved being my mom.

But the years passed and I entered college with lofty aspirations of becoming some kind of famous fashion designer. I wanted nothing to do with being a teacher. There was no way I was following in my mother's footsteps! I wanted to be as different as I could from my mom. I know now that I could have declared my major to be basket weaving and Mom would've given me her full support. When becoming a fashion designer did not exactly pan out the way I had planned, Mom gently suggested that I put my talent in art to use by going into art education. Little did I know that this small encouragement would lead me to the profession I would come to cherish. I guess Mom was teaching me then that it was okay to make mistakes, and that she would always be patient while I made the decisions she knew were right for me all along.

Mom's love and patience sustained me through a difficult marriage and divorce. She opened her heart and home to a bruised and scared daughter and granddaughter and tried her best to nurse us back to sanity. There were times when I am sure she felt emotionally drained, but I have never seen so much strength from one person in so many ways. She kept reassuring me that even though it was hard to see at the moment, God had a plan and a reason for everything.

Her most important lesson, however, was taught recently at breakfast. As I sat down with my nineteen-month-old daughter, I was determined that she would eat more than two spoonfuls of cereal. Of course, my daughter had other ideas. My mom realized the impending battle of wills that was about to occur, and her years of experience with a stubborn daughter, namely me, kicked in. Her sage advice was to let my daughter eat when she was ready! Well, to a novice this sounded ridiculous. Nevertheless, moments after I had given up, the struggling stopped and my daughter began to feed herself. I sat back, amazed, and again realized (regretfully) that my mother knows more than I do. My mother has been my teacher for almost thirty years. I hope she will continue her "lessons" to me for at least thirty more.

~Jessica Gauthier

The Pantsuit

I have seen my kid straggle into the kitchen in the morning
with outfits that need only one accessory: an empty gin bottle.
~Erma Bombeck

My mother and I are going down to North Carolina for my niece's graduation from medical school. A week before the trip, I get a phone call.

"Do you have enough clothes to bring?" my mother asks.

I sigh. "Yes, I'm fine." I'm sure my mother has packed and repacked her suitcase at least three times by now. The thought of what I am going to pack hasn't yet crossed my mind. Probably my ten-year-old black pants and my one decent jacket, a gift from my nieces, that almost goes with the pants. A couple of tops. Whatever.

As if she can read my mind, my mother continues. "Are you sure you don't need any blouses? Maybe a pantsuit?"

My sigh gets longer and louder. I'm surprised she waited this long to bring up the dreaded pantsuit. "I'm fine," I repeat, feeling the muscles in my jaw tighten. She's been trying to get me to buy a pantsuit for years. I've been resisting just as long.

"Okay," she says. Then a moment of silence. "Maybe I'll pack a couple of extra blouses for you, just in case."

I close my eyes and count to ten. "Better go," I say, "I think the cats are fighting." I hang up—gently—and glare at the phone for a moment.

Although I look like my mother, when it comes to style I am

definitely a changeling. My mother's years of tutelage on quality and fashion have fallen on deaf ears. She shops at higher end stores, I shop at thrift stores. Although I smile when she compliments me on one of my "finds," I don't admit to buying used clothes. Instead, I airily tell her that I bought it at a local store.

For my mother, the word "pantsuit" is not just matching pants and a jacket. It's a code word for wearing a presentable outfit, her polite way of telling me my style leaves much to be desired. That my pants are too baggy, my sweaters synthetic, my shoes at best serviceable.

My lack of style has become a family joke, one that I have learned to take advantage of. When I visit my mother, I leave lots of room in my suitcase, knowing I can "shop" in her closet, with her encouragement. She loves bright, oversized prints and florals which I loathe, so I head for the solid jewel-tone blouses, sweaters and turtlenecks. I seldom go home without a few new offerings for my wardrobe, though I make sure to only choose clothes she's worn for a few years.

"Now that's what I call shop-at-home service," I once remarked to her.

I remember her shaking her head, wondering how she failed to drum her love for good clothes into me.

Two days before the trip to North Carolina, I check my clothes, folded, piled and ready to pack. Pants—yes. Almost match-ing jacket—yes. Shoes—yes. I've put on ten pounds, so some of my—that is, my mother's—nicer tops are tight. I find one of my old, not too threadbare ones and add it to the small pile.

The suitcase is about half full, which is about right.

My mother arrives the next day to spend one night at my house before we fly down together for the graduation in North Carolina. Her suitcase is at least twice the size of mine. I heft it onto the bed in the guest room, not surprised when the mattress sags. Two cats jump onto the bed to watch, a third sits on a nearby chair.

She opens her suitcase and my youngest cat takes that as an invitation to jump in. My mother pushes the cat away, trying to defend her clothes against cat hair.

I pluck some stray cat hairs from my own pants and wait for the reveal.

For a minute, I worry she'll pull out a bright floral pantsuit for me. Instead, she hands me a black and white print blouse. "I thought you might like this," she says. Then she adds a short-sleeved black jersey, a three-quarter-sleeve gray top, and a deep red blouse to my pile. "Maybe while we're down in North Carolina, we can find you a pantsuit."

I grin. "You never know, Mom. This might be the year of the pantsuit after all."

~Harriet Cooper

Thank You
for Not Pushing

Don't handicap your children by making their lives easy.
~Robert A. Heinlein

G runt, creek, creek... grunt, creek, creek...

My legs swung back and forth. I was using all of my strength to get that swing into the heavens. It seemed impossible.

"Mom, can you give me another push?" I whimpered.

"Are you kidding me?! You can do it. Just focus and keep pumping your legs."

I looked around and saw all the other moms and dads in the park, pushing their little kids in the blazing heat of June. I wondered why my mom couldn't just do the same. But I was never one to try and question her. I did all I could to avoid "the look." You know, that look parental figures get in their eyes when they feel their authority is being questioned.

"Okay," I mumbled. I didn't think I could do it. But Mom never seemed to doubt me. I wrapped my small hands tightly around the metal chains, wiggled into position, tilted back and I was off.

"Now just keep pumping your legs back and forth kiddo! You've got this!" my mom encouraged me. It seemed like she wanted this more than I did. I didn't want to let her down, so I kept at it. Eventually I was so high up in the blue sky, the tips of my shoes were playing tag with the clouds. A grin stretched across my face from one ear to the other. I had done the impossible. I had flown.

I jumped off the swing and dug my feet into the warm sand. "Mom! Did you see me? Did you see?" I exclaimed.

"Of course I saw. I didn't take my eyes off you for one second!" she smiled.

Back then, I didn't understand why my mom made me do everything for myself. If I couldn't get my swing going, why wouldn't she just push me?

Throughout the years, my mother has given me the greatest gift a parent can give her child: tough love, freedom and independence. She has taught me how to face challenges myself. She has prepared me for my future. And she has shown me a great deal of love and compassion while being my teacher, two parents in one, and my best friend.

Every time she heard the words "I can't do it" a smile crossed her face because she knew I could. If she had pushed my swing, I never would have jumped off it feeling so wonderfully accomplished.

~Christy Barge

The Chest

A son is a son till he takes him a wife, a daughter is a daughter all of her life.
~Irish Saying

It has darkened with age, but the memory of receiving it has remained fresh in my mind—like it happened yesterday. I write of the hope chest that my mom bought me when I was still in college.

We took our annual summer trek to a beautiful little suburb far outside of Chicago that year. The small quaint town sat on a river, banked by lush trees. It had an inviting magical quality about it.

This was always a trip I looked forward to because it was just my mom and me. We would spend the day there, away from all of the testosterone within the walls of our home. I was her only daughter.

My mom and I went in and out of the stores, looking at clothes and trinkets, enjoying the warm sunny day. Typically, she bought me a piece of clothing. I always appreciated it, especially because I had been raised to understand the value of money.

On this trip, we ventured into a furniture store. Every piece in it was handcrafted. The pieces were lovely. I remember the thick smell of the rubbed tung oil, and the warmth of the late morning sun as it filtered into the store. Fresh shavings littered the old planked floor. I had little interest in the furniture, but followed my mom around as she took it all in. She slowed her pace and stopped in front of a simple rectangular chest. Made from rough hewn pine, it had plain solid footings and handles. It was utilitarian, but somehow attractive for its lack of decoration.

"Isn't that pretty? What do you think, honey? Do you like that?"

"It's nice, Mom," I replied, not sure why she was asking. "What is it?"

"Why, it's a hope chest." I could tell she was excited—and wistful.

"What's that?"

"Well, you store the things you collect before you get married, like linens and other items."

I was stumped because I had just started dating my current boyfriend in the fall. Here it was June and she had marriage on her mind. I really liked him, but love? I wasn't so sure. Marriage? No way.

She smiled. "I want to get it for you, honey!"

I looked at her with complete surprise and I said, "Mom, I'm not sure it will fit in the car."

"Sure it will," she said, with a reassuring smile.

And I nodded, accepting her gift, "Thanks, Mom."

She paid for it and we loaded it into the car. It just fit.

Through the years, the chest accompanied me as I went on to graduate school and then moved from state to state as I was relocated by employers. It was my first piece of furniture. It served as storage for many things—books, clothes, and odds and ends. It doubled as an end table, a coffee table, and a footstool. Careful not to stain it or mar it in any manner, I oiled and dusted it, watching it slowly mellow from the color of honey into a deep rich burnished yellow-cherry.

Eventually, I used it as my mother had planned, as a hope chest when preparing to marry the boyfriend I'd been dating when my mom bought it for me. She had somehow known he was "the one" before I did. Later, it was used to store our children's baby items as we waited for their arrivals.

The chest now sits in my bedroom, next to my reading chair—a reminder of the hopes and dreams my mom had for me. It holds treasures, items that represent memories of life and love of family. And the love of a mother for her daughter.

~Judy M. Miller

Just in Case

Safety isn't just a slogan, it's a way of life.
~Author Unknown

f "I love you" are the three nicest words in the English language, then "just in case" must be the three most irritating. They are often followed by those other three "you never know..." implying a whole bundle of horrors if you don't go along with the "just in case" idea.

The first "just in case" you heard was probably from your mother; do you remember "Always make sure your underwear is clean. Just in case?" You'd ask "In case of what?" and she'd say, "You never know...." If you kept asking she would finally utter the ominous words, "You could be in an accident." She doesn't say always make sure your underwear is clean, because that's how it should be, she had to use the "just in case" threat.

Through most of your school years, in addition to books, pens, etc., you carried around a heavy sweater, sunscreen, and a plastic cape, just in case it got cold, or hot, or it rained. You became paranoid. Thanks to Mom, "just in case" ruled your life. You walked around ladders, not because you were superstitious, but just in case. It was the same with Halloween candy.

"Don't eat it 'til Mom or Dad can check it out, just in case."

"In case of what?" you'd say.

"You never know."

"Know what?"

And then it came, the threat which ensured you would end up letting Mom and Dad eat all your candy, simply because they loved you so much and wanted to protect you from harm.

"There could be poison in it."

The fact that I know of no proven case of poison in Halloween candy since Ichabod Crane took up horse riding doesn't matter one bit. Nor can I find any authenticated, recorded cases of Halloween drugging or soda drink spiking, but that doesn't change the argument. It's solid as a rock and just as immovable.

As we get older the habit has become so ingrained we inflict it on ourselves. We leave for the airport to catch our flight half an hour before the aircraft leaves its previous location, just in case the traffic is bad. And speaking of flights, what about those hasty extra prayers uttered as insurance as flight takes off, or at unexpected turbulence... "just in case." The phrase is so much a part of our lives that we buy enough insurance to keep those companies in the lap of luxury for all eternity. I'm not talking about the everyday car and house insurance, but the little extras the agents talk us into, like the four dollar a week extra coverage, just in case we are attacked by a swarm of killer geckos, or are hospitalized with a particularly rare form of athlete's finger, (an affliction contracted from dirty holes in bowling balls, I believe). When the insurance agent clinches it with those immortal words "you never know," you're hooked and sign. Mom's lessons die hard.

I'm going to print up this article now, but I'll also save it onto my hard drive, and just in case my computer crashes I'll also save it on a disc, and just in case the disc gets contaminated I'll save it on my flash drive. Well... you never know. Thanks a lot, Mom!

~Ann O'Farrell

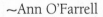

You'll Always Be "Mom"

I have fallen in love with American names, the sharp, gaunt names that never get fat.

~Stephen Vincent Benet

The first time I got lost at a grocery store was a very confusing day for me. When the store manager asked for my mom's name so he could page her, I told him that her name was "Mom." He said, "I know she's your mom, but what is her name?" I stared at him blankly. My brother and I both called my mom "Mom" and even my dad called her "Mom" as in "go ask Mom." I'd never heard anyone call her anything else.

Trying to help the grocery store manager I told him that her name was "Mom Hill" so he paged "Mrs. Hill." When she came to get me the store's manager told her that she needed to teach me her first name. My mom looked at me with amusement and said, "Becky, you don't know that my name is Kandy?" That confused me further. I knew what candy was, but why was my mom named candy? She said, "It's Kandy with a K." I didn't know how to spell yet so that didn't help.

On the drive home I asked if Dad's name was "Dad." She said no, that his name was "Don." I felt betrayed. Why had everyone been lying to me and using fake names? When we got home I asked if my brother Matt was really named "Matt?" My mom said, "No, Matt's name is actually Donald. Matt is his middle name." So all this time

I thought I was living with Mom, Dad and Matt but in reality I was living with Kandy, Don and Donald.

The next morning, I asked my mom if my name was really "Becky." She said, "No. Actually your name is Rebecca." I looked at her with great suspicion. My mom explained that "Becky" is a nickname for "Rebecca." It required a leap of faith, but I chose to believe her because this "mom person," this "Kandy with a K," whoever she really was, had always been kind to me and she was in fact my favorite, and most trusted, person in the world.

That was the first, but certainly not the last time my mom had to explain the nuances of life to me. Over the years my mom also had to explain that the flying monkeys in *The Wizard of Oz* were just pretend and that there was no way they were going to fly into my room and get me; she also had to explain that broken hearts do mend with time and that eventually I would meet a great guy, one who was much nicer and much cuter than the boy I was crying over; and most recently, she had to fly cross country to explain to me in person how certain medicines could, and in fact would, beat an auto-immune disease that was attacking my eyes. In all of these cases, it required a leap of faith, but again, I chose to believe her and (thankfully) in all of these cases, she was right!

So, I'd like to thank my mom for always being there to clear things up, especially when life was at its most confusing. As a forty-year-old I now know my mother's name is "Kandy" but to me her name, the one I will always hold closest to my heart, will always be "Mom."

~Rebecca Hill

Our Mother

My mother had a slender, small body, but a large heart—a heart so large that everybody's joys found welcome in it, and hospitable accommodation.
~Mark Twain

"Mom, is it painful to have a baby?"

Mom smiles. She takes a carrot slice and hands it to me. I take it as a treasure because it comes from her.

She knows something we don't know, our mother.

"Come with me," she says, carrying a full laundry basket. "Help me hang these." Diapers fill the clothesline in the backyard.

Teaching us responsibilities, our mother.

"Sit on the couch and you can hold him," Mom says.

Mom places her new baby in my arms. A wave of elation streams through me as her baby coos in my embrace.

Teaching us the joys of motherhood, our mother.

We empty all the toys from the closet, remove the shelves and make a train complete with bunks, seating and sound effects. Her eyes look past the mess. She sees us, smiles and calls us to dinner.

Nurturing our imagination, our mother.

She comes home from a date with Dad. I pretend to sleep,

leaving enough space in my eyes to see them tuck my blankets and hug each other.

Making us feel safe, our mother.

A vegetable garden, an apple tree, a pear tree and some pink petunias brighten our backyard.

"You get to pick the green beans and hoe the garden today!" Mom says.

Get to? I accept the privilege with honor.

Teaching us the joys of working hard and making it seem fun, our mother.

I bring my first baby home from the hospital.

"Look," Mom says as she rubs lotion on my little girl's arm and wraps her in a blanket. She hands my baby to me.

"You'll be a good mother," she says.

A positive attitude (wishful thinking perhaps), our mother.

Kneeling in church on Sunday, I see a beautiful new baby held by her mother. Tears fill my eyes as I am reminded of the baby I recently lost. Mom sees the hurt. I did not know love would hurt so much. Mom touches my arm and sighs.

"Let's go to a festival today!"

Finding some joy in times of sorrow, our mother.

My husband's mother dies at midnight. I wake my mother to tell her. We help the hospice nurse and say goodbye.

"Let's put some coffee on," Mom says. We bake chocolate chip cookies.

She knows what it is like to lose someone special.

Supportive in times of need, our mother.

Mom sits at Dad's bedside. He is weak and dying. "He likes Cream of Wheat." She carefully spoons it into his mouth. She turns him and gently kisses him goodnight.

Selfless acts of love, commitment to family, our mother.

It's a cold January morning. She makes pancakes and sausages. We visit with enthusiasm.

"Who's having this baby anyway?" she laughs.

She knows my husband and I will soon know the joy of being grandparents.

She will be a great-grandma, our mother.

Is it painful to have a baby?

WOW is it ever! The pain and the joy are in our hearts. Our children are our hearts walking outside our bodies.

Thank you for answering with a smile, our mother.

~Sandra R. Bishop

22

I've Got the Power

The troubles of adolescence eventually all go away—
it's just like a really long, bad cold.
~Dawn Ruelas

I never thought I would be bullied. All through my life, I had been the one sticking up for my friends, never stopping until the person making them upset had stopped. But when I entered high school, that all changed.

It was a typical night. I came home exhausted from lacrosse practice. After showering and hurrying through my homework, I checked my e-mail and instant messaged my friends. I glanced down my buddy list when one status message caught my eye. "Aditi = Opposite of Mary. Mary = Awesome person. So what does that make Aditi?" My eyes blurred with tears. It wasn't the first time Randy, who had been my best friend all through middle school, had posted mean status messages about me, but this time I hadn't done anything. I hadn't even talked to him in weeks. What could I possibly have done?

In a fit of anger I left my laptop open and ran to the bathroom to compose myself before I could cry. But while I was gone, my mom had passed by and seen Randy's message. She asked me what was going on, and for once I didn't give the standard excuse that nothing was wrong, and it would blow over. I poured out the entire story to my mother. The weeks of public ridicule. The months of teasing. I had absolutely no idea what to do.

My mom was sympathetic but also firm. It turns out she had to deal with a similar problem in high school and there was a boy who teased and humiliated her too. She told me to completely ignore him, and soon it would blow over. But I had been trying to for months and nothing had worked. Seeing the grief in my face, she decided to call Randy's mother, whom she was friends with. At first I protested, but finally I consented, realizing that I probably had no alternative.

After a heart to heart chat with Randy's mom, my own mother sat down and talked to me. She told me that Randy's parents had been appalled by his behavior and had left instructions to tell them about their son's misbehavior in the future. She also told me that no matter what, there are always bullies in the world. But it's my job to know that I am a better person than they are, and rise above all of it. The next morning before school, she handed me a necklace and a note. The necklace said, "Reach for the Stars." The note read:

Hi Sweetie,

Hope your day goes well. Nothing or nobody can rattle you unless you let them. Remember that. Be strong and think things through before you act on anything. Take care.

Love,
Mommy

Talking to my mother that day helped me put everything in perspective. Now the little things in life don't seem quite so overwhelming, because thanks to my mom, I know I can handle them. I can't say that Randy stopped talking about me behind my back or spreading false rumors about me, but I can say that thanks to my mother it doesn't bother me anymore. Nothing he can say or do can ever touch me, because I am above it. Thanks Mom, for teaching me that I do have the power to overcome anything. I love you.

~Aditi Ashok, age 15

23

Blooms of Wisdom

I'd rather have roses on my table than diamonds on my neck.
~Emma Goldman

My mother loves flowers. As soon as warm weather comes around, you will find her planting, mulching, watering, weeding and fussing over everything from tulips to mums. For a number of years we lived next door to each other, and she spent as much time in my garden as she did her own. After the blooms became plentiful each summer, she would cut colorful bouquets to enjoy inside the house—both hers and mine. I would often come home from work and find a beautiful arrangement of fresh flowers on my coffee table or bathroom vanity.

Shortly before Christmas one year, a local florist offered a bouquet-a-month special. It seemed to be a made-to-order gift for Mom, a great way to thank her for all of the flowers she had given me through the years. I couldn't wait until Christmas so I could give it to her!

After the holidays, in early January, I drove her to the florist to pick up her first month's bouquet. The small bunch of mixed blooms the florist handed her, while fresh and colorful, would hardly fill a small vase.

I was so embarrassed.

But, beauty is in the eye of the beholder, and moms are good at soothing their children's feelings. After we returned home, she began to arrange the half dozen stems she had received.

"Mom, I'm sorry," I told her. "I can't believe how skimpy that bouquet is."

She looked at me and smiled. "It's okay," she said as she adjusted the flowers. "It allows me to better enjoy the beauty of each one."

I was struck by the insightfulness of her remark, because it illustrated how much she loves flowers, each and every flower. Yet it also related, so poignantly, to life in general and helped me to realize something bigger and more important—that when we have too many good things we often fail to enjoy the beauty of each one.

Thanks, Mom, for helping me understand that less is sometimes more.

~Kathy Harris

Is Anybody Dead?

You may not realize it when it happens,
but a kick in the teeth may be the best thing in the world for you.
~Walt Disney

My mother will tell you that she's had a blessed life.

From one perspective, this is true. She has three healthy children and eight grandchildren who adore her, she has been very successful in her job, she has a nice home and friends who love her.

In another sense, this is an illusion. She was raised in a broken home. At age twenty-nine, she became a widow with three young children. She lost her second husband to a brain tumor. She broke her back when I was in college and it still gives her pain. She has diabetes, partially brought on by the stress of caring for her second husband during his illness.

But my mother doesn't focus on the negative. It's not that she doesn't feel the pain. She does feel the pain, very deeply. But it has never prevented her from living her life. Her greatest gift was teaching me to never give up, to keep moving forward, to know that while life is full of tragedy, it is also full of joy.

Only three years after my father died, my mother planned a trip for the four of us to Disney World. She was a widow with three kids, ages twelve, eleven and eight. She was only thirty-two herself. She made all the arrangements and got us ready to go without showing a single worry. We had a blast.

Even a broken rental car was something she could handle. We'd spent the day at Disney World and were very late leaving. By the time we reached our car, the parking lot was emptying out and we were exhausted and cranky.

And the car would not start.

So there we were, years before cell phone service; my mom was in a big, empty parking lot with three exhausted children and a car that would not work. And it was getting darker fast.

Not a problem.

She'd paid attention to the announcement on the trams about car trouble and how to request help from Disney staff. The staff acted quickly, reported the problem for us to the rental car company, and said to wait until they brought a replacement.

So we waited. And we waited. It was hours.

I remember being a little worried that it was very dark outside. It was also quiet, as the place was shut down for the night, and that seemed ominous. There was nowhere to sit but the car.

If my mother was scared, she never showed it. I don't remember exactly what she did to keep us occupied during that wait. I think she told stories. Or we played some guessing games. Or said what we liked most about the vacation so far.

I do remember that she kept saying, "No big deal... patience... this will get fixed." And when the car showed up, finally, we cheered.

The rest of the vacation, the broken car became a running joke, something we laughed about. She approaches every obstacle in her life this way. If it's a small thing that will eventually get fixed with patience, no big deal. If it's more menacing and looks insurmountable, she'll say, "Is anybody sick? Is anybody dead?" And, if not, well, then there are options, even if we can't see them yet.

I remember the day I announced that I would be a writer. I was a little kid and she probably heard her kids say this kind of stuff all the time. But she instantly said, "I think you'd be great." And she meant it. Sure, there were obstacles. We had little money. My parents were from families where no one had ever gotten a college degree. And I wanted to go into journalism, which paid badly then and pays less now.

But she never saw the problems as problems. I never heard one negative word from her about it. What I heard was, "You're a great writer, you're talented, you keep working, and you'll be great."

All she emphasized was that if I wanted to do something, I had to work hard; I had to never give up. I had to know that I would make mistakes, that practice was important and nothing would come easily. But the most important part is to keep going, to keep learning.

Even if the odds are against you, even if tragedies happen.

I have four kids now, and one of them has "special needs." We've had some serious issues over the years paying for medical expenses. But I think of what my mother handled and still deals with, and I ask myself: "Is anybody seriously ill? Is anybody dead?" And if not, I move forward.

People ask me sometimes how I deal with the things in my life. And I say, "I learned from my mom."

~Corrina Lawson

Chapter 3

Thanks Mom

Making Sacrifices

Seven Sticks

A mother is a person who seeing there are only four pieces of pie for five people, promptly announces she never did care for pie.
~Tenneva Jordan

Well, here it was... one of the most exciting days of my youth, my very first trip to college! Twelve years of school had led to this very important day. I am not sure who was more excited, my mother or me. Just being able to attend college was a miracle in itself since Daddy had passed away three years earlier.

I always knew that funds were scarce after he died. But Momma was somehow able to provide for us. I thought I had understood the extent of her sacrifice, but it was on this day, driving in the car with my mother to college, that I learned one of my life's most important lessons.

As we drove, she offered no profound advice—not about safety or financial responsibility or anything else of any importance. There really was no need for such conversations on this road trip because these talks had happened long before. Instead, the lesson came in the form of a few words spoken as we listened to songs on the radio.

My mother said, "San, do you have any gum?"

My mother never, ever chewed gum. Since I was the one driving the car, I told her to help herself to the gum in my purse. My surprise continued when Momma pulled the gum from my purse and said, "Oh, honey, this is my favorite gum. Even when I was a child, I always loved this gum."

Okay, now I was really, really shocked. Not only did she chew gum, but she actually had a favorite gum? How was it possible that this precious woman who raised me enjoyed such a simple pleasure in life, yet I never knew? As I watched my mother take the gum from the silver foil and begin to chew, I decided that I had to know the scoop about the gum.

"Momma, I have to ask, how did I not know that you chewed gum?"

Before giving her a chance to answer, I went on to reflect on what I remembered as a child. Whenever we went anywhere as a family, we would pile in Daddy's truck, Momma and Daddy in the front and all six of us in the back. Like a tradition engraved in stone, Daddy would always stop and get three Cokes in the bottle, one to share with Momma, one for the three girls, and one for my three brothers. In addition to the Cokes, Daddy always bought a pack of gum, and it was the very flavor that my mother had just taken from my purse.

After I finished rambling on, my mother just smiled and said: "Honey, the pack only had seven sticks."

It was at that exact moment that I realized my precious Momma had made a choice all those times years ago. She'd given each of us children a stick and then one to Daddy—seven sticks gone and the pack empty, leaving none for her.

To some, this may not seem like a large sacrifice for a loved one to make. But my realization that she spent years giving up even the smallest of pleasures forever changed my heart. I realized that day that, although my mother made huge sacrifices for us, that she also made a million small ones that went unnoticed.

People say being in the right place at the right time is the secret to success. All I know is that a single stick of gum opened a world of knowledge about someone I had known and loved all my life, and about the unspoken sacrifices she had made over the years.

To this day, I am very thankful for the college education I received those many years ago. But it is my momma who taught me lessons of the heart.

By the way, every year since that time, I always nestle a pack of that flavored gum in the bow adorning her Christmas gift.

~Sandy M. Smith

Believing in the Writer in Me

Fill your paper with the breathings of your heart.
~William Wordsworth

There have been moments in my writing career when I felt like a real writer: When I sold my first story to a magazine, when I saw my writing in print for the first time, when I published my first book. All these moments made me feel like I was more than someone who believed he was a writer; they proved I was one. But none of them would have been possible if not for the moment when someone else showed me she believed I was a writer.

I was twelve years old when I decided that I was going to be a writer. Not simply someone who wrote in a diary or kept a journal or even someone who wrote stories and put them away in a desk drawer, never to see the light of day. I was going to be a professional writer, someone who wrote and published stories in books and magazines. My brother and I both had the same dream, and every night we'd sit and write stories of space travel, mystery, intrigue and adventure.

Being so young, we didn't know anything about writing, or the rules of grammar, or about how to prepare a manuscript for submission. We did all of our writing with pencils and tablets, scribbling away at our literary masterpieces. After we wrote stories, we'd sit and read them to each other or to our sister and mom, hoping to get them, our first readers, excited about traveling across the cosmos in our latest science fiction story, or pursuing clues to find the culprit in our latest mystery.

We were smart enough to figure out that the place to publish our stories were the magazines that we loved to read. So we'd look up the mailing addresses of the various mystery, fantasy, and science fiction magazines. Then we'd take our handwritten pages, stuff them into an envelope, and send them off to the editors. Week after week, we'd rush to check the mail, hoping to find a letter from one of the editors telling us how much they loved our stories and that, of course, they wanted to publish them all. We dreamed of becoming overnight successes.

But that didn't happen. Instead, week after week, we'd find our stories returned to us with a rejection letter. Usually it was a preprinted rejection form that gave us no clue as to what we were doing wrong. Sometimes we'd get a handwritten note telling us to send typewritten stories if we were serious about being writers. Since we couldn't afford a typewriter, we simply ignored this advice and kept on writing and sending out our stories. The rejections just kept coming.

Our mom knew that we wanted to be writers. She also knew we were just kids, and that we had a long way to go before we'd ever be good enough to be professional. And she knew that we'd never get anywhere sending out stories written in pencil or pen on paper. She'd read one rejection we got that told us to wait until we grew up to follow our dreams. She could sense we were losing faith in ourselves.

Back then we had no money to spare on something like a typewriter. My mom was barely making ends meet for us. She worked hard to put food on the table and keep a roof over our heads. My brother and I decided we might just have to put our dreams aside and face the realities of life. There'd be time to dream about being writers some other day.

But my mom knew we were serious about that dream, and she could see the potential in our work when perhaps no one else in the world could. She had always told us to go after our dreams and not give up on them. She had watched us writing week after week. She had sat and listened to our stories. There must have been some glimmer of hope there for her to do what she did.

One day my mom came home carrying something in her hand. It looked like a miniature metal suitcase. She smiled when she set it on the table and snapped open the silver locks on either side. The top of the thing slid upward in her hand, and when she lifted it off, we stood there looking at a small, portable typewriter. The keys shone white and silver. I reached out and pushed down on the S key. The corresponding key flew up from the carriage and thwacked against the roller. It was the most beautiful sound I'd ever heard.

Our mom explained that she hadn't bought the typewriter. There was no way we could afford an extravagance like that. What she had done was found a place that rented typewriters, and then asked them for the cheapest portable manual typewriter they had. The little gray and white model that sat before us cost her ten dollars a month. I couldn't believe what she had done for us. I stood there looking at my mom, a person who had always told me how much she believed in me, and realized she believed in my dream as much as I did—so much so that she would use the meager money she worked so hard to earn to make sure I had a chance to follow that dream.

That one act, along with the constant support and inspiration that she has always given me, is the thing that made me the writer I am today. Here was someone whose opinion I valued more than anyone else's, and she gave me the means to make a go of it. My brother and I began typing up our stories and sending them out again. It took time, lots of time and experience, but now we both have the thrill of seeing our words in print in magazines and books. And it's all thanks to my mom, who believed in my dreams with all her heart, and gave me the chance to write about it.

~John P. Buentello

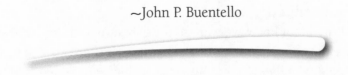

A Mother at Last

Christmas is not as much about opening our presents as opening our hearts.
~Janice Maeditere

I t was a typical Christmas day in western Pennsylvania—snow-covered ground that hadn't seen a speck of green for over a month and air that stung your cheeks when you stepped outside. My two sisters, mother and I had driven the fifty miles to spend the day with my grandmother.

My grandmother was my world at that age. She had been born Sarah RhuEmma, but was known simply as Rheuie. In her lifetime, she had given home and refuge to four children and seen that they grew into adults—yet she never did have a child from her own body. The oldest one called her Aunt Rheuie, as did the next two. She was no relation to the first, and the story of how he came to live with her and her husband was never clear. The next two were her biological niece and nephew. She and her husband had "rescued" them from a children's home where they had been placed. These children also called her Aunt Rheuie.

The youngest of her "children" was my mother. She had been presented this eight-month-old baby as a Christmas present one year. "She's yours; I don't want her," they said. Already in her fifties, Rheuie took to mothering the little one. This one did call her Mom, but there was always that nagging sense that the child's real dad was nearby, and the knowledge that there had been no official adoption.

That Christmas we entered her cozy home and shed our coats.

As usual, there was the smell of good food cooking and wood burning in the stove. There were presents exchanged, but there is no way I can remember any of them. The final gift given that day was to take center stage.

Grandma held the tiny blue velvet box in her hands and I saw how they trembled as she raised the lid. Nestled inside was a silver band with the word Mom on it and four brightly-colored stones representing the birthdays of each of the children she had so lovingly cared for over the years. Tears flowed freely from her eyes.

I didn't understand the tears then, but age and experience have helped with that. Sarah RheuEmma cried that day—not from sorrow, but from the pure joy of being acknowledged as a mother. That one moment made all those years of caring for others worth every minute.

~Joyce A. Anthony

My Mother, My Friend

The best substitute for experience is being sixteen.
~Raymond Duncan

For the longest time I thought I hated her. I was thoroughly convinced that she was wrong about everything, and I made sure that there was no misconception of that fact. I said the most hateful, awful, hurtful things. Things that a daughter should never say to her mother. I cannot count the times I told her that I couldn't wait to grow up and move far, far away so that I would never have to see her again. I remember once looking at a map and telling her that I was going to move to Australia because it looked like the farthest place on Earth from where she was.

I was sure that my parents' divorce was just another selfish act of my mother's. Why couldn't she put up with a man who refused to obey the law? Why couldn't she spend several nights a week lying awake waiting for him to come home? Why couldn't she just let it go? It had to be her fault, that even though she was married, she was pretty much raising three kids on her own. She had to have done something awful to make Daddy want to be away all of the time. And now Dad was crying and telling us that he didn't want to, but he had to go. It wasn't bad enough that we were poor; we had to be a broken family, too. And why? Because Mom didn't want to deal with it anymore? How selfish of her.

We fought, almost endlessly, through my teen years. I resented the life we had because she was a single mom. I had a lot of responsibility.

I spent many of my Friday nights babysitting my younger brother and sister because my mom had to work and she couldn't afford to pay a sitter. I hated that once she came home from work she only had enough time to make us a quick meal before heading out the door again to either her second job, or to school. I hated that I had to buy my school clothes at Walmart, when it seemed like all the other kids were shopping at the mall. I hated that she had to embarrass me by driving around in an old clunker of a car. I hated that we lived in an old trailer, with mostly second-hand furniture, and carpets that, although clean, still badly needed to be replaced. I hated that Dad wasn't around, and that Mom was always complaining about him and how, "We would have it so much better if your dad would just help out once in a while." I hated hearing her cry at night. What did she have to cry about when it was my life she was ruining?

It was a long time before I began to understand everything that my mother did to make sure that, one day, we would have a better life. In fact, it took becoming a parent myself to realize that everything she did was to achieve just that goal. She was often put down for all of her efforts. It's very easy to pass judgment when you're on the outside looking in. But each and every time, she pulled herself back up, dusted herself off and kept moving forward.

I once thought that my mother was wrong about everything. Ten years ago, if anyone had told me that someday I would miss being mothered, I would have laughed and said, "You obviously don't know my mother and me." I used to think that she was the world's worst mother, that she didn't do anything right. But I was so wrong.

With all that she had to fit in to one day, my mother still found time to keep house, do laundry and put dinner on the table every night. Even after a ten-hour workday, followed by four hours of class, she would still come home and tuck us in and sing to us until we fell asleep. Even when she only had one day off every two weeks, she would still take on an extra kid or two so that we could have sleepovers like all the other kids our age. On hot summer days, even if she'd worked third shift the night before, she would load us and half the neighbors' kids into the van to spend the afternoon at the beach.

When we would get sick, she was always there with a bowl of soup, a Popsicle and glass of ginger ale to try and make it all better.

There was a time when I could only hope for a couple of hours with my mother where we weren't at each other's throats. A couple of hours that we could spend catching up on the week's events without me throwing past arguments in her face.

As a parent myself, having been through the ups and downs of motherhood, I have a great deal of respect for my mother and all that she went through for us. I now know that she wasn't wrong about everything. Quite the contrary, she was right about almost everything. Today, I am lucky enough not only to have the most amazing, strong, smart and wonderful woman in the world as my mother, I am also blessed enough to be able to call her my friend.

~Elizabeth M. Hunt

First Anniversaries

Empty pockets never held anyone back.
Only empty heads and empty hearts can do that.
~Norman Vincent Peale

The night of my first wedding anniversary, I called my mom. I was planning to be strong, to hold myself together, but as soon as she picked up the phone and I heard her voice, I cracked.

"Hi," I said, holding at bay the knot that threatened to explode in my throat.

"Well, hello to my girl," Mom exclaimed.

I pictured her, a thousand miles away in Pinedale, Wyoming, spending a quiet Sunday afternoon in the La-Z-Boy working a crossword, her bare feet curled under her legs. In Lafayette, Indiana, two time zones away, I stared at the carpeted kitchen floor in our cramped apartment as dinnertime was fast approaching.

I had already talked to Mom earlier when she and Dad called to wish Bryan and me a special day. It had been a conversation filled with laughs and smiles. Now, less than twelve hours later, all those smiles seemed long gone.

"Is everything okay?" Mom asked now, an air of concern shifting the tone of the conversation.

"Mmm-hmm," I quivered, a lie Mom immediately detected.

"Okay, what's the matter?" she asked.

The story tumbled out. For months Bryan and I had prized a

gift certificate to a small, lavish Italian place downtown. The gift card was worth forty dollars, enough for a romantic evening under dim lights with thick, cloth napkins, two sparkling glasses of wine and plates heaped high with exquisite fettuccini Alfredo. We drove to the restaurant after church to check its dinner hours, only to find it was closed on Sundays. Our gift certificate was useless. With Bryan in school and me earning a meager writer's salary, our checkbook was too thin to splurge on a nice meal, even on our first anniversary. We would be celebrating our special occasion at home, over boxed pasta and cheap wine, sitting on bar stools pulled up to a stainless steel counter—the closest thing to a table we had.

Bryan, who had grown up in a family of five, was used to nights of canned vegetables and only enough food for one serving apiece. Sometimes, his dad even skimped on meals so his children got enough. A night at home for him, even on our anniversary, was no big deal. With a full afternoon ahead of him, he returned to school to catch up on some summer classes. I was alone, exactly one year after the most momentous day of my life, soon to start boiling water on the stove.

I knew Mom would be sympathetic. As much as I didn't want t to admit it to myself, that's why I had called. I was an only child in a family where money had never been an issue. I was used to getting everything I wanted. Now I cried into toilet paper, one-ply.

I expected Mom to soothe me with comforting words and remind me of what truly mattered—that I would still spend this night with the one I loved, my best friend. I wanted her to justify our splurging forty dollars on a night out, even though we couldn't afford it. Maybe she'd even offer to help us pay.

Instead, she told her own story:

On her first anniversary, twenty-nine years ago, she cooked elk steaks packaged from the elk that Dad shot the winter before.

It was old meat.

"Dad was only bringing home $300 a month from the shop, and I wasn't working yet," she said. "All of our money had gone to bills and rent. So on our first anniversary, I was the cook and cleanup crew.

The paycheck demanded it." Fresh steak from the store was not an option.

"I tried not to let it bother me," Mom said. "But as I took the paper off that meat, I cried."

I slid to the carpeted floor in tears at Mom's story. I had never known my parents to struggle. But being poor early on had no bearing on their love for each other. In fact, their first anniversary celebration had set the stage for a relationship that was still going strong after twenty-nine years.

Our first anniversaries had converged, two nights twenty-nine years apart. Mom and Dad did what they had to do, without the outward signs of glamour or romance. And it was our turn to do the same.

I was still in the kitchen wiping my eyes when Bryan came home.

"Hey woman," he whispered into my ear. "Get out of the kitchen. I'm cooking tonight."

~Kate E. Meadows

30

Role Model

Train up a child in the way he should go:
and when he is old he will not depart from it.
~Proverbs 22:6

They say that babies are gifts from above. I believe that mothers are gifts from above also. Mothers are gifts of love, happiness, joy, encouragement, care and support. We do not get to choose our mothers or the families that we are born into, but our mothers choose how they care for us. I am fortunate to have a mother who is everything a kid could hope for.

My mom had me while she was a sophomore student away at college in Nashville, Tennessee. She could have dropped out of school and returned home to New York City where her family was, but she did not. She once told me that I was her inspiration and motivation to finish what she had started. My mom remained a full-time student and worked part-time in order to support me while earning her degree. When I was an infant, she often took me to class with her until I was old enough to attend daycare. For her determination to be a successful role model just for me, I am thankful.

Each and every day I wonder what it would be like without my mom. Would life turn into misery? That question was answered for me one summer day. This was the day when my mom went into labor with my sister, Alexus. I was so excited that day! But the delivery went wrong and my sister passed away. I could have lost my mom as well and this forced me to take an in-depth look at what she meant to my life.

Shortly after my sister's death, my parents separated. This was even harder for me to deal with. Although I was only four years old when it happened, I remember the day as if it was yesterday. The break-up of my family was hard on me and I blamed my sister. If only she had lived, we would be one big happy family.

Although my parents separated, they continue to work together to make sure that they support me. My mom continues to provide for my personal wants and needs. She maintains a good relationship with my dad just for me. This experience is what encourages me not to take my mom for granted. This is why I am thankful for her.

Mom, through thick and thin, you are one of my best friends. You encourage me to follow my dreams and you teach me life lessons through your actions and experiences. Mom, I thank you for inspiring me to follow the right path in life and for helping me make the right choices and exposing me to incredible adventures.

I never realized how much you meant to me until I sat down to write this story.

I want you to know that I will always love you. I only hope that when I grow up I can be as good a parent to my children as you have been to me.

~Kiashaye Leonard, age 12

31

Bright Lights, Big City

There is nothing wrong with today's teenager that twenty years won't cure.
~Author Unknown

I n so many ways my mom was a saint. Maybe she wasn't unique compared to most moms, but she meant the world to us. She was someone who would always give up the last piece of cake for her kids. She would always make a special effort to make each of her six children feel like they were the most important person in her world. And her strength of character and compassion are attributes I have strived to emulate my entire life.

She came from meager means and endeavored to raise six children with even greater financial duress, never straying from her values. She proved time and again that she loved each of us to the depths of her caring soul. Nothing etched that in my mind more than an incident along the shores of scenic Lake Tahoe when I was fifteen.

There we stood atop the mountain amidst the pine-scented air, toe-to-toe in the light of a full moon, verbally duking it out over my future like so many mothers and sons through the ages. It is incredible how my mom's wisdom in those volatile moments would impact me for decades, and define my measure of success for a lifetime.

We had been living in a small town on the northern Great Plains for a couple of years. Financial struggles, and being newcomers, made us big targets for bullying in a little school. A summer road trip to visit family at Lake Tahoe was a welcomed opportunity to get away from an unpleasant situation. Growing up in rural Michigan, and then the Grain Belt, I had never seen a major city — much less one that was active twenty-four hours a day. I was absolutely mesmerized by the lights and sounds, and especially the money. There were millions of dollars changing hands within those glittery buildings. Coming from nothing, I desperately wanted a piece of it.

We enjoyed a glorious week of adventure visiting family and taking in the breathtaking beauty that is Lake Tahoe and its surrounding attractions. And then it was time to leave. I was utterly crushed at the prospect of going back to what I considered an insignificant town with mostly insignificant (and cruel) people. In my mind, there was no way I would consider returning, and I was willing to do virtually anything to avoid it. It was that conversation with Mama that gave me a permanent sense of her maternal devotion.

After explaining my feelings to her with conviction, she let me know that not returning home with the family wasn't really an option.

"I'm not going back, and there's nothing you can do to make me," I said, grossly naïve to the fact that millions of teens have uttered the same sentiment.

"You don't have a choice," she said, raising her voice. "You're part of this family whether you like it or not, and that's where home is. Besides, how do you think you would survive?"

"I'm tired of being poor. I'll find a way to fend for myself." And then I had one of those moments that seem to pass in slow motion, when you wish you could stop the hurtful words from leaving your mouth, but they just keep rolling. "I'm not going to be like you. I'm not going to be a fail...." I didn't finish the word, but she knew what it was and I knew I had hurt her. I felt bad immediately.

I expected her to lash out at the hurtful remark, but she remained composed. She looked me in the eye with a gaze that pierced my soul.

"You think I am a failure? Not even close!" she said. "I have six children who I love dearly. I take care of a husband who I love, and each one of you. I have what I want in life, and by that standard I am every bit a success... and it has nothing to do with money."

In the heat of the moment, I didn't believe her, but in my heart I knew she was right. It was a conversation that has stuck with me for more than a third of a century, and her words have always reverberated in my mind whenever I've been tempted to base my success on material measures. As it turned out, my sister and I were able to stay with Grandma at the lake for a couple of months and work to pay rent. The family moved to the nearby desert later in the summer. In the end, I never did have to go back.

My heart still aches from my mother's death, but whenever I pause to soak in the light from a full moon, her words come back to me and refresh my perspective on life. No matter where I am, I can close my eyes and see clearly across the lake to where her remains sit atop a mountain, and I feel the warmth of her love. I am no less determined to achieve financial security than I was standing at the lakeshore so many years ago, but as a Godly man and devoted husband and father, I thank my mother for her wisdom, and pray that I achieve a fraction of the success she measured with her heart.

~Tom LaPointe

32

A New Mom in Town

Call it a clan, call it a network, call it a tribe, call it a family.
Whatever you call it, whoever you are, you need one.
~Jane Howard

Our family doesn't label relatives as "step-this" or "half-that." Not since my father's remarriage to a Southern Belle, that is.

Truth is, the biological issue doesn't really matter. What's important is how you're connected inside; and once you're in, you're in. Period.

Our "extended family" began about a year after my father lost his beloved spouse of thirty-odd years to cancer. To say Dad was devastated by Mom's death would be an understatement. For more than three decades—and most of Dad's adult life—my mother represented everything to him, from partner to daily organizer. Mom was truly his rock, and once she was gone, my father seemed to become lost and alienated from life. Although the family tried to distract him from his depression and grief, Dad refused to take interest in any sort of activity, preferring to stay at home and watch TV.

Then Dad was introduced to Becky through my aunt. This wasn't a matchmaking scheme; it was simply an opportunity to help my father make new friends and to start socializing again. But whatever the motive, that casual meeting changed all of our lives—especially Dad's and Becky's. Within moments, they found themselves drawn to each other, thrilled that they shared many of the same hobbies: traveling, gardening, family gatherings, even raising dogs.

The blossoming romance shocked the entire family, especially since Dad had been extremely vocal about not wanting to tie the knot again. Nor, as it turned out, was Becky looking for another Mr. Right after her painful divorce. Having raised five children more or less on her own, she was beginning to settle into independence and liked being single.

Until she met Dad.

Sometimes people don't realize how lonely they are until they are given the opportunity to meet someone special and discover what they've been missing.

To our family, Dad's return to the land of the living was nothing short of a miracle. How we'd missed his smiles and laughter! We even teased him — lovingly, of course — about his newfound habit of waiting by the phone.

No one was surprised when, a few months later, Dad proposed to Becky. But before she accepted, she talked to my siblings and me.

"I'm not asking to be your mother," she told us. "I wouldn't dream of taking her place. I just want to be your friend."

Turned out, Becky feared we wouldn't accept her, an anxiety that was unfounded. Sure, there was a learning-to-accept-one-another process. After all, both sets of families loved their biological parents very much, and even as adult children, needed a bit of assurance that a new spouse wouldn't threaten that love.

Silly, isn't it?

Of course, Becky was wise, and respectful, in considering our feelings. After one huge family gathering in Alabama, the matter was put to rest. My siblings and I accepted our new mother, and Becky's children took to Dad. In fact, they quickly nicknamed him "Papa Chief" due to his Hispanic and Indian heritage.

But there were more miracles to come, since the marriage seemed to pull two lonely, fragmented families together. The bonding process was like something in a TV sitcom, only without commercials. Mom and Dad's new home in Alabama became the heart and the center of the family gatherings, especially during the Thanksgiving and Christmas holidays. A slave to tradition, Becky was the epitome of southern hospitality when it came to my siblings and me. Not once did we ever feel like the second-string family at her and Dad's new home. She welcomed us as if we were royalty, lavishing us with feasts and the best accommodations.

Two families had become one.

Still, my biggest debt toward my new mother was how well she took care of Dad when his health began to decline a few years later.

She called me regularly, day or night, and kept me updated on Dad's doctor appointments and medical conditions. From minor procedures to the more serious ones, she made me aware of each doctor's diagnosis (sugar-coating nothing), and helped arrange for me to travel from Oklahoma to Alabama whenever possible.

There were countless nights she would stay at the hospital, at Dad's side, until the doctor released him to go home. Throughout these vigils, not once did she consider her own health. Even family members knew better than to ask her to take a break from caring for Dad. That wasn't happening under her watch!

Looking back, I believe it was her love and willpower that helped him survive a series of strokes and a cancer diagnosis, which, thankfully, proved to be an error. Whenever Dad's health declines, I feel positive that Becky will somehow help him pull through, that her devotion to him exemplifies the bond between husband and wife.

Who could ask more of a mother, whether a biological one or not?

~Al Serradell

33

My Supermom

The phrase "working mother" is redundant.
~Jane Sellman

One night when I was a teenager, I walked by my parents'
bedroom and saw my mother soaking her feet in a pan
of water. Although it was only 7:30, she had already
changed into her pajamas and bathrobe. Why was she always so tired
at the end of the day? After all, my father went to work every morning, while Mom stayed home and did whatever she wanted.

I leaned against the doorframe, ignoring the box of Epsom salt
on the dresser, not even bothering to ask my mother if her feet were
sore. I was thinking about my best friend's mother, who worked as a
secretary for a construction company. That afternoon I'd watched her
answering telephones and typing contracts, and her job seemed so
important. My mother had been a secretary before she married Dad,
and I didn't see why having eight kids in the meantime kept her from
working now.

I blurted out, "Why don't you get a job, Mom?"

In a matter-of-fact tone, she replied, "Because I have one."

I frowned. Then I realized she meant that her job was being a
mother. "No," I said with a little sigh. "I mean a real job."

Mom's blue-gray eyes sparkled. "Wait until you have children of
your own," she said with the hint of a smile. "You'll see!"

Just as she predicted, motherhood looked very different to me
at twenty-one, when I brought my first baby home from the hospital.

My days and nights turned into an endless cycle of feedings and diaper changes. I couldn't rely on my husband for much help because he was in an intensive military program and was gone fifteen hours a day. We'd just moved across the country to Idaho, over two thousand miles from our parents in New York, so I was on my own.

Late one morning when my son, Brian, was napping, I caught my reflection in the bathroom mirror. I was still in my nightgown, and my long hair wasn't combed. My eyes had dark circles under them. Now that Brian was sleeping, I had to quickly pick up the breakfast dishes and put a load of clothes in the washer. He'd woken me up four times during the night, and all I really wanted to do was climb back into bed and take a nap myself.

I multiplied my tribulations by eight and wailed, "How did Mom survive?" She'd had it even harder than I, because women of her time weren't encouraged to breastfeed. That meant bottles to wash and formula to mix. Some years she'd had three in diapers at once, and disposables didn't yet exist. The diaper pail was a permanent fixture in the bathroom, and it filled up daily.

As my son grew, so did my appreciation for my mother. There certainly was more to this motherhood business than I'd given her credit for! When Brian started crawling, he put everything in his mouth, and I had to be incredibly vigilant so he didn't choke on a dropped paperclip or chew on a dirty sneaker. Before long, he was yanking on electrical cords and almost toppling over lamps. Most of my time was spent following him around and keeping him out of trouble. In the evenings, I rocked him to sleep, kissed him on his forehead and whispered, "We got through another day."

I made friends with a few other mothers in our neighborhood who had babies the same age as my son, but for the most part I lived in isolation. Only a year before, I'd worked full-time at a public library and actually seen people every day! The hours seemed long then, but I had breaks and lunch hours, as well as evenings and weekends, to spend however I pleased. That library job looked easy now, compared to being on call twenty-four/seven.

At ten months, Brian learned to pull himself up to the edge of the couch and inch along. I knelt behind him with my hands out, ready to catch him should he fall. Sometimes when he looked at me with his blue-gray eyes, my mother's eyes looked back at me. The conversation I'd had with her that night long ago, the one about her work not being a "real" job, haunted me. She must have worked so hard, with no paycheck at the end of the week. And when she went on "vacation," we children went along, the potty chair tied to the top of the car.

How did Mom manage to keep the household running with so many kids? Every morning, she laid out our school clothes on her bed so that getting dressed was a snap. To make lunches, she lined up two rows of bread on the kitchen table like an assembly line. She remembered who liked mustard and who liked mayonnaise on their sandwiches. In the afternoons, when my sisters and I got off the bus, she had glasses of juice and homemade cookies waiting for us.

I found myself overwhelmed with the responsibility of feeding one child who was hungry every few hours. Yet night after night, Mom had cooked enough to feed an army. She always served two vegetables with every meal in case someone didn't care for one of them. After dinner, we kids took turns washing dishes, but she helped. She'd look at the mountains of dirty plates piled on the kitchen counters, roll up her sleeves and say cheerfully, "There's really not many here." This, after twelve hours of vacuuming, scrubbing floors and trying to reach the bottom of the laundry basket. No wonder Mom was always so worn out at the end of the day! How did she even find time to soak her feet?

Every day that passed, I understood her a little more, how she put us kids before herself and went above and beyond fulfilling our basic needs. She kept a box for each child, filled with a baby book, vaccination records, school papers, report cards and photographs of milestones of our lives. She searched for Christmas presents that took into account our individuality, and even though my birthday was two days after my sister's, Mom always made another cake for me.

Because of the distance between us, I didn't see my mother for an entire year. Finally, my husband was transferred to a duty station on the east coast, and before reporting, he took leave so we could visit our families.

Returning to my childhood home was like arriving in heaven. I could smell roast beef as I walked in carrying Brian. Mom was peeling potatoes at the kitchen sink, and when she heard us, she looked over her shoulder, her blue-gray eyes smiling. She wrapped her arms around both Brian and me, and hugged us tightly. Then she said, "I have a room ready for you, beds with clean sheets and fresh towels in the bathroom." Here she was, my supermom, still mothering me!

~Mary Laufer

34

My Mom, My Hero

Being a full-time mother is one of the highest salaried jobs...
since the payment is pure love.
~Mildred B. Vermont

When I was twelve, my mom found out she was pregnant with my little sister. We were all shocked. Right after I was born, she'd had her "tubes tied" thus preventing any further pregnancies... so she thought! The humor of this is, the day she went to the doctor and found out she was pregnant was none other than April Fools' Day! Of course, we were all excited and couldn't wait until the day the new addition to the family arrived.

Around two o'clock one morning, my older sister burst into my room yelling at me, "Get up! Get up! Momma is going into labor!" Honestly, I rolled over and told her to go away. It was too early for Mom to have the baby. It was not until I heard my mom talking to someone on the phone and crying that I realized something was wrong.

When I got up, the house was in a frenzy, and the only thing I could see was blood. I was terrified. My mom and I were inseparable. She had always been a stay-at-home mom, classroom mom, always there whenever I needed her. And now it seemed to me, a girl of twelve, that my momma, my best friend, might have to fight for her life.

In the hours that followed, we got the news that my new baby sister, Kaytlyn "Nikki" Love, might not make it. My mom was alive, but had lost a lot of blood. She was unconscious for several days before she regained the strength to open her eyes and talk to us. Nikki was still touch and go and they didn't know if she would ever leave the NICU.

My mom came home first, without her new baby. When Nikki finally did come home, she was in a fragile condition. Her lungs were weak, and she had suffered brain damage at birth causing her to have cerebral palsy.

We had a short period of home nursing, after which my mom was thrown into the new position of caring for a sick child. There were some very long nights, and there were times when Nikki wouldn't sleep for days. Through it all, my mom stayed strong and never faltered. She never once complained.

Eventually, times got easier and Nikki became a bright, shining light in our home. Always smiling, she could melt anyone's heart simply by blinking her blue eyes. We were one big, happy family again. The fears of losing Mom and Nikki had passed and everyone seemed at ease. That is, until Nikki was sixteen months old. It was at this time when we were reminded of how every day is a gift and should be cherished like there is no tomorrow.

We were visiting family — the first vacation we had been on since Nikki was born. For the first time in a long while, I was wakened by the sounds of crying. Nikki's heart monitor began to sound when her heart rate dropped too low for the machine to detect. By the time the paramedics arrived, her heart rate was twenty-nine and her oxygen saturation was in the fifties. They airlifted her to a children's hospital where she spent six weeks in the ICU. My mom was right there by her side, never leaving, not once.

They told us that Nikki would not live to see her second birthday. And although my mom was completely distraught herself, she managed to break the news to my older sister and me. She was there for us while we cried on her shoulder. She told us that she and my dad were going to take Nikki home to live out her remaining days, so she would be surrounded by love. And my parents faced their worst nightmare... having to plan their child's funeral.

It brings great pleasure and joy that my little sister, the little angel who was not supposed to see her second birthday, is now fourteen! All of her doctors are dumbfounded and cannot explain it, but I can. I truly believe that my mom pulled her though it with unconditional love, devotion and prayer. To this very day, my mom takes care of my little sister 24/7. She delivers medicine and feedings around the clock. She lifts her and bathes her, and is constantly watching over her daughter, her life. If you were to ask my mom how she does it, she would most likely look at you with a confused expression on her face, because there is no other option for her. She would give her life for her kids and not think twice about it. I thank God for her every day.

~Brandy Widner

35

Surprise!

The heart of a mother is a deep abyss
at the bottom of which you will always find forgiveness.
~Honoré de Balzac

t's funny. I'm sure there were many times I was punished as a child but they have just about faded from my memory. What I do remember well are the times I should have been punished, but was not—especially the time I planned a surprise birthday party.

I planned the party for myself. I was in first grade and I wanted to have a party for my sixth birthday. I guess money was tight because my mother said firmly, "No party." Well, that didn't seem right to my still-five-year-old mind. So when I got to school I went up and down the aisles of my classroom whispering invitations to my friends. Apparently I didn't have the sense to reckon on what lay ahead when all those kids would appear at our door ready for cake, soda and pin-the-tail-on-the-donkey.

But they did appear at the door and my mother was, to put it mildly, the one surprised. We were living in Closter, New Jersey at the time, not far from the "downtown" which was a short strip of Main Street with a few stores on either side. One of those stores was a newsstand/candy store with a soda fountain. So, my mother did the best she could, solving the predicament by giving me money and having my older sister take us to the candy store to get ice cream sodas—a treat we didn't enjoy every day.

The kids didn't seem to mind—or if they did, I forgot. I do

remember getting gifts, including a copy of my favorite story, *The Poky Little Puppy*. It wasn't until years later that I thought about where the money had come from. Had my mother used some of the rent money or the food money... or did she have to go without something for herself? At the time, with the selfishness of a child, I didn't give that a thought. All I knew was I had my party... and I got my gifts.

My mother was not amused, but she didn't punish me either. Maybe she appreciated my tenacity or felt a little sorry for me. But she never berated me or seemed to include it in my ever-lengthening list of childhood sins.

I guess there are times a parent just can't punish a kid... even if the punishment is well deserved. Maybe it's the heart-melting innocence in a child's eyes or the good-natured devilment in her smile. Or maybe it's a reminder of the vulnerability of childhood, the poignancy. Whatever it is at the moment, it's surely based upon motherly love.

I know that I owe my mother a lot for all that she did do and also for what she didn't — for all those times when she allowed me to escape unscathed for my little acts of malfeasance.

~Carolyn Mott Ford

36

The Old Green Coat

*It's difficult to decide whether
growing pains are something teenagers have — or are.*
~Author Unknown

Children learn a great deal from their parents through the years, from the basics of walking and talking, to the more complex concepts of beliefs and values. Some of this information is taught through words, but most is simply learned by example. Occasionally, a lesson remains so vivid in your memory, that it dramatically influences your life. My mother's old green coat had that impact on me.

My mother and I never had one of those cutesy, "dress in matching mother-daughter clothes" relationships. But it was good — until my teenage years when my mother became my opponent in a battle of wills. In the confused, uncertain mind of a teenager, this translated to, "She doesn't care, understand or love me." As a matter of fact, I was quite sure that she had no idea what love was really all about. While she was mopping the floors, cooking meals, helping my father with their business and raising five children, I was listening to the music, reading poetry and experiencing the excitement of love.

As the winter of my sixteenth year approached, the tension between us grew. Looking back now, I realize that I took every opportunity to lash out at her in an effort to soothe my own insecurity. And that is exactly what I did when she unpacked that old green coat of hers. Well-worn and out of style, I bluntly told her that I could not believe she would wear it for another season. She began to say something about not having the money for a new coat, but I was already spouting phrases like, "When I'm older, I will have a beautiful coat, a rich-looking coat. I wouldn't be caught dead wearing a rag like that." She hung the coat in the closet and said nothing.

Christmas morning was always an exciting time in our house, and that year was no exception. The sound of laughter, kids yelling and paper ripping filled the living room. Though I tried to maintain what I thought was a sense of maturity, I was anxious to see what "Santa" had brought. One box way in the back caught my attention. It was large, brightly wrapped and it had my name on it. I quickly tore it open and lifted the lid. Inside was the most beautiful coat I had ever seen. Brown suede with a white fur collar, it was nicer than anything I had ever dreamed of owning.

Looking up, I caught my mother's eyes. I thought of the old green coat and, instantly, I realized how precious this gift really was. She knew what a coat like this would mean to me, and she was willing to make do with her old coat so that I could have it. And what was even more profound was what I saw in her eyes. They did not reflect resentment from her having made this sacrifice, but instead they gleamed with joy, as if it were she who had received the very best gift. Suddenly the true meaning of love was clear to me.

I wish I could tell you that our relationship magically changed into a loving and giving one after that day, but that only happens in the movies. We still fought and found fault with each other, but I always held a special place in my heart where I loved her and I knew that she loved me.

Eventually, the teenage years ended and mutual love, respect and friendship grew between us, and has remained there since. I now have children of my own and I love them with an intensity they cannot yet understand. It's the love my mother taught me the year she wore her old green coat—and I began to grow up.

~Kathy Smith Solarino

Chapter 4

Thanks Mom

Favorite Moments

Cape Towns

When I was a boy of fourteen, my father was so ignorant I could hardly stand to have the old man around. But when I got to be twenty-one, I was astonished at how much he had learned in seven years.

~Mark Twain

When I was seventeen... it was a very good year. That was when I first visited Cape Cod. However, and this is a very big however—I was with my mother. We stayed in Hyannis. I hated being with my mom. And she knew it. She made several references to my sulking. I snapped back with something sweet like, "I wish I was never born." Then we exchanged more clichés.

"Wait until you have a daughter of your own."

"I'm never having children."

"That's what you say now."

Mom tried to make our visit better by taking me to Provincetown. She figured I'd relate to a place that's not on the middle class map. You see, I wore beads and headbands back then. She meant well. What mother doesn't? But Provincetown? Oy, what a mistake.

This is not only a beautiful quaint artists' colony on the tip of Cape Cod. It's a wonderfully unique place inhabited by, as Marlo Thomas once put it, people who are "free to be you and me." Provincetown's folks live just like they'd like to live, in a community where they are accepted and welcomed regardless of their lifestyles. But my mother, from upscale Baltimore, never associated with anyone other than the conservative members of our synagogue. So when she saw a man in a dress, she had a conniption.

As we were strolling through the wild and wonderful carnival-like Commercial Street, she screamed, "Do you see that?"

Being seventeen, and definitely not into being uncool, I saw the person in the red chiffon dress. Then I said, "I don't know what you're talking about."

"Isn't that a man?"

Frankly, I wasn't sure. But I figured whatever she said in this phase of my life was most certainly wrong and worth arguing about. "Not every human being on earth is a middle class person from Baltimore, MO-THER."

Then she wanted to go in a store. "Let's find something for your Aunt Ruth." The shop's sign read, "Eros."

"Mom," I pulled her away. I knew they sold primarily erotic things, and of course mothers know nothing about any of that. "Let's go have a lobster."

She looked aghast. "Lobster?" she said way too loudly. "You should never eat a lobster. They eat sewage. When people on Cape Cod flush their toilets, it all ends up in a lobster."

"Mom," I sighed. "That's not true." I shook my head. "And lobster is the best thing I have ever eaten."

"It's not kosher. It's a bottom dweller—a scavenger. You know, like your Uncle Lou the leech."

There was no lobster on that trip. When we left Cape Cod, something haunting about it lingered in my mind. So after graduating from college in New York, Mom came to pick me up so she could help me move to the Cape.

As mothers often do in some divine miraculous way, mine still loved me.

First, she wanted me to live in elegant Sandwich, the oldest town on the Cape, where she saw the huge white captains' houses and stately inns. She figured I'd spend my after-work hours in quaint book stores among the intellectuals. I wanted to live in rural Eastham, where you can actually breathe the salt air since it's so close to the ocean on both sides. She didn't like Eastham. She thought I'd be too isolated. They didn't even have a Macy's and apparently, according to the local fishermen she harangued, had no plans to build one.

Then I saw the gorgeous cranberry bogs in Harwich and decided to live there. "I'm going to marry a cranberry farmer," I informed her, "and spend my days shucking berries."

"Cranberries don't get shucked," she said. "And besides, we're talking physical work here. Think about it."

I thought. We compromised on Falmouth.

"I'm going to live in a shack by the sea," I announced. "I'm going to decorate my shanty with nets and buoys and I'm going to get up at dawn and dangle my feet over the side of a lobster boat while my swarthy fisherman takes me out to Cape Cod Bay."

"You've never gotten up at dawn your entire life."

"Well, I'm starting now."

"No Jewish man is swarthy. What does it mean, anyway? I think it means somebody who hasn't taken a bath in two weeks."

"Oh," I looked up in a dramatic swoon, "it means devil-may-care. It means lust for life. It means..."

"It means I'm getting those heart flip-flops you gave me when you weren't wearing a bra at your cousin's graduation."

We found a lovely one-room apartment. And there, the most amazing thing happened. Mom, it turned out, could actually be fun. We traipsed all over Falmouth trying to find salt and pepper shakers in the shape of lighthouses. We never found any, but as they say, it's the journey that counts. While searching, we developed frequently occurring cases of uncontrollable giggles. That is, until we discovered steamed clams.

"Shellfish isn't kosher," I reminded her, as she looked over the menu at a seafood restaurant.

"There's something you should know," she said, solemnly. "It has been commanded that we can eat non-kosher food outside of the house."

"Who commanded that?"

"I did, and so did your Aunt Ruth."

The waitress brought us a bowl of steamed clams. Mom picked up a clam and pried it open. She looked at the gloppy gray insides for more than ten seconds. "Now I know why God made shellfish unkosher," she said. "He took a look at one of these. It looks like something in a specimen bottle."

I started laughing so hard that the waitress came over. "We're fine," I said, trying to catch my breath. "Do you have hamburgers?"

After two weeks, it was time for Mom to leave. I didn't want her to go.

"Can't you stay one more week?" I fought back tears. She was doing the same.

"Your father needs me." I knew what she was really saying was that she needed him.

"How do I thank you, Mom?"

"You just did. You always do. It never has to be said out loud, to me."

And so I waved, sad and frightened, as the taxi took her away from me. Soon she'd be back in Baltimore, among the red brick houses with their classic marble steps, and I was faced with the task of beginning life on my own on Cape Cod, the peninsula surrounded by sea.

Now, thirty years later, I still adore the Cape. I love the seashores, the sand dunes, the golden marsh reeds. The only thing that's missing is my mom. Last year, on the day which would have been her birthday, I took my husband to a gift shop. To honor Mom's special day, I bought salt and pepper shakers in the shape of lighthouses. The gal asked if I'd like them gift wrapped. I said I would.

To this day, the unopened gift-wrapped box rests on our mantle. When I look at it, I not only savor memories, I sense her presence. I guess the little girl in me still dreams she may someday open my gift. Now that she's gone, of course it's impossible.

But I can still dream, can't I?

~Saralee Perel

38

Taking Time

A daughter is a mother's gender partner,
her closest ally in the family confederacy, an extension of her self.
~Author Unknown

Mom stood in the small farmhouse kitchen, staring at the clean dust rag in one hand and the can of furniture polish in the other.

I sat at the dining room table folding laundry. I finished a towel and reached into the basket for another, never taking my eyes off her across the open bar that separated the kitchen from the dining room.

"Mama, do you want me to dust?" I asked.

"Hmm?" she murmured.

It was summer and the middle of the week, so I wasn't in school and Dad was working. My ten-year-old heart picked up its pace as I saw her gaze linger on the clock. I suddenly knew what was preoccupying her—Dad wouldn't be home for two or three hours.

She turned and looked at me.

"Let's read," she blurted, hazel eyes flashing with anticipation. "The dusting can wait."

"Can I bring in Ebony?" I asked, as usual. Ebony was the black cat I'd raised from a kitten. She had to stay outside because Dad didn't want animals in the house.

"Sure. You get Ebony and I'll make us some hot tea."

It didn't matter, summer or winter, Mom loved to drink hot tea.

She also read a lot of romance novels set in England, where they were always drinking afternoon tea. Maybe that's what whetted her appetite for it every time we read.

I quickly set the folded laundry in the basket and rushed outside, careful not to slam the screened door.

Ebony lay stretched out on the cistern, basking in the sun. I scooped her up and hurried inside. I was barely back in the dining room before she was struggling to get down and explore. I let her go and rested my elbows on the open counter to watch Mom in the kitchen.

She had set out her fancy teacups, the pretty white ones with pink flowers. Delicate, painted saucers rested beneath their rounded bottoms. A Lipton tea bag nestled in each cup, the white string and tag dangling over the side.

"Afternoon tea is good for the spirit. It's four o'clock somewhere, right?" she said, her eyes twinkling.

"Too bad we don't have scones," I said. I had no clue what a scone was, only that Mom said everybody in England ate scones with their tea. "What is a scone?"

"Some kind of biscuit, I think," she said.

The teakettle whistled, and Mom poured the hot water into the cups. Steam curled into the air.

I leaned over a cup and drew in a deep breath. The pungent scent of black tea filled my nostrils.

When the liquid was dark brown, we doctored our tea: sugar for Mom, milk and sugar for me.

"What are you going to read?" she asked, as we eagerly headed, teacups in hand, to the living room like two kids skipping school.

"*Misty of Chincoteague.*"

"Of course," she laughed, "I should have known. Another book about horses."

"What are you reading?" I asked. "Another romance?"

"Yes," she said, carefully hugging me with one arm. "We're a predictable pair, aren't we?"

Mom sat in her favorite, Early American rocker with the brown and gold flower print and ruffled skirt. With her cup of tea on the round end table, she picked up the latest Harlequin novel she was reading, perched her elbows on the armrests, and crossed her ankles on the small, matching footstool.

After depositing my teacup on the coffee table, I dashed upstairs to my bedroom and grabbed my book off the nightstand.

I kicked off my shoes and stretched out on the dark-rust sofa. Ebony wandered into the living room and jumped onto my chest. She curled into a knot, closed her eyes, and began purring.

The house was quiet except for the grandfather clock ticking in the dining room and the soft rumbles coming from Ebony. Mom and I disappeared into our books.

When we heard a truck coming down the gravel road, we snapped our books shut and jumped to our feet.

Mom rushed to the window and peered through the curtains.

"Dad?" I asked.

She nodded and hurried to the kitchen while I put Ebony outside. I came back in and started setting the table as Mom pulled out pans for boiled potatoes and peas and threw thick slices of ham in a skillet.

I don't know if Dad ever suspected us of whiling away afternoons reading. All I know is that those were some of the most special times I spent with my mom.

She taught me important basics of life: how to keep house, cook, be responsible, and care for others. But she never once said to me, "Take time to enjoy those things you love." Instead, she put aside the dusting, forgot the laundry and ignored the vacuum sweeper a few hours a week to indulge in tea, books, and a purring cat.

Today, I have shelves stacked with books and a houseful of cats. The hot drink at my side when I read is freshly brewed coffee with sugar, no milk. I give my mom full credit for the growing and keeping of these passions. She knew the things we have to do in life change through the years, but the things we love only grow more precious to us.

~Teresa Hoy

39

The Birthday

Adolescence is a period of rapid changes. Between the ages of 12 and 17, for example, a parent ages as much as 20 years.

~Author Unknown

After my brother and I began school, my mother got the first full-time job she'd had since getting married. It was important to her to regain some independence and meet some new people. Yet, somehow, she also managed to find the time and energy to keep our home looking immaculate and to make sure we always ate healthy, delicious meals.

Of course, having to live with three men wasn't easy. My father worked long hours and also spent time with his friends at the pub and the local bowls club. My brother and I liked to bicker and argue over every little thing. On top of that, there was the usual mess associated with a household of men — wet towels on the bathroom floor, clothes and toys scattered like confetti in our bedrooms and the tell-tale signs across a freshly washed floor that someone hadn't wiped their feet before coming inside.

"I didn't do it," I'd say.

"Well, I didn't do it, either," my brother would echo.

Mum wouldn't even bother asking Dad.

"It looks like it was Mr. Nobody again," she'd say with a sigh.

To my shame, my brother and I would sometimes be so aggravating that we would bring our mother close to tears, and I think we even succeeded a couple of times. Fresh arguments would then ensue.

"Look what you've done now!" I'd snap.

"You did it, not me," he'd counter.

"Will you two just SHUT UP!" my mother would scream, nearly going out of her mind.

"You two must really hate me," she said once.

"No I don't," we'd chorus, pointing at each other. "I hate him!"

It seemed my mother could never win, and no matter what she tried, peaceful times in our house never lasted for very long.

In my fourteenth year, Mum developed an interest in her origins and began researching our family tree. I don't know how many hours she put in writing letters to distant family members scattered all over Australia and around the world. We didn't have a computer then, so everything was at the mercy of the postal system.

And still on top of this, she kept a perfect home, cooked wonderful and interesting meals and put up with a moody teenager and a husband who spent even more time away from home.

Around this same time, I developed a modicum of maturity. I could appreciate how hard Mum worked for us and how difficult it sometimes was for her to live with all the tension that pervaded our house. It was then I decided to do something really special for her upcoming birthday. I wanted to show her how much I really loved her.

My grandparents lived across town and one day after school I rode my bike over to ask them a favor.

"It's Mum's birthday soon," I began, "and I was thinking of having a surprise party for her."

"What a fantastic idea," said Nan.

"I was wondering if I could have it here?" I asked.

Nan looked at Granddad and I knew from their expressions that I hadn't quite won them over yet.

"It's just an afternoon tea, but with a cake and presents. And I'll pay for everything," I said.

I meant it, too. I'd been working at the local supermarket for six months and had accumulated a few dollars, which would just about cover the goodies we'd need for the party. I wouldn't have much left over, but Mum was worth it.

Nan smiled.

"Of course you can," she replied. "Just tell us what to do."

Feeling as pleased as punch that my plans could now go ahead, I began to make a mental list of all the things I'd have to do. The first thing was to invite my guests. I rode my bike all over town, paying a visit to each of my mother's three best friends to give them the details. Then, over the following week, I bought supplies for the party, sneaking them around to my grandparents' house for them to keep until they were needed.

"But how do we get Mum over here without her suspecting anything?" I asked Nan.

Not much ever got past my mother. Her knowledge of the things that went on behind her back was astounding, sometimes baffling.

"I know," said Nan. "We'll tell her that a relative from the east is popping in to visit us and that they have some information for her family tree."

At that moment, I thought my Nan was the cleverest person in the world.

"That's fantastic, Nan!" I gushed. "That is just so... fantastic!"

The following day, Nan rang my mother to tell her the news. Finally, Saturday came.

"I'm going to hang out with Michael," I told my mother after lunch.

She didn't notice I was wearing my next-to-best clothes.

I raced around to my grandparents' house and found that Nan and Granddad had already set out the coffee cups, plates, snacks and had even bought a couple of bottles of wine for the occasion. The cake looked amazing with a ring of unlit candles standing up in the whipped cream. I blew up a few balloons to add to the party atmosphere.

One by one, the guests rolled up with their presents, but I was so full of anticipation that I didn't perform my duties as host very well.

I paid more attention to the front window, waiting for my mother to arrive, than I did to the people I'd invited to help celebrate her birthday.

"Here she is," I shouted, as I watched her walking down the path toward the house, her arm cradling a stack of files, notepads and photos. I could tell she didn't suspect a thing.

The doorbell rang.

Nan answered.

"Sorry I'm a bit late," I heard my mother say. She always said that even though she was never late.

Footsteps. Footsteps coming down the short hallway toward the kitchen. Then she appeared.

"Surprise!" we all shouted.

The look on my mother's face was worth a million dollars. Her mouth was agape and her eyes watered.

We started singing "Happy Birthday" as Mum choked back her tears. The smile on her face was wider than I had ever seen it before.

"It was all his idea," said my granddad.

I think I blushed.

"Happy Birthday, Mum," I said, giving her a big hug. "I love you."

~Wayne Summers

40

Our Evenings
with Alex Trebek

What we want is to see the child in pursuit of knowledge,
and not knowledge in pursuit of the child.
~George Bernard Shaw

t's been a very long day. But it's evening now and for the next
thirty minutes, I can put today behind me and enjoy myself with
a special hobby. When I enter our family room, the sound that
I've heard so many times before blares out from the television. "This
is Jeopardy!"

That's right—I love watching and playing the popular game
show. I wouldn't miss a single episode. I can't wait to see what new
suit the always-debonair host Alex Trebek will wear each night and
who the contestants are.

I always root for the contestants who are from my home state of
Massachusetts. And of course, I gloat when I get an answer right and
the contestants do not. There's a sense of superiority when I answer
a question correctly. For just that moment, you're the smartest kid in
the class and you know it. Oooh, that feels good. What a rush!

I have a partner in crime with this obsession. My mother is
also a big fan of the show. We spend the thirty minutes of the show
in a friendly competition, shouting out the answers as quickly as
possible.

Mom and I are evenly matched competitors. Our brains are full of useless bits of trivia that are necessary to excel at *Jeopardy!* Anything involving history or geography she aces—while my knowledge of trivia relating to politics and pop culture is solid. When it comes to a category involving television or movies, it's a draw to see which of us can shout out the answer first.

There are some good categories in tonight's show. "Good" meaning categories where we have a strong chance of knowing the answers. And the game begins.

"Advertising Slogans for $200," says a contestant.

"This product gets the red out," says Alex.

"What is Visine?" the two of us shout out simultaneously. This is going to be so easy.

"Name that Comedian for $400," says a contestant.

"This is Al Sleet, your hippie dippie weatherman," says Alex.

"Who is George Carlin?" I say.

"Origin of the Specious for $400," says a contestant.

"Altar-bound Jennifer Wilbanks's 2005 kidnapping proved to be less than true, so she was given this two-word nickname," says Alex.

"Who is the Runaway Bride?" says Mom.

"Origin of the Specious for $600," says a contestant.

"This Caribbean leader's reported baseball tryouts for the major leagues in the '40s never happened," says Alex.

"Who is Fidel Castro?" Mom says.

Mom was always a smart lady. She easily could have enrolled in college, but few women of that generation had that option. She married and had five children. There were more options for me so I went to college and pursued a career.

Despite our different paths, five nights a week, we have something in common. When we watch the show, we don't keep score. That's not the point. We simply enjoy spending some time together having fun playing *Jeopardy!*

"Swimmers for $800," says a contestant.

"Qualified Navy submariners wear these creatures on their uniforms; sonar operators sometimes hear them in the deep," says Alex.

"What are dolphins?" I say.

"Mamma Mea for $800," says a contestant.

"An early sign of this one-word disease is Koplik's Disease, which can be seen on the insides of the cheeks," says Alex.

"What are measles?" I say.

The minutes fly by and before we know it, Alex announces that it's time for final jeopardy. The category is Famous Names.

"The Grady Gammage Memorial Auditorium at Arizona State University was the last major public building that he designed," says Alex.

The familiar *Jeopardy!* theme song begins to play as the contestants try to remember the answer. Architecture is not my strong suit. Alex Trebek has stumped me. The seconds tick away and I haven't a clue as to what the correct response is.

My mother says, "Frank Lloyd Wright."

I smile at her. She didn't phrase it in the form of a question, but her response is right. I guess Mom can still teach me a thing or two.

• • •

My mother passed away in 2008. I still watch *Jeopardy!* although it isn't the same without my maternal competitor. But I feel close to her when I watch. Watching the show reminds me that the greatest gift Mom gave me was a passion for learning and to always have fun. These attributes help me in my travels through life every single day.

~Maryanne Curran

Dark Winter

Are we not like two volumes of one book?
~Marceline Desbordes-Valmore

I opened my eyes, only to see darkness. A cool whisper of wind drifted through my window. All was dark in my bedroom, except for my windowsill that was illuminated by a soft outdoor light. The black sky was decorated with snowflakes, each drifting toward the cold, waiting ground. Silence touched every corner of my room. Dawn was yet to come, so I decided to go and make myself a cup of hot chocolate. As the water boiled, I gazed out the kitchen window and quietly said, "Winter truly is my favorite season." I pressed my hand up against the frosty window. I poured the steaming water into my mug, along with a teaspoon of cocoa powder. I caught a final glance of my handprint as I dragged my feet along the cold tile floor toward my front door. I turned the metal knob, and took a step onto the damp, wooden porch.

A brisk current of wind pushed against my cheek. I sat down on the shining black bench, curving my neck backwards to stare at the stars. Their silvery glow reflected off my driveway's pavement. The bitter cold nipped at my ankles, but I didn't mind. Here, in this moonlit moment, I had no one to impress. The echoing stress that once filled my mind had drifted away, into the depths of the sky. I finished my hot chocolate and tiptoed back inside so as not to wake anyone.

To my surprise, my mom walked out of the kitchen, passing me by as I headed for the dishwasher to put away my mug. As she passed me, she shot a fierce beam of happiness straight from her eyes to mine, with the corners of her mouth pulling upwards. It was a short stare of hope and love, the kind you can't fake. I looked upwards to the kitchen window, and saw a second handprint, slightly larger than mine, placed beside the one I had made minutes earlier. Together, the two handprints started to fade into the dark night.

~Lucas Youmans, age 14

42

The Gift in the Plain Brown Wrapper

At fourteen you don't need sickness or death for tragedy.
~Jessamyn West

The ad jumped out at me from the pages of the teen magazine that had arrived in our mailbox that very afternoon. And suddenly, I knew I needed a fuller bust for the summer—just like the swimsuit-clad blonde in the ad proclaimed. From the looks of her, her wish for a fuller bust had already come true. All because of the fabulous Mark Eden bust developer.

I had a year's worth of teen magazines stacked on my bookshelf—all of them filled with similar ads. Next to the magazines was a coffee can that held the meager amount of money I'd managed to save from babysitting and my weekly allowance. Not nearly enough to order a Mark Eden. Glancing at myself in the full-length mirror that hung on the back of my bedroom door, I sighed. Fourteen years old, stick-skinny, and still wearing a training bra. If anyone in the world needed a bust developer, it was me. But I knew there was no way my mother was going to advance me the money to buy one.

"You know times are tough right now for your dad and me," she'd said when, months earlier, I'd tentatively broached the subject. "We can't afford to throw money away on something as silly as a bust developer. And besides, honey, that thing can't possibly work. It's nothing but a gimmick." She planted a kiss on my cheek. "You're perfect just the way you are."

"You're wrong, Mom!" I wanted to shout. "It worked for Jan. She's been wearing a size 36C ever since she started using her Mark Eden! And you're wrong about me being perfect. I'm not. I'm flat as a pancake."

Jan was my best friend. Last year, she'd saved up enough to buy a Mark Eden by skipping school lunch every day for weeks and pocketing the money. I was with her when she filled out the order form and was at her house the day the package finally arrived. With trembling hands, she tore open the plain brown wrapper to reveal a pink plastic clamshell-like device held together with a heavy-duty spring designed to provide resistance. Included in the package was a booklet describing in detail eight separate exercises that would soon result in a breathtaking bust line.

It wasn't long before Jan's body really was transformed. She and I credited her thrice-daily workouts with the Mark Eden, accompanied always by the mantra WE MUST, WE MUST, WE MUST INCREASE OUR BUST. Never mind that during that time, puberty hit Jan full force. Never mind that she quit the basketball team and gained ten pounds. Never mind that her grandma, her mom, and both older sisters were well-endowed.

Jan was a 36C because of the Mark Eden and we both knew it.

I, on the other hand, seemed destined to have a boyish figure for the rest of my life. Who could blame me for gazing longingly at the Mark Eden ad every time a new magazine arrived in the mail? And wishing that, just in case my mom changed her mind about it being a gimmick, Christmas and my December 29th birthday weren't several months away.

So imagine my surprise when I arrived home from school one day in late spring to find a package in a plain brown wrapper, addressed to me, in the middle of my bed. With trembling hands, I tore it open. Inside was a pink plastic clamshell-like device and a booklet describing in detail eight exercises that would guarantee me new curves in practically no time at all.

I snatched it up and ran out of the bedroom. "Mom!" I hollered. "Where are you, Mom?" I found her in the backyard taking laundry down from the clothesline. "Look what I found in my room!" I said, waving the Mark Eden at her.

"Well, my goodness," Mom said, trying her best to act surprised and knowing full well that neither of us was fooled. "I wonder where in the world this came from?"

I laughed and hugged her tight. "It's the best present I ever got."

•••

Forty years later, it's hard to imagine the stick-skinny girl whose reflection stared back at me from the full-length mirror in my bedroom. My mother is dead and gone now. My own two daughters are—thank goodness—so accepting of their own bodies that, growing up, they never once asked for a Mark Eden bust developer. Not that they'd likely ever heard of one. Because in 1981, amid allegations of mail fraud, the Mark Eden disappeared from the market.

But it will never disappear from my memory. Nor will the image of my mother standing beneath the clothesline in our backyard holding a pink plastic clamshell-like device at chest level, and squeezing with all her might. Say it with me, honey, she told me. WE MUST, WE MUST, WE MUST INCREASE OUR BUST.

Thanks, Mom.

~Jennie Ivey

43

A Different Kind of Experience

A daughter is a day brightener and a heart warmer.
~Author Unknown

I went into high school knowing that my experience would be different from many of my fellow classmates. My mother was an English teacher at the school that I would be attending.

I was immune to the nerves that many students must overcome their first year. Instead, I strode onto the campus with confidence. Not only did I have the added security of knowing that my mother was only a few buildings away, I also knew my way around. I had no fear of getting lost, or apprehension about my teachers, many of whom I had known for years through my mother. All of this was great, but the real surprise was when I got to see my mother in an entirely different light.

I will forever remember lunches with my mother. Instead of sitting out in the Arizona heat or in the crowded cafeteria, I chose to eat with my mother and a regular group of her students in her air-conditioned classroom. I enjoyed these times immensely, because I felt that we grew closer than ever before. I was able to see first hand how much her students—my peers—liked her. Why else would they voluntarily opt to spend their lunch hour with a teacher?

I also learned how comfortable other people felt around my mother. Students and other teachers would constantly come to my mom to reveal personal problems they were experiencing, while also seeking advice. Her kindness and generosity became apparent to me.

Still, the most altering experiences for me were the two opportunities I had to be a teacher's assistant for my mom. When not grading papers or performing other tasks, I would sit in the back of her classroom and just watch her teach. Not only was she an excellent presenter of information, she also incorporated comedy into her lessons. She would tell stories about our crazy relatives and make jokes that even teenagers today would understand. This was the most shocking revelation to me; I learned that my mother was aware of what was occurring in my generation, perhaps more than I was. As a result of her masterful teaching, the students responded in a positive way. They were learning while also enjoying my mother's wonderful sense of humor.

In what seemed like an instant, my high school graduation arrived. I could not believe that four years had really passed. This unique experience with my mother was at an end, and I was sad.

People warned me that going to the school where my mother taught would be a mistake. But throughout high school I never once regretted attending my mother's school. Looking back at my high school years, I recall the new students that I met and a few exceptional teachers that I was given the privilege to know. But the most extraordinary part of high school was having my mother right there with me.

~Christina Flaaen

Duck and Cover

There can never be enough said of the virtues,
dangers, the power of a shared laugh.
~Françoise Sagan

My mom and I are super close. Not only do we look like sisters (seriously, I'm her carbon copy—it's freaky), but we share everything. Every date I go on, bad or good, I promptly tell her all about it in gory detail. She gives me the benefit of her years of experience with men, providing top-notch advice, even if I'm not always thrilled at the time with what it is. She's my go-to-gal for all things male. Which is why I was shocked when my sometimes... ahem, interesting... dating experiences prompted my mom to start dating again too. Honestly, I was proud of her. It's one thing to endure the soul-crushing, ego-bruising of the dating world as a young, single thing. It's another to subject yourself to it post-menopause. So, I gave Mom the full support she always gave me as she re-entered the dating world.

A few weeks into it, Mom and I found ourselves at the mall, and I asked how the dating life was faring.

"Ahn." She shrugged.

"Hmm. Just ahn?"

"Well, okay, there is this one guy...."

So, I dragged out of her that she'd met a retired former Navy captain. The first date went okay, and he asked her out for a second for that coming weekend. "But," she said, "he wants to go hiking."

Normally, hiking would be fun. But when a gal first meets a new guy, it's probably best not to go out in the wilderness alone with him until you really know each other. So, I agreed with Mom, hiking was not such a hot idea. As we strolled through the department stores, I offered up some alternatives. A stroll through the park? (Kind of like "hike-light.") A walk through downtown? (Like hiking, but with window shopping.) Dinner and a movie? (Okay, nothing like hiking, but always a good reason to snuggle.)

We were making our way through men's wear, and I was running out of ideas, when Mom stopped mid-step, abruptly veered right, and power-walked in the opposite direction.

Okay....

I jogged after her, catching up just as she shoved me around the corner into housewares.

"What was that about?" I asked.

Mom pointed over my shoulder. "That was my date!"

I turned around. "Who?"

"The captain. The hiker wanna-be. He's here!"

No. Way. What are the chances? So, I peaked around the corner just in time to see a tall, blond guy paying for a pair of gray slacks. He was slim, with a thick head of hair, strong jaw. Not bad, really. So, I said, "Let's go say hi."

Mom shook her head. "No way. Can't."

"Why not?"

"I'm wearing the same outfit I wore on the date!"

I looked down. She was in flat-front jeans, black shirt, white cropped jacket. Pretty cute date outfit, actually.

"If he sees me in this again, he'll think I don't have any other clothes!"

I did a giggle/snort thing. But, I had to agree. In her situation, I'd totally duck, too. No one wants to be a fashion one-hit wonder.

So, we hid out in housewares (picking up a new set of margarita glasses and a nacho bowl along the way) while waiting for him to finish shopping. Finally the coast looked clear and we emerged, making our way back through the mall.

Only we made it just three stores in before Mom grabbed my arm and veered left again.

I looked up.

The blond guy was dead ahead, coming right toward us.

Mom propelled me into the nearest store, shoving me behind a rack of A-line skirts.

"Oh, no. Oh, crap. Do you think he saw me?"

I peaked out. He was making a beeline for the exit, no sign of recognition on his face.

"Doesn't look like it."

She sighed with relief. "Oh, thank God." Then her expression relaxed and she let out a little laugh. "You know, maybe I will go on that second date. We're obviously a lot more alike than I thought."

"Because he likes the mall, too?" Hey, I gotta admit, a Navy captain who does power shopping is almost too good to be true.

But Mom shook her head, the laughter growing now. "No. Because he was dressed in the exact same outfit, too!"

Thanks, Mom, for your amazing sense of humor in any situation!

~Gemma Halliday

Secret Stash

A daughter is a little girl who grows up to be a friend.
~Author Unknown

Our household looked like a North Wales Library annex. There was a stack of kid books for my five-year-old sister, Lori. My brother, David, age ten, enjoyed sports and adventure novels. At age fifteen, I devoured Dickens, Agatha Christie, and any young adult novel in reach. Medical novels captured my mother's eye, and finally my father nabbed the latest *Car and Driver* magazines. It was an eclectic mix, and my mother kept our books in circulation. The old green Ford station wagon must have logged a million miles between our Oakland Place home and the library on Summit Street, especially during the summer when school was out.

"Mom, may we stop at the library on the way?"

It didn't matter the location of "on the way." It could have been to the YMCA, the grocery store, or to my friend Joan's house. The answer was always, "Yes, but we better get a move on so we have enough time." My mother, all five feet of her, moved quickly and efficiently. Her graying reddish hair, short and neatly combed, waved over her forehead and she was crisply dressed in slacks, a blouse and Keds sneakers. She rounded up shirts for the dry cleaners, a grocery list, her pile of books, and all of us from upstairs, downstairs, and the basement. Green eyes flashing, she brokered no nonsense and we dutifully piled into the car with minimal elbowing.

The North Wales Library was located in the basement of the

ancient elementary school. We didn't walk down steps to enter. Basically the school was built on a bit of a hillside and the library was tucked into the hill. So we walked to the side of the school and opened huge, heavy wooden doors. Slender dirty windows at the ceiling allowed in a hazy light, and being underground, the library was always cool, even on a steamy August day. As the doors thudded behind us, we strolled in quietly with only a squeak of our sneakers announcing our arrival.

Mrs. Schultz's cloud of white hair and her smiling face emerged from behind the heavy oak library desk, a dark contrast to this tiny woman. I remember her as shorter than my mother and as the loudest librarian on Earth. Her cheer and hearty laugh distracted many a scholar.

"Mrs. Crowther," she said to my mother. "I'm so glad you came by because I was going to call you. I have the latest Irwin Shaw." She bustled to her desk and opened a huge drawer. That's where she held the newest books aside for her favorite readers. At that time, there were no reserve lists or computerized requests. Popular books were distributed at Mrs. Schultz's discretion. Like Christmas, you wanted to be on her Nice List.

We turned in our old books and disbursed to corners of the library while my mother thanked Mrs. Schultz and chatted. I helped Lori with her picture book selections and then wandered aimlessly, sliding out some titles to read the blurbs. "Joanne, I think I have something you'll like," boomed the librarian. I scurried up front and Mrs. Schultz pulled out *The Thorn Birds* by Colleen McCullough. "Now, you have to share," she said with a wink.

Looking at my mother, Mrs. Schultz continued, "It's a tad racy in parts, but Joanne is one of my advanced readers. You'll both enjoy the book." I hugged it to my chest after she finished her card stamp process and handwritten log out.

"Thank you so much. I can't wait to begin," I said. She finished checkout for David and Lori and we all waved goodbye. Mom dropped me at my friend's house and we agreed she'd pick me up at five. I hated to relinquish *The Thorn Birds*, but knew I'd begin reading it that night.

My afternoon was full of laughs, and then at home, dinner was the usual family chitchat over meatball sandwiches. After cleanup, I went to my room, checking the bed and my desk before hollering downstairs, "Hey Mom, where's my library book?" I heard a muffled reply and bounded down the steps to find my mother sitting in her chair, with her feet up, reading *The Thorn Birds*. Her sheepish smile said it all. She'd come home, begun the book and now was hooked. Uh-oh.

This was the first of many reading battles—a friendly tug of war over *Rich Man, Poor Man, Love Story*, etc. She'd read during the day, neglecting a few chores. I'd read at night or on weekends. I knew when my mother was at an exceptional turning point in a book, because she'd stall me. "Joanne, how about if you help Lori with her leaf collection?" she'd suggest. Or, "Joanne, your turn to clear the table, please." No point in protesting. Her back was turned and she was down the hall in a flash to get to a chapter.

Reading was certainly a joy she passed to all of us kids, not to mention the art of disappearing. *The Thorn Birds* set the standard for stealth. It also opened up a new dialogue between us, since I now could read some popular adult fiction. "So, have you read the part where Meggie does...?"

"No, don't give it away," I said and covered my ears. Later we could talk about Australia, the priest, and forbidden love. I think we both set a world record for reading that book, and were reluctant to see it end.

That Saturday morning, Mom appeared in my doorway and said the magic words. "We need to return your *Thorn Birds*. Want to go to the library and see what Mrs. Schultz has stashed for us this week?"

~Joanne Faries

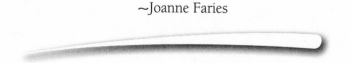

Walking with Mom

Making the decision to have a child is momentous. It is to decide forever to have your heart go walking around outside your body.
~Elizabeth Stone

I took my first steps holding a basketball-sized kids' play ball, the plastic kind you buy at the supermarket. It was painted with a picture of Grover from *Sesame Street*, my favorite TV show character at the time. We called it my "Magic Grover Ball" because I didn't think I could walk unless I was holding it. In fact, I wouldn't even try to walk without it. It was as though the ball was filled with helium to hold me upright.

Then one day, the unthinkable happened. My Magic Grover Ball popped.

Oh no! What would I do without my safety net? I would never walk again. I was doomed to a lifetime of rug-burned knees from crawling too quickly across carpet floors.

Then my mother stepped in. After drying my tears, she positioned herself a few feet away from me—miles away, in my fifteen-month-old eyes—and spread her arms wide.

"Dallas," she coaxed. "Come here. Come to Mommy."

I stood there on my wobbly legs, still not quite believing my Magic Grover Ball was really gone. Didn't Mommy see that? Didn't she realize there was no way I could walk to her without it?

"Come on, Dallas. Walk to Mommy."

As my parents tell the story, I looked my mother square in the eyes and took a few hesitant steps that turned into a few more-confident steps that turned into walking all the way across the floor—without the assistance of my Magic Grover Ball. Yes, I was walking all by myself. Well, along with a little helpful encouragement from my mom.

My mother and I went on almost-daily walks around the neighborhood. As I learned to walk better, I would climb out of my stroller sometimes and walk beside her for a bit, holding her hand. Later, of course, we ditched the stroller altogether.

My memories of these walks are filled with a sense of comfort and peace: Gentle sunlight filtering through the leaves of trees above, the warm security of my mother's hand in mine, the sound of her voice as we sang songs together. Who could ask for anything more?

As I've grown older, things have changed, as things always do. Life has grown more hectic. A college student now, I take a full load of courses, run my nonprofit literacy foundation, volunteer as a tutor for grade-school kids, and work as a freelance writer. My mother, Lisa, is the head of her planning department at work, does volunteer activities and keeps our household running. But, no matter how busy we get, one aspect of our lives has remained the same over the years: our shared walks.

Whenever I come home from college to visit, Mom and I take our family dog for a one-mile stroll around the neighborhood, just as we used to do every evening when I still lived at home. Now, as then, we talk. We laugh. We bond. I know when I have something to say, Mom will always listen. If I have a problem, she will always help me figure out a way to fix it.

After all, Mom and I have struggled through our share of problems together. Born three months prematurely, I weighed a mere two pounds, six ounces, and at the time, the chances that I would survive were extremely small. My mother was stricken with preeclampsia, a terrifying collection of syllables that threatened her life as well as mine. A team of surgeons flew me to the Neonatal Intensive Care Unit in Fresno, California because the small Santa Maria hospital where I was born didn't have the specialists or NICU equipment to care for me. Meanwhile, my mom stayed put in the Intensive Care Unit in Santa Maria for three days and wasn't well enough to come visit me for a few weeks.

Miraculously, both my mother and I are portraits of health now, twenty-one years later. Perhaps that is in part because of our walks. A ritual that started when I was in preschool has evolved into a passionate bond for us.

Together, we have hiked up to the peak of Mt. Whitney, the tallest mountain in the contiguous United States at 14,500 feet, and down to the bottom of the Grand Canyon. We have walked through shopping malls searching for the perfect dress for my prom; we have walked through college campuses searching for the perfect college. And, at my college graduation this spring when I walk across the stage to receive my diploma, I know I won't be walking alone. Though physically cheering me on from the stands, in spirit my mom will be right there alongside me as I step across the threshold into my future.

It's funny. Looking back now, I realize that my special first steps weren't because of my "Magic Grover Ball" after all. The real magic came from my mother's love and encouragement. I know her magic will remain with me as I walk along life's winding paths, and even when I have a little wobbly-legged toddler of my own one day. Thanks to Mom, I'll know just what to do.

"Come on," I'll say. "Let's go for a walk."

~Dallas Woodburn

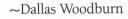

Thanks Mom

Mom to the Rescue

Driving Me Home

When you have brought up kids,
there are memories you store directly in your tear ducts.
~Robert Brault, www.robertbrault.com

t was a cold New England night. I hurried out of work, then ran the few blocks from my office to the subway, barely catching the uptown train. I was bundled in a wool suit and overcoat and lugging an enormous briefcase, which was weighed down by an inordinate amount of paper. I remember sitting on the train as I caught my breath, my cheeks burning from hot blood beneath cold skin, and sweat seeping through my silk blouse. The train was crowded. Not an inch to move, to remove a layer of wool for the long ride to Grand Central Station. So I sat there and let the thoughts I had left at my desk catch up and resume their hold.

I was several months into a two-year position as a financial analyst at one of the best investment banks in the world. The job had been my trophy after a lifetime (short as it may have been at the time) of arduous work. Competitive skating, straight A's through high school and college, a major in economics. I was following in my father's footsteps, only taking even greater strides. I was making proud my immigrant family on both sides that had struggled through poverty and unemployment. This was the job I had coveted for as long as I could recall, since before I even knew what it was. And I was absolutely miserable.

The train arrived at Grand Central. I shuffled through the masses to a second track and a second train. I lived in New York, but tonight I was heading out to Connecticut to shop for a dress with my mother. I can't remember what the dress was for. I rarely wore dresses outside of work, and I was far too busy to date, try to date, or do anything remotely social. In fact, I was too busy to be visiting my mother in the middle of the week. I worked in Mergers and Acquisitions, and the department's reputation for inhuman hours had been fully confirmed. For sixty, seventy, eighty hours a week, I put together financial models, traveled to client meetings and fed on a constant diet of stress and anxiety. This night "off" would surely be paid for over the weekend. But we had made the plan and I needed the break. More than that, I needed to see my mother.

She picked me up in a station wagon, one of many she drove over the years. With five children nineteen years apart, she had been mothering since she was nineteen herself. I was the second oldest, just twenty years younger than she, and our relationship had become more of a friendship now that I was an adult. It was odd, then, that I had not confided in her about how miserable I was. I hadn't kept it from my friends or older sister. In fact, I was so unhappy that I probably told half of New York by the time it was over. Even when my parents expressed their concern over the hours I was putting in and the family gatherings I was frequently missing, I shrugged it off as no big deal.

So I drove with my mother, first to the house to say hello to my dad, then to the nearby mall. We talked about the event I was attending and which shops we would hit. At a certain point, it was just my mother who was talking while I listened and nodded. And held back tears. I was at a breaking point. It wasn't just the hours. I can see that now, being the mother of three boys, divorced, working every free minute I have. My life now laughs out loud at what I thought was a hard workweek as an investment banker. The real problem was that I had chosen the wrong profession. I could not find an ounce of passion for the work, even in the face of tremendous financial rewards down the line. Having now found that passion, it is so clear. Hard work doing something you love is bliss. Hard work doing something else is misery.

We pulled into the garage at the mall and I got out of the car. But that was as far as I could go.

"Mom," I said, tears now streaming down. She looked at me from across the top of the car and her face changed in an instant.

"Wendy! What's wrong?" She was suddenly everything a mother becomes when her child falls apart—shocked, worried and frantically pulling together every resource, every weapon and shield she can find to go to battle with the enemy that dares hurt one of her own.

She rushed to my side of the car and pulled me into her arms. I cried, she comforted. Then, when the rush of emotion subsided, I told her.

"I don't know if I can make it another year and a half."

She didn't have an answer then, except to quickly call my father from a payphone and tell him she wouldn't be home for a while. She had to drive their daughter back to New York.

I told her it wasn't necessary, that I could just take the train. But she wouldn't hear of it. We didn't shop that night, and I honestly don't remember ever buying a dress. Instead, we got back in the car and drove the hour and a half to my apartment in the city. Along the way, I told her every detail of my misery and every plan I had to escape when my time was up. I told her how I thought I might want to be a lawyer, to practice in a field that I felt passionately about, even if it meant struggling financially. She listened, chiming in now and again to mirror both my anger and excitement. "That's outrageous!" she said. Then, "Oh, that's a great idea."

I have no idea what she was thinking that night. Given our family's long journey to financial security, I imagine there was some fear lurking within her. After so many years of hard work, their parents', theirs, and mine, I was now talking about swapping a golden ticket for civil service. Still, none of that, if it was present, came through.

When we arrived at my apartment, my mother parked the car and walked me all the way to my door. I think about that night often.

Not because it was the only moment when my mother went above and beyond the call of duty. Far from it. Those moments are infinite. I remember that night because it represents to me the essence of being a mother, a parent, a family. Those two years were a dark time in my life, and for the most part, I got through them on my own. But sometimes just knowing someone is there to drive you home from the mall is the very thing that makes it possible to face the greatest challenges life hands out.

I will always be thankful to my mother for that night, and for all that it represents about her and the kind of mother she has always been.

~Wendy Walker

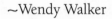

Pretty Baby

A daughter may outgrow your lap, but she will never outgrow your heart.
~Author Unknown

"Are you sure you'll be okay?" my mom asked.

"Yeah. At least, I think so."

I said goodbye and hung up the phone, discouraged and sad. Never before had I longed for my mother to be with me as I did at that moment. I inhaled deeply, but it didn't stop the tears. I was facing yet another medical test, and I really wanted my mom.

At twenty-four, after completing graduate school, I moved from my home state. I hadn't been in Colorado long when the stomach pain returned. Several years of tests and inaccurate diagnoses hadn't solved them. Now it was clear that the doctors' latest ideas, which held such promise and had worked for a while, had failed. I dried my eyes and tried not to think about the colonoscopy I'd face the next week. My first one, an intimidating prospect. The relatively short test challenges nearly anyone. But, the test simply wasn't worth my mom taking off work and driving or flying so far—not for a quick outpatient procedure. I wouldn't let her do it. Nevertheless, I felt incredibly alone.

"Honey. I'm sending you something," Mom said at the end of the call. "Watch for it."

She's such a mom, I thought. The gentle teasing, even in my own mind, made me smile a little. But, really, what could she send that could make this better?

A few days later, just a day before the test, a box arrived. I opened the package and gently shifted the tissue paper. Glancing inside, my eyes watered. Pretty Baby? My very first childhood friend—the treasured doll with the cuddly soft body and plastic head. I caressed the brown, molded hair, and looked into the blue eyes that really blinked. My fingers touched the line of marker I'd somehow tattooed her with when I was little. I'd named her Pretty Baby when I was two. I thought it a perfectly appropriate name for, well, such a pretty baby.

I held her close, taking the hug I knew Mom sent her to carry to me. Through the tears, my heart found strength. I dried my eyes and chuckled. Really, this is ridiculous, I thought. Aren't I supposed to be grown up?

But Mom knew, as moms somehow do, exactly what I needed. Right then, I needed support, even as I grew into a stronger, more independent woman. I set my doll on my bed, where she remained for a couple of days before being carefully packed away again. Giving her one last pat, I smiled, knowing I could handle whatever would come... and that I wasn't alone.

~Diane Gardner

Loving Hands

A mother's arms are made of tenderness and children sleep soundly in them.
~Victor Hugo

I lay confused on the crinkly white paper that covered the emergency room bed. The circuits in my brain weren't connecting properly. I was aware that a man had walked into my apartment in New York City through my unlocked front door and brutally attacked me, but I couldn't absorb it. In raping me, he seemed to have eviscerated me, too. I was empty, a shell.

"Hi, Sweetheart," I heard someone say through the haze. I turned toward the door. It was Mom.

Suddenly tears surged.

"Hi, Mom," I said, my voice cracking.

How did she find me? I knew that my mom must have driven into New York City from where she lives, a suburb about an hour away. I didn't know how she knew where I was, in what hospital, in what room. The last thing I remembered is that I had called her from my apartment while waiting for the ambulance to arrive. I had called and left a tearful message on her answering machine, something to the effect of: "Mom, I've been attacked. Come quick."

When I was growing up, my mom and I had a bedtime routine. As an only child of a single mom, most nights were the same. Mom would open my closet door and an automatic light would offer a sliver of brightness. She would turn off the two lights in my room while I jumped into bed. She would pull up my covers, or if they were already up, she would tuck in the sheets around me. If I felt sick or sad, or sometimes just because she wanted to, she would sit down on the edge of my bed—a simple sign that she would stay a little bit longer. Oh, how I loved that! She would smile and tell me that she loved me. She would push the hair from my eyes and look at me in a special way. She'd cock her head, silently measuring how much she loved me. These were also the times she would easily agree to give me a back rub when I asked. I would quickly turn over, smiling inside, plump with her affection, her hands filling me with love.

The night I was attacked, after I had been swabbed, tested, vaccinated and had six vials of blood drawn, Mom took me back to her home—my childhood home. It was almost midnight when we pulled into the garage. I climbed out of the back seat and closed the door. How long had it been since I was driven in my mother's car, she in the driver's seat and me buckled safely in the back? These were the things I could think about.

After we entered the house, she offered me food. Silently, I shook my head and walked straight to my old bedroom. Exhaustion, shock, adrenaline, and the various medicines given to me at the hospital had depleted me.

In bed, I rolled onto my side, pulled up my knees, and turned into the smallest human ball I possibly could. I wanted my body to disappear. All the rest of me was seemingly gone. Yet in all the quiet and emptiness, pain exploded within me. Darting through my veins, weaving through my mind, it was only physical weakness that kept me inert. I begged God to let me explode so that I did not have to feel the pain.

I became aware of Mom's hand gently moving across my back. I thought about her sitting there, on the edge of my bed, just like she always had. Slowly I unfurled myself from the fetal position. Instead of the pain, I focused on her hand. A hand that connected us. A hand that somehow eased the hurt. I realized then that the awful man had taken so much from me that day, but not everything. Not my life, and not my mom. And, like always, mom knew just what to do. It might have been a few years, but I was still her little girl, and she remembered.

~Jennifer Quasha

A Mother Takes On Big Tony

When you are a mother, you are never really alone in your thoughts. A
mother always has to think twice, once for herself and once for her child.
~Sophia Loren

"Can you do me a favor?" asked Bobby, a seventh grade classmate at my junior high school. "Hold this extra pair of shoes for me and I'll pick them up right after the final bell."

Now I had a dilemma. I was new at school and Bobby was one of the first friends that I had met. But I had a dental appointment after school and my mother said that she would pick me up in front of the school building at the end of the day. What was I going to do?

My mother was always late. So I told Bobby that I would wait for him at my locker with his shoes for a few minutes after the final bell. We agreed that if he did not show up at my locker after ten minutes I would just leave his shoes in a brown bag on the floor in front of my locker. He thanked me and said, "That would be perfect."

When the final bell rang at 3:15, I ran to my locker. I turned the corner of the hallway where my locker was located, expecting to see Bobby waiting for me. But Bobby was nowhere in sight. I opened my locker and took out Bobby's shoes. Still no Bobby. One minute, ten minutes, twenty minutes. No Bobby. It was 3:45 and the hallways were empty. Only the school janitor remained.

I put Bobby's shoes in a brown paper bag and put the sack down next to my locker. I then bolted to meet my mother, who told me she had been waiting for me since 3:13. Probably the first time she hadn't been late in my entire life.

The next day, I saw Bobby at school.

"Where are my shoes?" he asked.

I explained to him that I had left the shoes in a brown paper bag on the floor next to my locker. I reminded him that he had agreed to this plan.

Bobby screamed, "THOSE SHOES—THOSE SHOES—THEY WERE NOT MY SHOES! THEY WERE TONY'S SHOES!"

I swallowed and meekly said, "You mean Big Tony?"

Bobby did not have to say one word. The look on his face told me I was right. I was your typical thirteen-year-old: Five-foot-two, voice cracking, poor complexion. But Tony, well, basically, he was a big man. He was over six feet tall, bearded, with an Afro that had a metal rake in it.

I ran all the way home, surprising my parents.

"What's the matter? Are you feeling okay?" my mother asked.

I explained the problem with Big Tony's shoes and begged my parents for help.

My father was quick to respond: "We'll just buy Tony some other shoes. Mike, find out what size he wears."

But before my father could finish his sentence, my mother erupted, "We're not buying any shoes for Tony. This is ridiculous. Mike told the boy if he wasn't at his locker he would just leave the shoes and that's exactly what he did. I don't want to hear anyone saying anything more about buying shoes!"

I was shocked. My mother had always been so passive with everything, but now when her son was probably going to be murdered, she was standing up and being assertive. I did not know what to do.

My mother quickly replied, "Mike—you go back to school this instant and I don't want to hear one more word about any kind of shoes!"

As I slowly and meekly exited from my house, I heard my mother's remark as I closed the door: "Ridiculous!"

I was petrified at school when I returned. I pondered which would be worse: Getting punched by Big Tony or facing the wrath of my mother.

I could not concentrate on anything that day except the sounding of the final bell. At half past two, the door to my classroom creaked open. I was even more petrified as I looked to see who was on the other side.

Thankfully, it was just Mrs. Brown, the frail sixty-eight-year-old school secretary, who whispered something to Mrs. Johnson, my fifth period math teacher. Mrs. Johnson quickly told the class, "Boys and girls, it seems Mr. Watson (the school assistant principal) wants to talk to Mike."

I walked with Mrs. Brown to Mr. Watson's office. As I sat in the chair outside his office, I could feel my knees shaking as I wondered which was worse—being punched by Big Tony, facing the wrath of my mother, or being questioned by the assistant principal.

Mr. Watson exited from his office and motioned me to join him there. I rose from my chair, entered his office, and sat down—but my knees refused to stop knocking.

However, I was so surprised by his meek voice when he began speaking: "Mike, I understand you're having some problems with a Tony Peterson. Ordinarily I don't condone students fighting, however I'll make an exception in this case. Mike, you can fight Tony."

As he said those words, my mouth dropped open. Was he kidding? How was I going to fight Big Tony?

I left Mr. Watson's office feeling petrified. I could not concentrate on anything, except avoiding Tony. However, as the days went by Tony did not even say anything to me. In the ensuing weeks I realized what must have happened: my parents must have called Mr. Watson and threatened dire consequences if I were hurt. In turn Mr. Watson must have persuaded Tony to leave me alone.

True, if my father would have had his way, I would have been able to sleep much easier that eventful evening when Tony lost his shoes. However, because my mother got her way, I learned many lessons, including that money cannot buy everything. For that, and for so much more, I say, "Thank you, mom."

~Michael Jordan Segal

From Mama to Mom

Grandmother—a wonderful mother with lots of practice.
~Author Unknown

On more than one occasion, my mother shared with me the story of how she was the first to know when she was pregnant. At the age of forty-four, my mother sat nervously in the doctor's office awaiting her results. As she waited, she wondered what on Earth she would do with a baby at this time in her life. Her oldest two children were almost twenty-three and twenty, and her youngest child was a junior in high school.

She knew right away she was pregnant with me even though the doctor didn't think that could be the case. He very gently explained to my mother that she had reached that magical age where things begin to change for a woman. The doctor was a renowned physician in this small community in Texas. His medical knowledge and experience were highly respected. He was confident of his diagnosis.

Mama, on the other hand, was a non-assuming, non-assertive woman, but, on this day, she openly disagreed with the good doctor. Although it had been quite some time, she knew how she felt when she was expecting a baby.

After what seemed to be an endless wait, the doctor came into the office with an apology for doubting my mother's wisdom and then gave her a congratulatory hug. He informed her that she was about three months pregnant.

My mama was the most nurturing person I have ever known.

She was always kind and gentle but, when needed, she could draw a strong and bold line that I knew darn well I had better not cross.

As a young kid, I realized my parents were much older than my friends' parents. It wasn't too hard to figure out. None of my friends' parents had His and Her denture cups in the bathroom or arthritis creams lining their shelves.

Not to mention, when someone was introduced to Mama, the first thing they would ask her was if she was my grandmother. She would always blush and answer them with, "No, she is my daughter, my very own little blessing from God."

When I got old enough to understand the ways of nature, I had the awful realization that my parents might die before I was grown. That thought scared me senseless. I finally decided to ask my mama what would happen to me if something happened to her. She did not hesitate and answered with an emphatic, "Never worry about that. God will always take care of you. Long after I am gone, God will still take care of you."

At the time, I felt my mother might have been giving my question the slip. Like the doctor who delivered me, I did not realize how wise my mother was.

I lost my mama too soon. A massive heart attack stole her away less than three months after my husband and I were married. I was only twenty and I was not ready to let her go.

I thought it was poor timing on God's part. I had just gotten married when he took her. What should have been one of the happiest years in my life had become the saddest.

My new mother-in-law, whom I call Mom, checked in on me regularly. She called and came by to see how I was doing.

People often complain about their mothers-in-law. I hear about how bossy, nosy, and interfering they can be. Mom is not like that and I have never complained about her, not once.

I remember a time when we were at a community function. As I sat at the table with Mom, an elderly man walked up and said, "jak sa mas" which means, "How are you?" in Polish. These words happen to be the only words in Polish that I understand. Mom replied quickly with, "Please speak English. My daughter-in-law does not understand Polish." I will always cherish my mother-in-law's response. It demonstrated such respect for me.

Then there were the births of our three sons. Each time Mom came to stay a few days to help me. I always appreciated her being there.

I was especially appreciative of her when my first son, Grayson, was born. Mom came in carrying not only her suitcase but also invaluable experience in caring for a baby. Being the eldest of six siblings and having ten children of her own definitely prepared Mom for mothering.

I, on the other hand, did not have that kind of experience, so when I brought home my newborn baby boy, I felt incompetent. In fact, I was scared to death.

Over the course of three days, I asked her hundreds of questions and watched every move she made with my baby to learn from her words and her actions.

On the fourth day, Mom announced that it was now time for her to go home. I clung to her arm as she tried to leave, pleading while she walked toward her car. "Please don't go. I don't know how to care for this little baby." She promptly replied with, "Yes, you do. You will do fine," and then added, "But if you have any questions just call me."

Ben and I have now been married for thirty-five years. During those years, Mom has given me all of the motherly love and care I needed.

My mother-in-law is now ninety-four years old. She lives in a nursing home. Physically, she has some challenges, but she has an incredible memory and an alert mind. She ends every call with, "I love you."

Now I get it. The timing of my mother's death was not wrong, nor was it unfair. I can hear, again, my wise mother saying, "God will take care of you. Long after I am gone, God will still take care of you."

~Jane Dunn Wiatrek

Fear

... mother is one to whom you hurry when you are troubled.
~Emily Dickinson

"Here we are." My mother held my hand as she led me through the front door of the shop into a small, cramped room. I'd been taking piano with my mother for two years and I was really excited about learning how to play the recorder. At least, I had been excited.

Now that I was here at the studio, I was a little nervous. Make that a lot nervous. Okay, I was terrified.

We sat on plastic chairs facing a large black curtain. From the other side of the curtain, the instructor yelled at a student for not practicing enough. I shrunk down in my seat.

My mother leaned closer. "I'm not sure I agree with his teaching methods. I'll understand if you want to leave and find a different instructor."

I licked my lips. What if the next instructor was worse? Sure, my mother never yelled at her piano students, but she was my mother. Maybe all other music instructors were mean or maybe it was just those who taught the recorder.

"No. I'm fine." I clenched my knees together.

On the wall clock, the minute hand slowly crept toward the twelve. I couldn't decide whether I wanted time to move faster or stop all together. I told myself that I was a big boy and that I could handle this.

The curtain parted and a smaller boy stepped out, a recorder clutched to his chest. He stumbled across the floor, dropped onto a nearby seat and stared at the door we'd entered earlier.

I said, "Hello," but he didn't even nod.

My mother squeezed my hand.

The instructor poked his head out from behind the curtain and barked he'd be ready for me shortly. The curtain closed.

My mother gave me another squeeze. "Good luck. I'm sure you'll do just great." She paused. "Once your lesson starts, I'm going to run across the street to the bakery to buy some decorations for your birthday cake."

What? The room dimmed and I felt my chest pound. The thought of being trapped here made me want to cry. "No. Please stay."

"I'll stay if you want, but then you won't have any decorations on your cake. This is my only opportunity to get them."

"I'd rather you stayed."

She kissed me on the top of the head. "Okay, honey. I'll be right here then, waiting for you to come out."

I no longer remember that first recorder lesson, or how many more I attended before finally quitting. I don't know what decorations my mother had intended to buy, or recall anything about the birthday cake I received the next day.

What I do remember is that when I suffered a crisis of confidence and asked my mother to stay with me, she did so with uncritical love.

Her kind words were music to my ears that still warm my heart.

~Stephen D. Rogers

53

To Keep Me from the Rain

Sweater, n.: garment worn by child when its mother is feeling chilly.
~Ambrose Bierce

Sometimes it's not the huge sacrifices that mums make, or even the countless things they do day in and day out that make you realize what really special people they are.

It was just a typical, dull and windy January day here in the North East of Scotland. When I left home for the office where I worked in the next town, the weather forecasters said, "Windy and cold, but no rain." Naturally, by the time I was about to leave work in the early evening, it was absolutely pouring!

My office was close to the bus stop so that was no problem; I just shot out the door and onto the bus. Unfortunately, once I got home to Montrose, I had about a mile to walk from the bus stop to my home. Normally on a night like that, if my husband were home, he would get into the car and come and get me. That morning, he had told me that he was putting the car in for a service and it would be in overnight.

As I stepped off the bus that night to walk home, I struggled to get my tiny umbrella to go up in the strong wind. It had a sunny pattern on it and was obviously designed for a very light shower somewhere on the Mediterranean, not a Scottish downpour! Then, suddenly and to my amazement, I heard my mum's voice.

"Quickly! Come under here, before you get soaked!"

I nipped under my bigger umbrella and stared at Mum in surprise. "What on Earth are you doing here in this weather?" I asked her. My mum was eighty-three that year, and although fit and healthy, she didn't normally like going out in strong wind and heavy rain. In fact, if we got a few days like that, I usually nipped round to her house to make sure she didn't run out of anything.

"You said to come round for tea tonight, but I came early before the rain got too heavy. Eric told me that your car was in for a service and I saw your big umbrella lying on the chair. I guessed you had taken it out to bring with you, but had forgotten it. Eric was on the telephone, so I just picked it up and came out so that I could meet you and you wouldn't get soaked!"

My mum passed away the following year. This simple act remains embedded in my mind, and reminds me how completely my mum loved me. She wouldn't have gone out in the wind and rain for herself, but, at eighty-three, she never gave a second thought about braving the elements so I wouldn't get wet.

I just stopped and gave her a hug. And, as the umbrella shook all over the place, she asked, "What on Earth was that for?"

Only she could possibly have asked me that!

~Joyce Stark

54

With Ears Wide Open

One good mother is worth a hundred schoolmasters.
~George Herbert

At my ophthalmologist's appointment, the doctor stood across the dimly lit room. A powerful overhead bulb illuminated the eye chart.

"Carol, please tell me the letters on this line," the physician said. Suddenly, my stomach felt queasy. Since I viewed objects like a person looking down a gun barrel, I tilted my head to find the best position. My head began to ache from frustration. The tedious eye exam became more uncomfortable. Over and over again, the doctor flashed light into one eye and then the other. My anxious parents sat quietly nearby.

"Hold still," the doctor said, as he looked into my eyes with an instrument. I watched him as he rubbed his chin. He seemed to be thinking hard. Then I leaned so close to hear what the doctor told my parents that I almost slipped off the leather seat. Mom reached out and pushed me back on the examining chair. Her helping hand was always there.

The doctor cleared his throat and sighed. "One day, Carol's sight may get worse," he told my parents. "The disease in her retina can lead to blindness."

"Does everyone in this room think I am invisible?" I thought. "They're talking about me like I'm not here."

On the way home, no one said a word. In the back seat of our

1960 Buick, I pulled off my expensive cat-eye glasses. I had pleaded with my parents to buy them so I'd look cool. Now, I played with them like they were a toy since my hands would not keep still. I squeezed my eyes closed and turned my head toward the window. One day, would I only imagine the scenery beyond the glass rather than see it?

That September, I entered middle school. Most nights I had homework that included chapters to read. This wasn't elementary school where the sight-saving class that I attended protected me like a cocoon. I wanted to be the butterfly spreading my wings, but these teachers might not understand my limitations. Could I keep up with the other kids? The armful of books I lugged home made my shoulders sag.

Still, a good report card brought plenty of praise at home. Determined to read, and with my nose a couple of inches from the page, I tired easily. When I read a chapter on my own, the words slipped off the page into inky pools. My head throbbed. Teardrops fell on each page, blurring the words even more.

Studying alone seemed more grown up, but then I did not have audio books and electronic devices like kids do now. Instead, Mom volunteered to read out loud. I sat on my bed frowning, with my arms folded over my chest. Mom sat across from me. She ignored my "sour puss" and kept reading. Who wants their parent to read to them at thirteen?

I bit my lip as I wondered what Mom would rather be doing. She worked part-time, cleaned the house, cooked and spent time with Grandma. In spite of being so busy, she showed up in my room like clockwork, "Let's hit the books." I knew that Mom would have to rush to get ready for work that evening. Before I could make an excuse, a smile spread over her face as she sat next to me. She put on her reading glasses. Mom always thought those glasses made her look old. To me, she looked like a teacher.

As Mom turned the page of my textbook, I heard the beat of music coming from my brother's room. Loud rhythms and pounding drums shook the walls. I sighed. The weird music meant that David had finished his homework. In my room, Mom's voice competed with the ticking of the clock. We spent the next couple of hours working on my assignment.

Then, Mom's voice picked up a rhythm as she read aloud. My mind focused on the description of the story. Reading about people, places and descriptions of other times in history took me out of my funk. Instead of brooding about my failing sight, empathy for others seeped into my soul. English and history books made me curious about other people's challenges and how they coped.

My mother asked, "Carol, do you know the meaning of resolute?" My head jerked up.

"I think it means not to give up, but we'd better check." The fat dictionary sat nearby.

"Having a brand new dictionary should help us with our reading," Mom smiled.

Suddenly, the "reading bug" bit us, so we read on. To me, even though I could not use my eyes to fix on each passage, my mind lit up with every new book.

Being forced to concentrate on listening, I found a way to keep my marks up and compete with the other kids. When the teacher asked a question, I raised my hand with confidence. I learned that my ears were as powerful as the eyes of a person with perfect vision. Teachers praised me for having a good memory.

Most of all, friends often shared their problems with me. My talent for listening made me popular. Teenage "sleepovers" had a different twist. My friends and I had "read overs" with freshly baked cookies supplied by Mom. Of course, the gossip we read about Hollywood movie stars in fan magazines couldn't have been the literature Mom had in mind.

The dread of losing my sight has become a reality. Now that I've lost all of my vision, I realize that Mom's reading created a world with 360 degrees of sound. Thanks to Mom, my sense of hearing now allows me to see. Hope has replaced my helpless feelings. This was the most precious gift from mother to child.

~Carol Chiodo Fleischman

55

The Day My Mother Took On the Principal

Courage is what it takes to stand up and speak;
courage is also what it takes to sit down and listen.
~Winston Churchill

When I was growing up, I was ashamed of my mom. She dressed funny, talked differently and wasn't like other moms in our neighborhood. She always wore an apron over a cotton housedress that was faded and sometimes patched. She spoke broken English with a German accent. While other mothers had perms and wore high heels when they dressed up, Mom wore her hair in braids around her head, and her dress shoes were sturdy black Oxfords. But I was proud of her when she stood up to a haughty principal who had accused my brother of damaging school property.

My nine-year-old brother had come home crying one day because he'd been blamed for carving names on a locker room bench.

"I didn't do it, Mom," he said, "but Mr. Johnson won't believe me."

My mom was furious. She took off her apron, put on a better dress and told me to come along. We didn't have a car, so we walked the three blocks to school. The principal kept us waiting, which made her even angrier. When she finally got to see him, her voice was in high pitch. I stood behind her.

"My son is innocent," she announced loudly. "I teach my kids right from wrong. I want to see the damage."

"Now, Mrs. Mayer, please sit down," Mr. Johnson said, forcing a smile. His face was flushed as he closed the door. He ignored my presence. "Let's talk about this calmly."

"You accuse my son of bad things and you want me to be calm?" My mother spat out the words, glaring at the man who provided her a chair.

"Several people say they saw your son do it," the principal said, sitting down behind his desk, peering over his glasses. He shuffled some papers.

"What people? They are liars!"

"We found the knife in his desk," Mr. Johnson folded his hands over his waist.

"Roland doesn't own a knife. Somebody else put it there. He would never do such thing. You are crazy to believe he did this."

Several teachers had gathered outside the principal's office. They could hear my mother from the hall. They watched her storm out of the office. One of them stopped her.

"Mrs. Mayer, I'm Miss Sweeney," the teacher said softly. "I don't think Johnny was responsible for the damage," she said. "I'll try to find out who is."

"Oh, thank you," my mother said, squeezing the teacher's hand. "Please help me."

When we got home, my mother didn't say a word. She started peeling potatoes with more than her usual precision. She heated some water on the stove. After a while, she called Roland and told him what she had done.

"Aw, Mom, you're just going to make things worse," he groaned. He dug his hands in his pockets. "Now all the kids'll call me a Mama-baby."

"They're not going to punish you for something you didn't do. Miss Sweeney's going to find out who did it."

"Well, I know who did it."

"What? You know? How come you don't say?" Mom didn't understand the tattletale concept.

"Because if they knew I told, they'd beat me up." Roland buried his head in his hands. I felt sorry for him, even though he sometimes aggravated me.

"What kind of a country is this that kids beat up kids? If your father were here, this would not happen." She shook her head in disgust and checked the potatoes on the stove. My father had died when we were babies so we never really knew him. I only knew that the picture of him in my mother's bedroom showed a tall, serious-looking man with a black mustache and a receding hairline.

The next day at school, the principal called Roland to his office. I agonized with him as he waited in the outer room. I hung around the hall where he couldn't see me. He stared at the clock as it inched toward 3:15, his appointment time. I knew he was afraid he would be suspended and have to pay for the damage. He had no way to get the money and I dreaded what my mother might do. Finally, Mr. Johnson opened his door.

"Roland Mayer? Come in." The principal looked at him sternly. Roland followed him into the office and stood in front of the large desk. Mr. Johnson left the door ajar.

"Sit down," Mr. Johnson said, motioning to a chair. He leaned back in his chair, folded his hands on top of his potbelly and eyed my brother. "Your mother speaks her mind pretty strongly."

"Yes, sir," Roland said quietly.

"Well, you know we have witnesses."

"I didn't do it. The knife wasn't mine and anyone who says I did it is lying." Roland's voice was steady, even though I'm sure his knees were shaking.

Mr. Johnson was silent for a long time. Then he heaved a deep sigh. "I'll continue to investigate the incident," he said. "You may go."

The next day, Miss Sweeney spoke to her classes about the responsibility a person has to reveal what they know about any wrongdoing so that innocent people are not punished. There were whispers in the halls all day, but no one came forth. Then, the following morning a note appeared on the teacher's desk with the names of two boys who had been seen with knives the day the benches were damaged. She gave Mr. Johnson the information and when the boys were confronted, loopholes in their stories convinced him of their guilt. The chagrined principal later apologized to my mother and brother. I was glad my mother stood up to Mr. Johnson, even with her lack of education and poor English.

Roland was embarrassed at all the attention he got from the teachers and kids the next few days. But things soon got back to normal and he was as aggravating as ever. The experience, however, gave me a new respect for my mother.

~Barbara Mayer

56

Lifeline

There is no instinct like that of the heart.
~Lord Byron

t was only when the voices inside my head became so loud that they drowned everything else out that I admitted this was a battle I couldn't win. Not alone. I needed help, but in addition to the auditory hallucinations, I was suffering acute paranoia. I trusted no one. They were all out to get me, stealing my energy, my life force, plotting to kill me.

Over the last few months, the paranoia had grown. Malevolent whispers murmuring through my psyche insisted that my food was poisoned. The simple act of sharing a meal with another human being had become torture. How was I to playact, behave as if nothing was wrong, when I knew what they were all up to? I had no stomach for such charades, and I began to withdraw deeper and deeper into myself, shunning company, becoming a recluse.

Naturally, my friends and family knew something was wrong. They kept calling and dropping by, but this only convinced me more that they were out to get me, trying to get close enough for the kill.

I was heartbroken. Even as the voices insisted there were murderous plots underfoot, a part of me didn't want to believe, refused to believe, the very people I loved could be trying to destroy me. However, the voices couldn't be ignored, not when they were inside my very head. The repeated warnings raised doubts, and I didn't know what to believe. It seemed easiest to retreat into solitude, even though I was never alone. The voices were always with me.

Psychosis crept up on me, and within a few months, I had completely unraveled. I could no longer carry on a conversation with another person. The noise in my head was simply too loud. I could no longer fake normalcy. Throughout the last few months, I'd been showing a mask to the world, hiding how I was coming undone.

But I couldn't fool her, not my mother. No matter the excuses I made to not see her, she kept calling and coming by. She'd bring food, and I'd pretend not to be hungry, promising to eat it later, but secretly waiting until she left so I could throw it in the trash without tasting it.

The voices spared no one. No connection, no bond was sacred. I grappled with pained disbelief. How could my mother be trying to poison me? She wasn't she. She was an imposter. Somebody had made a switch. I was powerless. Everybody I loved was at risk. They, my secret enemies, were striking through the ones I loved. I had to play along. Having a breakdown was what they wanted. I knew my thoughts would be considered crazy. I was terrified of confiding what I was thinking to anyone, terrified of being locked up.

I kept up the charade for months, but then came the day it became too much. My mother showed up at my doorstep. I could barely hear her. I couldn't fake normal anymore, and this time she wouldn't be put off. She kept asking me what was wrong. I claimed I didn't feel well. She insisted I see a doctor.

But I couldn't see a doctor. Of course, they would use my doctor to get to me. He'd prescribe me poison. He'd have me locked up. It was a trap.

I battled my demons while trying to hold a normal conversation with my mother, trying to put her off with plausible excuses. Finally, I broke down. Once I started crying, I couldn't stop. The whole story came out. I rambled. I raved. My mother called the doctor and told the secretary it was an emergency so we could get in right away. She drove me down there within the hour. I had no more energy to fight. Soul weary, I decided to take a chance, to trust her.

I was prescribed anti-psychotics, and some guardian angel watching over me whispered in my ear that I should take the pills. My mother took me home with her. For the next few weeks, she made sure I took my pills and she took care of me.

The madness slowly receded. The voices stilled into silence. The delusional thoughts started to seem absurd. I was told I'd had a schizophrenic episode. No amount of willpower, no commands to myself to act normal had worked. By trying to be strong and handle things myself, I had slowly descended into hell, and no matter how hard I tried, I couldn't claw my way out.

I had needed help, and help came. My mother. My lifeline. She never gave up on me. She wouldn't take no for an answer. Thank you.

~Kiran Kaur

A Quest for Answers

Biology is the least of what makes someone a mother.
~Oprah Winfrey

Many things in our lives go unexplained. Some things we wish we could find reasons for, mainly the times in our lives when we feel desperation and sorrow. Sometimes we need a scapegoat, somewhere to put the blame. And some of us spend years trying to find answers that are unattainable.

The quest for answers can lead us down a dark and narrow path, many times alone and afraid, with the walls closing in. The "why" and "how" become more than just questions, they become our only source of motivation to do anything in life. Without those questions hammering at our conscious mind, we have nothing.

Then there are the other events in life that go unexplained. Wonderful things happen to us and we praise the heavens, exclaiming our thanks without wondering how they came about. We find ourselves blissful and become afraid to even ask the questions. Should we test fate? It has handed us something amazing; who are we to ask "why?" We revel in our happiness, enjoying it, knowing it could end at any time. The bad stuff could be just around the corner.

When I was but a few months old, my mother took me to a social gathering at the home of a relative. The gathering brought together women of all ages and relations to the hostess—some sisters, some aunts, some friends. As a saleswoman presented her plastic wares, passing bowls with airtight lids, my mother passed me to open arms that would rather examine the cooing bundle before them than the latest trend in food storage.

The years passed after that simple gathering of women and my young life changed so much. At the age of three and a half, it was missing one major component: a mother. The woman who once cuddled me and smiled at me found herself in need of answers, leaving me in search of them. Did she feel desperation and sorrow? Was something missing in her life that she needed to find? In her search for the "what" and "why," she left my father in need of his own answers. How would he raise a child all by himself? How would he make a happy and complete life for us?

Our resolution came in the form of a woman. She entered into our lives when we needed her most and was more than willing to step into the roles of wife and mother. She cared for us both with compassion and love, giving us what we were missing, and more. She guided me as a child, bandaging my wounds, cooling my warm head. When I was a young adult, she helped me through the awkwardness and guided me on the right paths. I owe so much of who I am to her. She has taught me firsthand how important it is to love unconditionally and how a family is not necessarily made by blood. A family consists of the people who care for you without hesitation or limitation.

As an adult, many times I wanted to ask my mother why she left, if she found what she was looking for. And if she did, was it much better than what she left behind? But the more I wondered about the answers, the less I really wanted them. I wasn't going to become one of those people on a never-ending quest for the truth. I was happy with my reality. How could the answers really help me? I felt they wouldn't. My life was forever changed when she left, but because of one amazing woman, it became the best life for me.

Not too long ago, my family was reminiscing about old memories and talking about how my father and stepmother met. I had heard the story several times, recalling how his brother and her sister, who'd been friends for years, introduced them at a summer cookout. I was also told that she, the woman who raised me and has loved me for most of my life, the one I call "Mom," was at that same social gathering of women when I was but a few months old. She came to the party out of friendly obligation, like so many of us do for girlfriends who host candle parties, home decoration parties and the like. She came expecting to purchase a new bowl or kitchen gadget and in addition, got the chance to hold the party's tiniest guest. She held me in her arms that day, the future unknown to her as well, in a moment of unsung serendipity. A connection was made between us, I am sure of that, and that force is what brought her to us some three years later. That connection has kept our family strong for more than twenty-five years.

As I look forward to the future, with her as a grandmother to my children, I feel warmth and happiness that they will also know her generosity. We are a family, through all of life's turns, bends and loop-de-loops. I know that if a time ever comes when we find ourselves in need of answers, we'll find them together.

~Stephanie Haefner

Carrying Me Forward

Pain is inevitable. Suffering is optional.
~M. Kathleen Casey

Dear Mom,

Thank you for carrying me. Not just in your womb, but thank you for carrying me to the ambulance when I was six. Thank you for carrying me emotionally through an ordeal from a split-second accident that would change the course of our lives. Thank you for carrying me through life as an amputee.

It was many years ago and you and Dad had just bought your dream apartment on Central Park West. I remember on the weekends we had so much fun at our farm in upstate New York. The horseback riding, snowmobiling, bike riding, fishing, swimming in ponds and playing with all the farm animals was amazing.

Until that fateful summer. You must regret ever letting me sleep at a friend's house that night. But who could have known? Kids do crazy things. I have often wondered how you coped with that phone call telling you I was stuck in a farm conveyor belt and that it looked like your precious six-year-old daughter was going to lose her leg. How did you watch rescue workers spend three hours sawing free my mangled, manure-ridden leg? How did you watch me screaming and scared, not knowing if I would live or die? How courageous you were when the rescue squad told me to stop screaming and you, instead, whispered in my ear, "Keep screaming, darling."

How did we endure three long summer months in hospitals

trying to ward off the gangrene, trying to save my leg? I remember when you had to go to the bathroom. I was so scared that you had to leave the door open so I could see you from my hospital bed. I remember your friends taking turns bringing you changes of clothing. Together we survived many operations, oxygen tents, hyperbaric chambers and many painful bandage changes. We endured a nightmare with you begging the nurses to wet the bandages before the doctors came to rip them off. When the ripping began and the pain was unbearable, you would bite my thigh to divert the pain. Imagine that, the horror of such a scene. Thank you for never leaving me. *Thank you.*

You tried your best to save my leg, but by August, we had to have my foot amputated. How great you were when you told me I would be like the Bionic Woman! You set the tone for what happened next. When they removed the rest of my leg, the emotional impact was minimal because of how you handled me. Being an amputee was not, and has never been, a dominating factor in my life. You did not allow me, or anyone, to dwell on it. You treated me like every other kid, encouraging strong academics, music, and a healthy social life. You never accepted anything less than my best effort. Thank you for never treating me differently.

Despite my bulky, below-the-knee prosthetic leg, you had me swimming in the ocean, running to parties, and cheering for my high school football team! You instilled in me confidence and security, which served as armor to thwart strange looks, uncomfortable questions and pity. Thank you for giving me the skills to cope.

When I grew up, I attended Vassar College, visited Paris and graduated from law school. I could have never done any of this without the support, love and security you gave me. I always felt like the luckiest girl in the world. I always felt so pretty, so beautiful, despite the leg.

Today, I am a proud mother of three children close to my age when I slipped into the conveyor belt. I wish you were here to help me raise them. Being a mother, I find myself with a true and profound understanding of what you endured. Your pain must have been agonizing and unbearable — far worse than mine. Throughout it all, you were elegant, stunning and graceful, inside and out. You were the purest and most honest example of a lady. If I can be one tenth of what you were as a woman, wife and mother then I will have realized my dreams. You were one of a kind.

Mom, this letter is to let you know that I am okay. Somehow, you paved a life for me with minimal suffering from this ordeal. Thank you for making my profound loss feel like nothing. Thank you for allowing me to live, love and grow up normally. Thank you for never letting me see your sadness, depression, fear or rage. You led by example. Thank you for giving me the strength and courage that I am now able to carry forward to other amputees in need of help. Thank you for teaching me that it is life's imperfections that make it all the more beautiful.

~Aviva Drescher

Chapter 6

Thanks Mom

What Goes Around

Chicken Soup from the Heart

Leftovers in their less visible form are called memories.
Stored in the refrigerator of the mind and the cupboard of the heart.
~Thomas Fuller

The icy February wind cut a path across the cemetery and bore a hole straight through my heart. As we turned away from the grave and headed back toward the car, snowflakes began to flutter down around us. Mom hated the cold but we left her behind, under a blanket of snow. I was powerless to reverse the weather, as I was powerless to reverse the cancer that had taken her from me in the first place. Hours after we were home, a frosty wind still chilled my heart. How would I ever replace the warmth of my mother's love? She was gone, and it was gone with her.

Over the next week, I drove back and forth from Mom's apartment sorting and distributing her belongings. On the last day of her lease, I brought a picnic cooler with me into which I deposited the contents of her freezer. At the end of the day, I closed the door on her apartment, turned in the keys at the front desk and started down the path of my life that would never again lead me to Mom's front door. I cried all the way home.

The dismal winter days that followed found me navigating on autopilot. I shuttled back and forth from work, muddling through tasks and daily chores with little enthusiasm for any of it. The endless loop of "Mom" tape that played over and over in my head distracted me from being able to concentrate on anything but my aching heart and how empty my life was without her.

When I woke up one Saturday morning with the sniffles and a fever, it seemed quite appropriate to be just as miserable physically as I was in my heart. Thank goodness I had the whole weekend to pull the covers up over my head and lock out my husband, my friends and anyone else in the world waiting for me to emerge from the cloud of grief that had swallowed me whole.

On Sunday afternoon before my husband left to do the food shopping, he mentioned that there was a pot of warm soup on the stove should my appetite return before he did. As I ventured down to the kitchen, the scent of Mom's legendary chicken soup got stronger with every step I took. This broth was renowned for working wonders on the common cold. But how could this be? Sure enough though, I lifted the lid on the pot and Mom's steamy chicken soup all but called my name.

I breathed in deeply, allowing it to penetrate every pore. Then I walked over to the sink and spied the empty container with a label marked, "Chicken Soup—January," in Mom's shaky handwriting. It was probably the last batch she made. I must have brought it home in the cooler the day I emptied her freezer.

Sitting at the kitchen table, I savored every drop of the broth and left all the wide egg noodles to the last. Then I placed a small dollop of butter on top of the noodles and, as it started to melt, I gently coaxed it through the bowl, watching it glisten on each noodle and anticipating the goodness of every bite.

My mother took no shortcuts when it came to feeding her family and everything we ate was always made from scratch. Though I grew to have great appreciation for her kitchen skills, I remember as a child begging her to let me have a thermos full of canned soup and maybe some apple sauce from a jar, because that's what I saw all the other kids pull out of their lunch boxes at school. Mom would roll her eyes and say, "Not while there is breath in my body," with a Katharine Hepburn kind of dramatic flare and an "absolutely not" tone in her voice.

When I finished the last noodle, I looked over at the stove and imagined Mom standing there stirring the pot and adding the carrots and celery as I had watched her do so many times in my life. Then I noticed something. I noticed that I was warm and full of chicken soup and, of all things, I was smiling—something I hadn't done since the cancer word was uttered only ninety-nine days before she passed away.

"Not while there's breath in my body." Those words replayed in my head several times until, finally, I laughed out loud. Leave it to my mother to find a way to care for me long after breath had left her body forever. For the next six months or so, whenever I was most lonely for Mom, I would slip a surprise package out of the freezer, heat it up, and bask in the pleasure of one of her homemade specialties. Every bite made me stronger and encouraged my appetite for the joy of living.

Mom is gone five years now, but her famous soup lives on. It was just last week that I finally got the courage to try and reproduce that delicious taste. As I gathered the ingredients, I reached for the bay leaves, remembering how Mom insisted this was the item that set her chicken soup heads above the rest. "Don't be shy with the bay leaves," she would say. "Add three or four good-sized leaves to the pot. That's what gives it all the good flavor." Bay leaves do give it a distinctive flavor, but they also impart an unmistakably delicious aroma that beckons anyone nearby.

My memories of all the wonderful meals we shared around Mom's kitchen table kept me company as I chopped the carrots and onions and placed them into the pot with the chicken. Soon after the broth began to simmer, the comforting and familiar scent of homemade chicken soup filled my own kitchen and I could hardly wait to serve it.

When we sat down to supper, I ladled the soup into a bowl for my husband and passed a warm, crusty loaf of bread across the table to him. After one taste, he dropped the spoon into his bowl and said,

"Please don't tell me I'm eating soup that's been in the freezer for five years." Oh, how I laughed when he said it, but I glowed with pride on the inside. Just before I went to sleep that night, I whispered a thank you to Mom for tucking safely into my heart, not only the recipe for her delicious chicken soup, but also the lasting memory of her enduring love.

~Annmarie B. Tait

Mom's Jewel

The most precious jewels are not made of stone, but of flesh.
~Robert Ludlum

When I was a little girl, I loved to look through my mother's jewelry box whenever my parents went out for the night. There were glittering treasures hidden inside, like the gems in a pirate's chest. I would try on each piece of Mom's jewelry and create a story to go with it. A rhinestone-studded pin in the shape of a crown seemed to give me a queen's permission to indulge my imagination. Slithery golden chains wrapped themselves like snakes around my arms so I could pretend to be Cleopatra. Mom had more rings than I had fingers and I wore each one in turn, assigning them individual magical powers that I could activate with a mere touch. There were earrings galore; some dangled halfway down my neck and swayed as I became an Egyptian dancer, while those with tiny pearls rested delicately on my earlobes, making me royalty for the evening.

What I loved best of all, though, was a bracelet with milky stones that my mother called moonstones. If I was lucky, and my mother wore something else that night, I could have the bracelet for myself until I went to bed. I would pretend that I reached into the sky and captured the moon's light, which I tucked carefully into each stone. Then I would hold the bracelet up to the window to compare it to the moon. The moon was always bigger but the stones were brighter. They seemed to glow more brilliantly as the moon got larger until, at full moon, they were so beautiful I had to hold my breath in wonder. One day, when I was grown up, I decided, I would wear the moon on my wrist whenever I wanted, even during the day. And I would be an elegant lady. At that time, the most elegant lady I could think of was my mother.

I had a grown family of my own when my mother was diagnosed with Alzheimer's disease. By that time, her jewelry box was forgotten and my fantasies were long transformed into more realistic possibilities. My mother, too, had been transformed. There was no elegance in the slow passage into dementia or in the anger of her despair. There was nothing elegant about having my mother, the woman who had so carefully tended to her hair and her nails, looking dirty and unkempt. I saw no beauty in the wildness of her eyes.

When Mom died, the moonstone bracelet became mine. I sent it to a jeweler to be polished and thought that it would be one of my treasured possessions, a part of my mother that would shimmer with my childhood memories. It came back with the same lustrous glow I remembered. I looked at each perfect stone linked in its place along the old-fashioned silver setting. All these years later and it was still beautiful.

But I couldn't wear it. It was tied up not with my mother's elegance, but with her disappearance. Her physical body survived into her seventies, but Alzheimer's claimed her personality and spirit. I could not separate the two images. The little girl was too devastated, and the adult too traumatized, to be comforted by the moon.

I put the bracelet into a plastic bag with some of my mother's other jewelry, none of which I could wear, and stashed it in my closet. It was there that my daughter found it one day when she was visiting.

"Ooh," she said. "When did you get this?"

"It was Grandma's," I said, surprised by the catch in my throat.

She held up the bracelet and let the light shine through the translucent stones the way I had all those years before. As I watched her, I saw the bracelet again through my child's eyes. I remembered my mother in her glamorous days with her exotic wide smile, rolling her dark hair up and back into what she called a chignon as she was getting dressed for an evening out. I could almost see her turn toward me again as she once had, hold out her arm, and ask me to help her put on her jewelry. I would reach out to lock the clasp on the moonstone bracelet around her wrist and be rewarded with a hug when it clicked into place.

I snapped back to the present when my daughter asked, "Can you help me, Mom?" Her arm was outstretched in the same way my mother's had been. I fastened the bracelet around her delicate wrist. It looked perfect on her, elegant the way it was supposed to. My daughter and I found the earrings that matched and scavenged through the other pieces, taking out whatever attracted her. We cleaned them and packed them for her to take home. Now and then I will see her wearing something from Mom's jewelry box and I am glad.

I know that one day I'll be able to wear my mother's jewelry again. In the meantime, I will try to remember not my mother's craziness, but how she tried so hard not to be crazy. How in her last days in the hospital she fought to regain the physical strength she once had and struggled fiercely against the haze that washed over her. It was a royal battle worthy of a queen. And like a queen, she bestowed a most precious gift; she roused herself from a semi-conscious state, her vacant eyes suddenly coming into focus and her mind reclaiming clarity long enough to say, "I love you," the last words she spoke to me before she lapsed into a coma.

That, I realize, is the true jewel she gave me — the understanding that each of us has an inner strength. Whatever comes, I will look for my own elegance as a woman grown and tested, as a mother passing on life skills to her children, as a person discovering her value as the decades unfold. And when I turn toward the moon, I will know that no matter how beautifully a jewel glows, it is the human spirit that truly shines.

~Ferida Wolff

Just Like Mom

Mothers and daughters are closest, when daughters become mothers.
~Author Unknown

"ou are going to be just like your mother," my father would tell me when I was younger. I am pretty sure that he did not mean it as a compliment, since he would only say this to me when I disagreed with him or was being stubborn. Since I was about fifteen at the time, I was more afraid of this than anything else in my life: Even more than pimples, dating, and high school.

I was determined to never let myself become my mother. I was sure that I was going to mature into a much cooler person than my mother could ever be. I resigned myself to never judge people based on how they looked. (So what if I had a penchant for bringing home strays that were not of the small, cute, or cuddly nature?) I knew with every fiber of my being that I would never tell my daughter she couldn't stay out with her friends, or that she needed to put more clothing on before leaving the house. I would never be so stuck up about things. At least, that is what I thought at the oh-so informed age of seventeen.

My independent streak only grew as I got older, went to college and moved out on my own. I was even more determined to do things differently than my parents had. I was going to get it right. How hard could it be? I was living on my own, and yet my mother was still attempting to control my behavior.

"Shannon," she'd say each time I would tell her about my plans, "you're being stupid about this." I wondered what was stupid about wanting to go to the beach for spring break. I decided to stop telling her my plans, hoping to eliminate the motherly input.

By the age of nineteen, I was convinced that I had everything figured out. I married my high school sweetheart, and for once my parents were pleased with one of my choices. At the age of twenty-two, I gave birth to my first child, a girl.

A beautiful little girl, who owned my heart from the first moment she looked at me. Before that moment, I had strived so hard to not be like my mother. I did not want to nag, to hover, to smother. This was not to be.

As the months and years passed after my daughter's birth, I came to realize how wonderful my mother was. She loved with every fiber of her being. She protected me with a fierceness that would rival that of any mother bear. She gave up all of her dreams and wants in order to provide for me. She nagged because she knew the world was not "all puppies and roses," as I had blindly believed. She knew that loving her child was the most important gift she could ever give. And she was right.

After spending twenty-plus years striving to be the polar opposite of my mother, I realized how much I wanted to be just like her. I wanted to love my daughter the same way my mother loves me. I was no longer afraid of becoming her; I was scared to death of not being enough like her! I wanted to love, laugh, live the same way my mother had. I wanted to give my daughter the same things my mother sacrificed to give me. I saw the love of a mother from an entire different light. My mother became my hero.

My father still jokes with me, saying I am just like my mother. I smile and thank God that I am living my life in a way that allows me to fill those shoes. I still bring home strays, but I stick to those of the mammal nature these days. And now my mother laughs heartily when my daughter tests me with strays of her own.

~Shannon Scott

Finding Joy in a Time of Loss

A daughter is the happy memories of the past,
the joyful moments of the present, and the hope and promise of the future.
~Author Unknown

I grew up in an instant. No, it was not as I walked across the stage as a high school graduate or even as I walked down the aisle with my new husband. I was twenty-eight and my mother had just died. The cancer had won and I had lost. I stood there in her hospital room with one hand on her arm and the other on my growing belly. I was three months pregnant with my mother's first grandchild. At that moment, my tiny world changed forever. Despite having a wonderful husband, a large extended family and supportive friends, I felt alone. The one constant in my life was gone. Without her advice, I was unsure of my next move. Without her guidance, how would I ever be the mother she had been?

I have spent endless hours examining the relationship I shared with the incredible woman I called my mother. She was my best friend, my biggest fan and the only home I had ever known. I was her only child and she was a single mother. We were a team, and though we were not the traditional family, I would not have had it any other way. Even as an adult, I enjoyed her company above all others. We shopped, traveled and had deep conversations in which my mom would share intimate stories about her life. These talks always involved at least one bottle of wine!

My mother's pregnancy was an accident. It was not until after a near miscarriage that she realized just how much she wanted the baby she was carrying. My mother started preparing for the arrival of a daughter. She never had an ultrasound. She somehow "just knew" that I would be a girl.

My pregnancy was a little different. After learning that my mother's cancer had spread from her colon to her lungs, my husband and I decided to try for a child. I desperately wanted my mother to be a part of my child's life. I saw us taking her to our favorite clothing shops and to the spa for the first time. I saw us swimming with her in the ocean and sharing all the incredible gifts that two generations of women could provide. Yes, in my mind, my child was always a girl. I saw a daughter who would allow me to continue the traditions I had shared with my mother.

For the weeks following my mom's death, I remained focused on the baby I was carrying. I kept busy with baby preparations. I deliberated forever over which jogging stroller would be easiest to take on runs with our two dogs. I paced the aisles of Babies"R"Us for hours trying to pick out the right breast pump. I stayed busy and tried not to let my mind wander. I felt that if I allowed myself to fully comprehend the situation I was in, I would sink into a depression so deep I might not be able to return. I tried not to think about what I had lost and I attempted to ignore the void that was now a part of my daily life.

During this time, my thoughts once again turned to the sex of my unborn child. In my mind, a daughter would help replace what I had lost. I knew that I would love my child regardless of the sex, but I clung to my dream of having a daughter like it was my lifeboat in a sea of emotion that was now my life. My only comfort came from knowing that I would take on the mother role in the mother-daughter relationship. I would provide to a daughter the same guidance, unconditional love and friendship that I experienced with my own mother.

My ultrasound to determine the baby's sex was exactly one month after my mother's passing. The day brought mixed emotions. The appointment was scheduled months in advance and my mother had planned to be there for the occasion. Instead, my husband and I sat alone in the waiting room. It is an unsettling feeling to be excited, nervous and sad all at the same time. I tried not to think about her absence. I tried to focus on the magnitude of the day. I was about to see my baby. I would finally know if I should buy that pink or blue receiving blanket.

The appointment seemed to drag on endlessly. I searched the doctor's face for a sign that would tell me what I was having. And then I heard her slip as she referred to the little peanut on the ultrasound image as a "she." My heart stopped as I waited for her to confirm the prediction. She smiled and finally said we could expect a baby girl in about four months. I could no longer hold in my tears. I cried happy tears at the thought of becoming a mother to my little girl. I cried tears of sadness because I desperately wanted my own mother at that moment. My husband held me as I sat on the examining table. The doctor was confused by my breakdown and made me laugh through my tears when she said, "I'm sorry. Did you want a boy?"

I now have my little girl and my love for her is stronger than I ever imagined it could be. My mom used to say that I was the best thing she did in her life. While my life is not over, I am positive that delivering this perfect creature into our world will be my crowning achievement. I will provide to her the same unconditional love and support that helped see me through the most challenging of times. I look forward to introducing her to new places and experiences. And when she is old enough, I will share with her the intimate details of her grandmother's life so she can know the legacy that she carries within her.

~Megan Dupree

Turning Into My Mother

Of all the haunting moments of motherhood,
few rank with hearing your own words come out of your daughter's mouth.
~Victoria Secunda

kay, now it's official—I am turning into my mother! On a recent airplane trip, not only did I put all the liquids in my carry-on into the required quart-sized Ziploc, I decided to carry my other toiletries in two other plastic bags. In my defense, I was moving my purse contents hurriedly into a laptop case, which had no dividers for small items. Even as I did it, I could remember recoiling in horror when my mother used to reach into her purse and pull things out of the plastic bags she carried regularly (in public!), so much so that I bought her a set of attractive cosmetic bags she could use instead. Sigh.

My relationship with my mother has never been black and white. I don't know about you, but I've got separation issues. Being close is a double-edged sword, I think, for girls and their mothers. All the years I was growing up, Mom was prominent in our small town, civically and socially. Townspeople were always calling me by her name and telling me I looked just like her, which I found unnerving.

As an adolescent, I could not understand why my friends tolerated, and even invited, her presence when I would rather crawl under a rock than be seen in public with her. She even dragged me to a meeting of a new teen group. Okay, so the kids there ended up becoming a wonderful group of friends. Don't you just hate it when your mother's right? Still, after finding my way through some rocky middle school years and through high school, I eagerly broke away from her sphere. After college, I moved hundreds of miles away to be clear of her influence.

Flash forward twenty years. Mom moved down here to my town and started going to the church of my newfound faith in my neighborhood. She started studying at our local college with the same undergraduate major I once had. I had an instant resurgence of the push-pull emotions of my childhood, of feeling eclipsed by her once again. My bristling defensiveness was magnified by the fact that I had my own child by then. And we had very different ideas about parenting—hers, typical of her generation, involved playpens and schedules and discipline. Mine, well... not.

My son, Sammy, knows that the single most effective way to push my buttons is to compare me with his Nana. Like when I was flipping the remote one day as we sat before the TV and I tried to stop on the *Meerkat Manor* show on Animal Planet, which my mom watches for hours at a time. He teased me mercilessly.

Like Mom's, my hair has thinned so that I now sunburn on my scalp. But I refuse (so far) to wear a hat every time I go out, partly because of my own personal sense of style, partly because Mom wears one. Shall I admit that sometimes now, when people are still saying I look like her, I can actually see the resemblance?

Recently, I have been caught phoning her about something special on TV I think she'd enjoy, though I roll my eyes when she does this to me. I still have a visceral spasm of distancing once in a while—like when I had to use a cane before and after knee surgery last year, and hurried to give it up so I would not seem like Mom. She used one regularly before graduating to a walker. Mother and daughter matching props—that was just too much, and hey, I'm twenty-eight years younger than she is!

All the defenses against turning into my mother that I have spent an adolescent and adult lifetime building are crumbling with age—hers or mine, I cannot say. What I do know is that I am grateful that I inherited her strength and resilience, even if it comes with the rest of it. And who knows? Perhaps one day I, too, will be a tough old broad.

~Karen Kullgren

Tunnel Vision

The trouble with being a parent is that
by the time you are experienced, you are unemployed.
~Author Unknown

I slumped listlessly in my favorite chair, a plush worn brown relic rescued on one of my garage sale expeditions. The breakfast mess left by my six kids leered at me from the little dingy kitchen. Huge piles of laundry lurked behind the door of the utility room. Unmade beds and cobwebs in dusty corners taunted me to the brink of depression.

"What the heck!" I thought. "I am going to make a cup of tea and get that candy bar I have been hiding." I snatched the new *Reader's Digest* beckoning me seductively from under a pile of unpaid bills.

Two hours later, I read the last page of the digest and resurfaced. "Oh, God!" I exclaimed, "I'll never get that wash out. The kids will be home from school before I get the house cleaned." I rushed around attempting to catch up on my chores.

I was getting nowhere when my mother walked in. "Hi," she called cheerily and grabbed the broom and began to sweep. "Looks like you got a late start," she commented. Not bothering to answer, I stomped into the laundry room. I mashed an unsorted load into the washer and sunk onto a pile of dirty sheets. Depression rushed in like the water pouring into the tub next to me.

After wallowing in my misery for half an hour, I slipped back into my kitchen. Mom was elbow deep in sudsy dishwater washing my dirty dishes. The floor was swept and counters were wiped clean. I sat down at the now clean table and burst into tears. Mom grabbed a cup of instant coffee and sat down opposite me.

"Okay, what's the matter?" she asked calmly.

"Mom," I gulped, as I wiped tears on the sleeve of my bathrobe, "when is it ever going to get better? It seems I can never get ahead with the housework. I'm tired of getting up early and staying up late and never having any time to myself. It is so hard to make ends meet. Every time we seem to get ahead someone has to go to the doctor or the car has to be repaired. This house is old and dumpy and way too small."

My mother listened patiently to my tale of woe. "Norma," she told me, "I remember feeling like this when I was raising twelve children. Trust me. Finances will ease and things will get better. You may not see it, but there is a light at the end of the tunnel. In two years your oldest child will be eighteen years old. Enjoy today—this moment with your children. Yesterday is gone. You only have today."

I looked up and there were tears in her eyes. Like a bolt out of the blue it hit me! Mom was talking from experience. She had reached the other end of the tunnel and was remembering those precious years. Maybe she had some regrets, too, and didn't want that for me.

"I will seize the moment," I thought to myself. "I'm not going to agonize over mundane things."

Later that afternoon, I watched my kids devour fresh baked cookies. They argued over who got the last one. Crumbs were scattered over the table and even on the floor. No matter. I was enjoying every minute.

Thank you, Mom, for what you taught me that day, for that moment and your sage advice and wisdom. I am grateful.

~Norma Favor

The Magic of the Mess

The woman who bore me is no longer alive,
but I seem to be her daughter in increasingly profound ways.
~Johnnetta Betsch Cole

After my mother died, I kept one of her treasures: A pale gray, marble-like paperweight that proclaimed in shiny black letters, "Lord, Bless This Mess." This item represented a mysterious notion about my mother. What, precisely, I couldn't place at the time.

I didn't know the story behind my mother's acquisition of the paperweight, but I could imagine her reaction when she first saw it. With an impish look she would have said, "Oh, that's what I need!" Then she would have burst into giggles.

For all the years I can remember, the paperweight graced the mammoth wood desk in the corner of the dining room of the house where I grew up in Kansas. Occasionally, one of my parents moved it from one spot to another, but it remained prominently displayed on the desk's surface. Sometimes my mother sipped iced coffee from a colorful tumbler while she sat at the desk. She did bookkeeping for my dad's company or executed personal business. At her fingertips she had her adding machine, her Rolodex, and her supplies.

The top of the desk strewn with ledgers, stacks of papers, and miscellaneous objects looked chaotic, but Mom had the key. She knew the order of the disorder. Usually. Blessing the mess must have been her secret, because orderly mayhem worked. Things got done.

Letters sent. Expenses logged. Bills paid. Decisions made. Occasionally, when an item escaped her, she methodically lifted each neatly placed stack and searched through it until she found what she needed. The delay didn't faze her. She plodded ahead with a formidable faith that the item would turn up.

"Oh, for heaven's sake, here it is!" she'd proclaim with glee when she discovered the errant object. Then, she'd return to her task until she smelled aromas from the kitchen reminding her to stop to wrap up supper. At other times, the stove alarm buzzed, signaling her to leave the desk to finish the laundry or to tackle gardening chores.

Now, as an early retiree and a writer, I preside over an unruly landscape where chaos has grown roots. Deep, tangled roots. I've straightened piles and tried organizational tricks, yet I wallow in the midst of every writer's nightmare: Messy stacks, piled-high tables and crammed bookcases.

Undeterred, I reinvent my situation with a different slant. I envision the daunting disorder as my mess of blessings. The gems that drive my writing to new levels hide within the disorder. When I doubt my direction, I caress the infamous "Lord, Bless This Mess" paperweight, willing its magic to rub off on me. I think: "What worked for my mom can work for me, too."

I press on as I remember my mother's faith, her mysterious magic touch that worked wonders on her messy desk. "I know it's here somewhere," I say.

I search, buoyed by the thrill of a treasure hunt. With a loving eye, I rifle through the piles of writing notebooks, journals, drafts, scraps of paper with jotted lists, scribbled quotes, notes on observed scenes, and accrued clippings. I tenderly lift my books of inspiration and writing craft, then leaf through them, letting their wisdom flow through me. I putter with my stash of keepsakes or monkey with my mountains of photos. At some point on the hunt I find it—the word, the image, the object, or the memory that had stirred me to put words on the page. My voice speaks up once again.

"Here it is!"

Sometimes I catch myself imitating my mother when I preface my proclamation with "Oh, for heaven's sake!"

Like her, an ordinary object's simple message grounds me. "Lord, Bless this Mess!"

The gem, the blessing found, portrays the deep untamed edge of life that, once named, captures the reader's heart. The once chaotic mass of words spins into a recognizable shape to ignite interest and harness hope for life understood.

Without mess there would be no order, no new way of viewing life. Embracing the chaos—digging into the swirling mess—sparks a change in viewpoint, a fresh description, a tidbit of untarnished truth.

Thanks to my mother and her magic, embodied in her paper-weight, I've learned to accept what is, including the mess that textures my environment. Claiming my mess and blessing it moves me forward into the world of wayward words and crafty characters frolicking on the page that, once befriended, lead the way.

My mother's magic still works wonders and I'm grateful. I've gained perspective and staying power from her premise that life pans out, one way or another.

~Ronda Armstrong

66

Dusting Off Memories

The happiest moments of my life have been the few
which I have passed at home in the bosom of my family.
~Thomas Jefferson

As a young girl growing up in rural Alabama, I never understood why my mom spent so much time baking bread from scratch, and making my brother and me help her. One day every other week was dedicated to making bread. My brother and I were in charge of grinding the wheat into flour while Mom prepped the remaining ingredients. One of us would pour the wheat, a little at a time, into the hopper while the other turned the handle, and then we would trade positions as our small arms tired. The grinder was attached to a metal desk in the corner of the dining room, and occasionally the vise-like grip would loosen and we would have to stop and tighten it.

Eventually, Dad bought Mom a motorized grinder and our routine changed from pouring and grinding to grinding and keeping the flour dust from settling on everything in the kitchen and dining room. Despite our best efforts, the flour dust always went everywhere. So at the end of the day, while the bread was baking in the oven, we dusted the white off every coated surface.

While I went about my bread baking chores obediently, I chafed at the hours spent in the kitchen. I would wistfully look out the window as my horses grazed contentedly in the nearby pasture. I preferred to be outside with my horses. Looking back, I never appreciated my mom's idea of quality family time with my brother and me, at least when it came to time in the kitchen.

Years have gone by and I have become a mother myself. Home is now North Idaho. I handle kitchen chores with more grace as an adult, but I prefer to leave most of the cooking and baking to my husband. He's quite good at it, too.

It was on one such occasion that my husband, Christopher, was preparing dinner. I was at the kitchen table going through the day's mail when our two-year-old son, Cody, asked his Papa if he could help him cook. Christopher smiled and tried to explain that the stove was hot and it wasn't safe for him to be near it. Undeterred and resourceful, Cody grabbed a chair from the nearby table, and with all his effort began dragging the chair toward the nearest kitchen counter several feet away. While he struggled with the chair over the carpet, he made fast progress on the linoleum and soon had it placed in front of a counter centered between the refrigerator and the pantry. I sat there amused at his determination.

Cody climbed up on the chair and reached for a glass on the counter containing two dozen or so wine corks that Christopher had collected. With corks in hand, he pointed to the coffee pot on another counter. His Papa handed him the unplugged coffee pot. His final request was a wooden spoon. I put the mail down and watched as Cody carefully removed the glass pot from the brewer and placed the corks inside the pot. He stirred the corks with his wooden spoon for several minutes before returning them, and the pot, to the coffee maker.

"What are you doing?" I asked.

"Helping Papa cook," he replied with a big smile on his face. "I'm making cork soup!" It didn't matter that Christopher was behind him tending food in the oven. He was in the kitchen helping his Papa and that was all that mattered to him.

At that moment, something from within me stirred. I thought back to all those times as a kid when my own mom asked for help in baking bread, and I had grudgingly, but obediently, complied. Perhaps she was trying to create something more than just fresh baked bread.

Maybe Mom was trying to instill a sense of togetherness through family time. Maybe she was trying to create a few lasting memories.

As I watched Cody take the corks in and out of the pot and stir them with all the dedication of a two-year-old, I realized that he had created a forever moment for me, a moment in time in which Christopher's willingness to let him "help" in the kitchen created a profound sense of family for our son. When the wine corks were sufficiently stirred to Cody's satisfaction, I got up from the table and offered him the small counter scale. Weighing the corks would let the moment linger even longer as I savored my newfound appreciation for the experiences my mom had given me years ago in her kitchen, a place where I was welcomed and belonged, flour dust and all.

~Jenny R. George

67

The Letter

My mother was the making of me...
someone that I must not disappoint.
The memory of my mother will always be a blessing to me.
~Thomas A. Edison

The most pervasive memory I have of my mother is her long struggle fighting, and dying of, cancer during my adolescence. While it is my memory now, it was not my reality then. Like all good moms, she seldom allowed me to see the face of death. Instead, she wore a mask of humor and hope. In her final year, however, the mask was getting worn and transparent—the burden too difficult to carry.

Ultimately, one Mother's Day weekend, alone, pen in hand, she decided to unleash the thoughts and feelings she had so carefully locked away behind the gracious façade. In an empty journal, she wrote what later became her most precious gift to me—a heartfelt message from mother to child. The letter is unfinished. Perhaps the flood of emotion was too overwhelming. I will never know. But this is what I do know.

I read this letter almost every year on the day she wrote it. Although my mother did not live to see another Mother's Day, she continues to teach me through her well-crafted words.

As a teenager, her words said she was proud of me when I needed the affirmation. As a victim, something she knew a little about, her words were honest about her own struggle to cope and I no longer felt alone in my circumstance. My mother did not attend church. She did not want to feel hypocritical by seeking God in her final days, only when she needed him, she wrote. The closest she could allow herself to get was to volunteer at the local church nursery. There, she befriended the pastor, took notes and, I believe, came to know our loving God after all. In her transparency about her own pride, she taught me humility and planted her own seeds of faith in my life.

But the most powerful epiphany I had while reading the letter was on the Mother's Day I discovered I, too, was going to be a mother. On this day, and every day since, the paradigm was changed. I was no longer the child, the victim, the student, but the mother—and, in fact, older than she was when she sat in her room and readied herself to pen this most incredible gift. As the tears streamed down my face, I experienced a shift in perspective. How difficult it must have been to write this letter, to tell your child you are not going to live. To try to summarize all that she means to you and all that you want her to know in a lifetime, all that is important to you, and all that you wish you had said but never did. The letter is unfinished. Of course it is.

My mother taught me to write—not the craft of it, but the value in it. Not for profit or fame, but so my child will know me not just through my actions and interactions, but through my words as well... someday, when I am no longer here to tell him myself.

Thanks, Mom.

~Kathy Marotta

Lasting Impressions

A daughter is a gift of love.
~Author Unknown

ome of our more daring conversations happened while my mother was applying her make-up—a morning ritual, complete with coffee, that also served as an invitation to chat.

"Have a seat," she'd say, pointing her wand of color at the chair across from her. I'd join my mother at the kitchen table amidst a vast array of cosmetics—pencils, powders, lipstick and blush—serious stuff, setting the tone for serious talks. Girl stuff. Our conversations were intense, personal and I always came away from them feeling deeply connected, reassured and loved. What I remember most are the answers I found in the long silences, when she'd stop to paint her lips, or curl an eyelash, or make a point, or to smile at my teenage dreams.

My mother died a few years ago after a courageous battle with cancer and I inherited, among other things, her beauty supplies—a wooden treasure chest to be gone through with my own daughter. I took the abandoned chest from the closet, set it on the bed, and invited Brittny into the room.

"Have a seat," I said, patting the spot next to me. "This box belonged to your grandmother." Captivated by the colorful contents—foundation and powders, tubes and wands, lotions and ointments, polish and files, spritzes and sprays—my bedroom soon became a salon, a place of mystical transformations. A place for girl stuff.

We "played" in the make-up. We rubbed foundation into our faces. We rouged our cheeks with corals and pinks. We lined our eyes with pearls and frosts. And we pondered surprising lipstick shades. Some tubes were worn down to the rim, while others seemed fairly new. Sleek, delicate and sometimes broken wands of color. Our painted and filed nails flashed with enamels—reds and whites, purples and blues. We impersonated the top models, promoting the cosmetic companies while wearing heels and practicing our walk. We laughed, we giggled and as the excitement wore down, we talked.

Some of our more daring conversations happened during the long silences, while we brushed and styled our hair. We talked about choices and changes, school and boys, life and death. It was my chance to reach out to my daughter, and her chance to let me in. We came away from that evening with a stronger, renewed relationship. We felt connected, reassured and loved. I knew the make-up would wash away and our curls would fall flat, but the memories, the bond we created, would last forever.

I realized the important lessons my mother had taught me—trust has to be earned, relationships have to be built, and love will outlive death. I lifted the neatly folded tissue we found at the bottom of the make-up chest and handed it to my daughter. It was stained red, and imprinted with my mother's last kiss.

~Janine Pickett

Happy to Be You

The mother-daughter relationship is the most complex.
~Wynonna Judd

Most women I know have knee-jerk "Not me!" reactions when told they're just like their mothers. If my husband, Bob, said, "Those slacks aren't flattering," I'd just go change. If my mother said the very same thing, I'd snap, "These are fine, MO-THER."

There comes a time when we learn that most moms are not being any more judgmental than our best friends. But we often interpret a mother's advice as controlling and meddlesome rather than helpful. What sounds caring and supportive from a friend can sound overbearing and insulting from a mother. It doesn't matter how old we get. This seems to remain true.

Long ago while visiting my mom, we had a big fight. She waited until we were alone, then asked about my financial situation. She knew Bob and I were poor.

"We're fine, Ma," I said, dismissing her rudely.

"But that same old car keeps breaking down," she said patiently.

I was embarrassed. Defensively, I said, "Don't worry."

"I do worry."

The reality was that she wanted to help. But I took her concern as a put-down and felt that she was meddling in my business, where she certainly didn't belong.

I stormed off to the same bedroom that I had as a little girl and, still acting like one, slammed the door.

I was fuming when she slowly opened the door and sat next to me on the bed. "If you don't have enough money to pay your bills, we can…"

I interrupted and stood up. "I'm twenty-eight! I can take care of myself."

Then she broke my heart. Quietly she said, "It hurts me when you're unhappy."

And although she had, in fact, said that before, I was always too wrapped up in my defensive anger to hear her. But this time, I saw her sitting on my bed with her hands in her lap and I realized that the look on her face was not one of condemnation, but of pure maternal love. It was a pivotal moment, seeing the situation from her point of view rather than mine. It was then that I felt her tender compassion and finally understood what a mother's love means. It was then that I finally said, "Thank you, Mom."

So, I think we should re-consider our mothers' true intentions when we think they're being critical.

When mom used to say she was unhappy that I lived far away, I felt smothered. But the reality was that she wanted me nearer. Is that so terrible?

And when she gently offered to give us money that day, my response was one of foot-stomping resistance. I thought, "You think I'm a failure." But the truth was that she didn't want to see her daughter going without anything. And my happiness mattered to her as much, if not more, than her own.

Bob and I have rules we follow when we argue. One is—no sarcasm. Another is—no mind reading; we need to explain what's wrong.

And one was that he could never say, "You sound just like your mother."

That's no longer on the unfair fighting list because, if he said that to me today, I'd hug him, thank him from the bottom of my heart and tell him he couldn't have given me a lovelier compliment.

~Saralee Perel

Thanks Mom

Chapter 7

One of a Kind

How to Be Special

Always be a first-rate version of yourself,
instead of a second-rate version of somebody else.
~Judy Garland

Olivia Mai rocks. She's my mom, and because of her, I learned that fashion is powerful. Mom's daring, playful and unconditionally loving personality taught me that being attractive has nothing to do with good looks, but everything to do with great style.

Growing up was a show with my mom. We glittered it up for grocery shopping, gave makeovers to friends who stopped by, and had fun with style for the sake of creativity, not for money or because of trends. Mom believed looking good said two things about a woman: First, that she cares about herself; and second, that she wants others to care about themselves. And she was right. Taking the time to dress yourself builds the confidence to feel good, therefore making you give your best to everyone. People will see your positive energy through your style. Fashion is powerful.

For the first few years of my life, everything was cupcakes and cashmere. I had no problem being myself, and had the most enjoyable time decorating my moods each day. Then came my first day of school.

All month, Mom and I had been preparing for this day and I had everything set the night before to walk in and make new friends. I had decided my first-day color had to be a powerful purple, and sprung out of bed that morning ready to throw on my purple and gray plaid jumper with my favorite T-shirt underneath that spelled "J-E-A-N-N-I-E" in bold black letters. I had also chosen funky, fresh pink fishnet stockings and glossy purple rubber galoshes that my mom had purchased for rainy weather. (It was seventy-four degrees and sunny that day.) She helped me with the finishing touches of sparkly bangles to my wrist, gave me a wet kiss on my cheek, (careful not to smudge my glittery lip gloss), and walked me into school.

The moment I walked into my classroom and took off my coat, every single kid stared. Parents, too. Mom saw Mrs. Clark, my new teacher, and left my side to say hello. I immediately felt the eyes all over the room pan head to toe over my outfit. Several of the parents raised an eyebrow, while many of the kids pointed and laughed. For the first time, I felt insecure. Even scarier, I felt like I'd rather be anybody else but me. I saw that everyone else had slicked smooth hair, barrettes, matching dresses and socks and appropriate sandals and shoes. I sat down wishing I could take off my galoshes and hide.

By midday, I was known as Jeannie Weenie Wild. At lunch, nobody sat by me and at the end, where new friends waited in pairs to be picked up, I waited by myself. When Mom rolled up, I lunged into the backseat, kicked off my boots and headband, and slouched low in my seat. I didn't even wait for Mom to ask what was wrong. Through tears, I wailed about how she let me go to school looking like that and why didn't she buy me clothes like the other kids and why did she name me something that rhymes with Weenie and why...?

Mom immediately pulled the car over, took off her seatbelt and turned around with such a thrilled, elated expression of joy that I wondered if I was in the right car. "They already know your name? What did they say? That's WONDERFUL!"

I sat there dumbfounded. "Did you hear what I said? NO! I don't want them to know my name! I hate school! I'm never going back! Everybody is too mean and I hate my clothes!"

I never forgot the next words my mom said: "Con (which means "my child" in Vietnamese), this is the best day ever. I raised you to stand out and be something to talk about. I don't care what they're saying. You were noticed and unforgettable. You are my daughter and I am so proud!"

Those words changed my life forever. The very second her words slipped into my ears, I understood the difference between "owning it" and "being owned," a philosophy I advocate today when adopting new styles. Never again would I let anybody else tell me who I was. She spent those years teaching me to celebrate myself, and now was my turn to learn how to make a statement. This lesson has built the wall of protection I need in this business. As long as my actions come out of love and a fun spirit, I'm a "Do" all the way.

Thanks to Mom, I use that confident foundation to influence others through fashion.

And just so you know, I wore those purple galoshes the next day, too.

~Jeannie Mai

71

My Blessing

Men do not quit playing because they grow old; they grow old because they quit playing.
~Oliver Wendell Holmes

"97, 98, 99, 100..."

I count while Mom, lying on the floor in front of the TV, does her Marine Corps crunches. With a baby pillow under her head, she performs this nightly ritual designed to allow her to sleep a full six or seven hours before she wakes up between 6:30 and 7:00 AM. At that time, she will lace up her walking shoes and go for her daily five-mile walk.

In the snows of winter, a mailman asked her if she wanted a job.

I don't go with her at that hour. I have learned that I can't keep up. She is eighty-one. I am sixty-two. She walks fast. Too fast for me.

"178, 179, 180..."

She is a marvel, this mother of mine. Her shapely tan legs are in shorts. She has no extra fat on her body. Her fitness routine has been her job for the last forty years. Many high school girls would kill for her shape. Wrinkles she has. Fat she doesn't.

She has four children, four grandchildren, and six great-grand-children. Few can keep up with her. My sister and I took her to Hawaii. It was a good thing we both went, because we took turns resting. She wore us out.

We never saw her sleep. She said she could sleep when she got home. When she's in Hawaii, she wants to take it all in. We rested when we got home. Mom was busy looking at all the pictures, putting them into collage frames for her wall and telling everyone about her trip—the water ballet, the luau and the flowers.

"249, 250, 251..." Her crunches continue.

Mother finishes her daily walk and follows it up with an exercise routine done in the clubhouse of the senior mobile home park in Bend, Oregon. That starts at 9:00 AM, and she is never late.

Everyone knows not to telephone during her exercise times.

Later in the morning, she will go to Curves. Her photo is pinned on the wall there as the winner of the hula-hoop contest. She kept the hoop going longer than anyone else. The photo is frayed but she isn't. She will wear her "Curves-600 sessions" T-shirt.

"323, 324, 325..."

She works crosswords puzzles at night to keep her mind sharp. She has won 987 games of Yahtzee against me in the last three weeks. We have also played Skip-Bo and cards. Unless I am lucky, she slaughters me.

The only area of loss might be her short-term memory. New words that she doesn't use every day escape her. Computer terms? She has no need of those. ATM machines? She doesn't use those either.

iPods and Nintendos? Forget it.

"363, 364, 365..."

I took her to Costco today and as we were standing in line, I asked her if she wanted an iced mocha or a freeze. She didn't. She watches what she eats. I opened my wallet and gave her two dollars and asked her to go get me an iced mocha. The line was long and I knew that she would want to pay if she stood there with me. Her income is minimal but she knows how to stretch it. This trip is my treat.

Everyone in line was watching her. She was all color-coordinated in pink earrings and size six shorts. She returned too soon and asked me the name of "that thing" I wanted again.

"An ICED MOCHA."

The lady behind us in line smiled.

I was next in line for the cashier. When she came back again... what was that name? ICED MOCHA... "Mom," I said, pointing to the huge sign with the foot long hot dog.

"See the hot dog, well, on the left of the hot dog is an iced mocha. That's what I want."

"Okay," she says, "but that line is awful long."

The cashier interrupted saying that it moved really fast.

She left and the cashier laughingly asked me, "Do you really think you will get your iced mocha, or do you think she will come back with a hot dog?"

"You know what, she's eighty-one years old, and I'm just so glad to have her that I really don't care what she brings back."

I heard the lady behind me in line gasp. The stooped little old man in front of me turned around and said, "How old did you say she was?"

"Eighty-one."

"She sure doesn't look eighty-one."

"397, 398, 399, 400."

She is finished. She does not look eighty-one. She does not act eighty-one. And she can't stand to be around old people who constantly talk about their aches and pains. "Take vitamins and exercise," she tells them.

When I count my blessings, my mother's good health and zest for life top the list. She cleans her floors on her hands and knees and defrosts her freezer and plays Bunko. She loves to bake and always takes treats to pinochle on Tuesdays and bingo on Fridays.

That's why I want to be just like her when I grow up.

Thank you, dear God, for giving me the best role model. She is truly a blessing.

~Linda Burks Lohman

72

My Mother's Legacy

If you break your neck, if you have nothing to eat, if your house is on fire,
then you got a problem. Everything else is inconvenience.
~Robert Fulghum

My ninety-four-year-old mother squinted at me across the breakfast table.

"I don't understand," she muttered, a shadow darkening the cornflower blue of her eyes. "My daughter in America always calls—usually every second day. And now it's been quite a while since I've heard from her."

Stunned, I leaned forward. "Mutti, look at me. I'm right here. I have come all the way across the ocean to be with you. That's why I haven't called."

"Oh." A distrustful little smile danced across my mother's lips. "I see."

Then, just as I hoped that she had recognized me, she proceeded to tell me about my personal history in the third person.

Listening to her rendition of my past, I was reminded once again of the incredible odds this strong, loving, and very funny woman had to overcome to turn my childhood into the happy adventure it was.

I was only four when WWII came to an end and my mother fled with thousands of other refugees from the Polish Corridor into Austria, before finally being settled in a small village at the foothills of the Bavarian mountains.

Although the government provided us with a small room in the back of an old farmhouse, finding something to eat was a daily challenge since food was scarce even in the remote countryside.

Whenever she got the chance, my mother helped in the fields, always hoping for small handouts from the harvests. When that wasn't enough to feed us, she had to resort to begging—and I helped.

In contrast to my mother, whose Eastern German speech pattern marked her as an outsider, I picked up the local dialect within a very short time.

Feeling like "one of them," I went cheerfully from door to door in the village to present a schmaltzy hymn my mother taught me to up my chances of finding a way into the farmers' hearts and food supplies. I still wonder what really got to them: The heart-wrenching theme of the song or my whimsical delivery.

It worked. I often left a farmhouse clutching a loaf of bread and other goodies.

My mother also taught me how to "semi-legitimately" harvest apples that belonged to others.

In the village, common law and social mores dictated that the yields from the fruit trees falling on the owners' side of the fence were theirs, but the apples falling onto the village street were common property.

Always one for putting her immense repertoire of proverbs into action, my mother concluded, "Well, it doesn't hurt to lean a little." It was a very effective way to get hold of some delicious vitamins.

Taking into account her own advice of, "Even a blind chicken will find a kernel eventually," my mother was relentless in finding ways to make things better for us.

She tried her hand at growing her own vegetables and experimented with cooking, sewing and knitting. But since she had to work with whatever was available, she gave up on following standard instructions.

I almost never saw her consult a cookbook or study a recipe. She measured any given ingredients by eyeing them or guessing their weight. Then, in order to season the dishes, she used her taste buds until it was "just right."

Her creations often came up a bit flawed, but instead of being rattled, she seemed to delight in the challenge of fixing the things that were less than perfect.

In that way, she was a pioneer in "thinking outside the box."

After lifting a lopsided birthday cake from the oven, she would apply enough icing and decorations to even out the shape. Then, with the cake being cut, everyone at the table received an individually shaped piece with either a lot of cake and little icing or the reverse.

Then there was my high school graduation dilemma. Mom insisted on sewing my dress from a nylon fabric with large red roses on a cream-colored background. The garment had a tight waistline and a widely ruffled skirt, perfect for dancing to the rock-and-roll type rhythms of that era.

Unfortunately, just before I got dressed, my mother decided to press the dress. When the iron touched the nylon, one of the large red blooms disappeared and my wonderful dress had a big hole in it. Unperturbed, my mother cut another rose from an unused piece of fabric and—using her hot-iron method in reverse—she melted the patch across the opening and tugged the seams of the fix-up under a large ruffle. Needless to say, I had a great time at the party.

My mother was also very generous and little concerned with material things. Having seen so many people lose so much during the war made her quite indifferent to worldly possessions. She would often say, "You can't take it with you," or, "Even a rich man can only eat until he's full," and, "Your health is much more important than stuff."

She always put me first, no matter what. So, when it was time for me to get a better education than was available in that tiny village, she decided to send me to another school in a town about ten miles away. To pay the tuition, she took a job in a nearby sausage factory.

I still remember how tired she was in the evening after putting in a long day of work on an assembly line, in addition to commuting on a lightweight moped that exposed her to all kinds of weather conditions.

Swinging it, laughing at life and joking about its idiosyncrasies, she was always there for me, doing whatever she could, and taking great pride in her efforts.

I will never be able to repay my mother for her love, her devotion and sacrifices. I can only hope that the way I live my life—swinging it, embracing it, taking imperfections in stride, worrying little about stuff, and trying not to take everything too seriously—shows my gratitude and honors her.

~H.M. Gruendler-Schierloh

Mom's Many Hats

*A child embarrassed by his mother
is just a child who hasn't lived long enough.*
~Mitch Albom, For One More Day

ost mothers wear many hats. My mother, literally, had a closet full. And, to my great embarrassment, she wore them in public.

Mom adored hats of all kinds—the bolder the better. She had rows of tissue covered hats overflowing her closet and spilling onto attic shelves. Vibrant red straw peeked through one bundle, chocolate-colored felt from another, and an occasional ribbon or bow escaped the wrapping. Another child might have found Mom's hat fancy intriguing or exciting. Not me. In the small Midwestern town where we lived, practical, plain clothing prevailed. My goal was to fit in. Mom had a flair for standing out.

One frigid winter in my tender junior high years, Mom and Dad came to a basketball game where I was a cheerleader. Parents streamed in the doors, unwinding knitted scarves and popping off woolen caps. They wrangled their way out of sturdy parkas and canvas farming jackets. The crowd was similar—bland and comforting. When my parents arrived, it wasn't hard to spot them. Mom was sporting a white rabbit fur hat with a leather bill (and it was "Belgian rabbit! On sale even, from Esther Kirk Boutique!"). It snuggled on the top of her head like a woodland creature trying to beat the cold. I hid behind my pompoms, waiting for Mom to find a seat and remove her hat. Nope! Too chilly in the gym—the rabbit stayed in place all night.

A vacation photo memorializes Mom's favorite summer hat. The picture was taken on a road trip west, and we are posed in a Nebraska wheat field. Mom is wearing an avocado-colored short set that looks earthy in contrast to the waving wheat at our knees. On her head, however, is a bright orange straw hat with a bill wide enough to slice your jugular if you got too close. In the picture, Dad is keeping his distance. That hat thwarted my goal that vacation, of "not looking like a tourist." To this day, Mom sighs when she sees that photo, looks wistfully into space and murmurs, "I always loved that hat...."

Easter, as you can imagine, was the Academy Awards of hat exposure. One of Mom's favorites had a high, hot pink crown, completely engulfed with magenta flowers placed every quarter of an inch. The flowers carpeted the entire hat. Glorious! That Easter marked Mom's only attempt to pass on her hat obsession to my sister and me. She had purchased flower-encrusted headbands for us to wear. My sister and I remember that day as living proof that one's brain can be perforated by headband spikes. We swear that blood pooled on our scalps underneath the celebratory flowers. On the upside, I only have vague memories of the obstruction that Mom's hot pink extravaganza created in the pews that Sunday.

The mustard-colored English Bobbie hat was perhaps the most radical and surely the most embarrassing. Accented with leather braided cord, it exuded an authority that only a woman of confidence could pull off. Lucky for me, Mom was up to the challenge.

I did not inherit Mom's flair for flaunting a fancy hat. I still, much like in junior high, prefer to fly under the radar. However, I have grown to appreciate Mom's courage in wearing hats she loved, even if they elicited public stares or groans from her family. More importantly, I have received the powerful message of Mom's action: Be yourself. Don't worry what other people think. When people are looking at you, hold your head high. Even if there's a rabbit on top of it.

~Gail Wilkinson

74

Fish Lips

Nothing encourages creativity like the chance to fall flat on one's face.
~James D. Finley

When my brother and I were growing up, we spent most of our time outdoors riding bikes, roller skating or climbing trees. We took turns playing Good Guys and Bad Guys, Cowboys and Indians and any one of our favorite movie heroes. We both loved Tarzan. With the help of our father, we built a tree house in the nearby tamarack trees; a rope made the perfect vine for swinging. We would spend days acting out new adventures and would practice our Tarzan yell, bragging that one was better than the other, yodeling until we were nearly hoarse.

One summer, our small town was sponsoring its annual marina parade. All the local fishermen would decorate their boats with tissue paper flowers, sea shells and other nautical themes and tow them around Main Street to announce the beginning of a new fishing season—a good source of tourism income for the town.

Excitement filled the air as talk spread about who would be the master of ceremonies that year. Mothers began working on costumes for their children as men washed and waxed their boats. A picnic was planned for the city park where the parade would end. A variety of goodies, including hot dogs, potato salad, cookies, chips and root beer would be waiting as the boats lined up for judging in the fire station parking lot. Everyone had something to do as our small town prepared for the event.

Our mother was thrilled. She loved to make costumes for my brother and me. I stood by and watched as a beautiful sequined mermaid suit was fashioned by her talented hands. At one point, she had to stop and go into town to the store to pick up the remaining ingredients for her famous potato salad. Tagging along beside her, half listening to conversations between other housewives while staring through the candy counter glass, I couldn't help overhear my mother ask about the progress of the other little girls' costumes. Back in the car, she drove the short ride home, slightly distracted and not really paying much attention to my rambling. Once home, she returned to her sewing and I went outdoors to play with my brother.

The day of the parade, we heard that the real Tarzan was coming to be our master of ceremonies. The air was filled with excitement. My nine-year-old brother stood proudly before the mirror on the closet door, admiring his pirate costume from every angle, turning his foil sword back and forth as it shone in the hall light. Mother helped me into my suit, sewing down the sides of my legs to make a perfect fit, and then began to pull my long hair up, pin-curling it to my head. At that point I began to suspect something was very wrong. She pulled a rounded cap down; tucking my errant curls inside and fastening a strap under my chin to keep it in place. Now I knew for sure that something was not right.

"Mama, this doesn't fit right. Isn't my hair supposed to be down with flowers and shells like a mermaid?" I asked. She smiled at me and continued fussing with my costume. I knew I was doomed when she brought the black poster paint out and began to paint huge black circles around my eyes. The final touch was when a tube of bright lipstick was produced and she very carefully traced the outside of my lips in orange.

I stood in absolute horror as she shoved me in front of the mirror to approve of her handiwork. My older brother was snickering the whole time. "No," I cried to myself as I stared at my reflection. That's not a beautiful mermaid! The funniest sight stared back. My mother had turned my pretty mermaid costume into a goldfish suit! I stood in shock as I tried to tell my mother a fish was definitely not a mermaid and that I would be the laughing stock of my school if I even dared to wear it in public.

I remember her reassuring me that I would have the best costume there. After talking with the other mothers in town, she decided there would be too many mermaid costumes and she wanted me to stand out. Why couldn't one of the other mothers change her daughter's costume? Why did I have to be the one who was different?

The ride into town seemed as if we were in a time warp. When we arrived in the parking lot and I looked out of the car window, everywhere I could see were festive decorations, boats scrubbed and shiny, boys and girls scrambling to sit on the bows of the boats, all ready for the parade to begin. Grandpa's boat was the first one, pulled by his Jeep, and to my horror—sitting on the front seat—was none other than my brother's and my favorite hero, Tarzan. He was right there in person!

As we got out of the car with my brother pushing me all the way, we were brought straight up to the Jeep, both of us totally speechless, my brother in shock, and me completely embarrassed! Introductions were made and my brother climbed up into the boat, raising his sword proudly, waiting. I, on the other hand, had a problem. Mother had sewn my costume on me. With a fish fin and flippers, I definitely could not climb. I couldn't even walk. But Grandpa had a solution for that; he just lifted me up and set me on Tarzan's lap in the front seat.

"All set, Sisser?" Grandpa winked at me.

Mortification, embarrassment and shame all went out the window. I was sitting with Tarzan, my hero! At that point, I didn't care who saw me in my ridiculous fish suit. Grandpa started up the Jeep, pulling his boat forward. The rest followed. Mother ran alongside, coaching me to make "fish lips" by pursing my mouth together and opening my eyes wide.

The parade was over far too quickly. I must say that one of my best moments in that dusty small California town was sitting with Tarzan, making "fish lips." It was an honor I would carry the rest of my life, and it was all due to my mother's quick thinking and creative touches.

~Terri L. Lacher

75

Making Her Own Way

When we are no longer able to change a situation,
we are challenged to change ourselves.
~Victor Frankl

When my mother set out to rule the world, it was not the most popular or likely road for a woman, much less a single mother, to travel. She had been a stay-at-home mom for my sister and me until her divorce, so when she struck out on her own, she didn't have any experience.

She got a job as a secretary for an insurance agency and worked very long hours to make ends meet. She had been at the agency for a while when she started to notice something. Her boss referred to her as a secretary only and didn't allow her to do any more than answer the phones. She would speak to customers and have the answers to their questions right in front of her, but was not allowed to give them. Any and all calls had to be forwarded to her boss when he was in the office, which wasn't often, as he liked to play golf. Consequently, she took messages and told the customers that he would call them back, all the while knowing that she could just as easily have helped them. She begged him to allow her to study to get her insurance license but he denied her the time off and, again, made it clear that she was only a secretary, only a woman, and should know her place.

One morning, my mother went into her boss's office to ask him a favor. She wanted to see if she could get an early lunch. I had been named to the honor roll in school and an assembly was being held to honor me and five other students. She desperately wanted to attend, but her boss pointedly refused her. My mother quit right then and there. She said she could take him talking down to her, she could take him mismanaging the place, but she could not take him keeping her from her family.

She went back to school, got her license to sell insurance and started her own agency. She went around taking employees from the most bizarre places. One was a door-to-door copier saleswoman, another a night manager at a local pharmacy. She hired two new employees with zero experience in the insurance industry and began training them. She wanted them each to get a license to sell insurance. She encouraged them to speak to the customers, so that she was no more important than any of her employees. She got her master's degree online and hers became one of the top agencies in the state. Her employees (mostly women) are now all required to have their licenses. She instills in them the confidence that they know as much as she does and are just as important to the business.

Both of her original employees have been with her for more than ten years. Of the ten employees she now has, only two have been with her for less than five years. She allows them time off for family events whenever they need. She has just published her first book, which was a labor of love for her for more than eight years. My mother showed me, from an early age, the value of family, of working for what you believe in, and knowing above all else that you are important and that you can make a difference.

~Kara Townsend

Beauty Never Fades

Everything has beauty, but not everyone sees it.
~Confucius

Once a week, no matter how busy I am, I take an afternoon off and just sit and stare at the clouds.

It's not always easy to rearrange my schedule or put my deadlines on hold to carry out this weekly ritual. In fact, there are many times when I almost talk myself out of it. But in the end, once I park myself on my usual bench and turn my head skyward, my cares and troubles just seem to drift away as the clouds work their magic.

"Look! Look at that one," my mother will say. "Look how soft and fluffy it is. And it reaches clear across the sky."

My mother is eighty-eight years old and it is she who draws me to this weekly meeting with the clouds. Ten years ago, her doctors diagnosed her with dementia. But in her present state of constant peace and happiness, it's hard for me to see her as demented. To me, she seems transcendent.

I've spent a good part of my life trying to reach a state of complete mental calm and peace. My mother has reached it. I struggle with daily demons of guilt and insecurity and fear. My mother has none. No matter how hard I try, I sometimes focus on the negative and ugly elements of life. But not my mother. All she ever sees is beauty. And she's eager to share it.

"Mmmm, feel that breeze," she'll say. "Nice and soft."

I realize that, if she hadn't mentioned it, I probably would have let the breeze go unnoticed. But her words slow me down and I feel that gentle brush against my cheek, feel the slow-motion movement of my hair in the wind.

Every now and then she'll turn to me and say, "But nothing is better than having my favorite daughter beside me. You are even more beautiful than the clouds."

This time with my mother is bittersweet. She always had an eye for beauty. She always took the time to stop and gaze at the clouds or appreciate the wonder of a full moon. Her home was full of artifacts from nature that held intricate patterns and designs so miniscule that they would have gone unnoticed by a lesser mind—a mind that didn't realize that life is short and full of infinite beauties to behold. But she saw them and she savored them and she collected them to point them out to others who didn't take the time to stop and see. People like me. Too wrapped up in my jobs and my romances and even things as mundane as books or movies or television. I was too busy to see all that beauty around me, but also too busy to really notice how much of it was there, in my mother.

And so, each week, no matter what I am doing or how busy I am, I stop and visit my mother and we sit and stare at the clouds.

"Look! Look at that one," my mother will say. "Have you ever seen anything so beautiful?" And I turn and look at her and realize that, until this precious time in my life, I don't think that I have.

~Betsy S. Franz

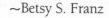

77

Mom's Heart

When you look at your life, the greatest happinesses are family happinesses.
~Dr. Joyce Brothers

There were at least six inches of snow on the ground that Valentine's Day morning. My brother and sister and I sat on the couch together, watching cartoons as if we ourselves might suddenly join the ranks of Captain Planet and go on to save the world from the evil of polluters. Mom urged us to leave the couch and told us to put on our winter clothes. We grumbled a little, wondering if this was going to be like that time Dad's tractor broke down and we had no way of plowing the quarter-mile drive, meaning we had to shovel two paths all the way down. Mom assured us the tractor wasn't broken; all we had to do was follow her.

Out in the field, she told us to walk in single file behind her, and for a moment I wondered if it was going to be some weird version of Simon Says. But what we soon began to realize as we looked back at the shape of the tracks we were forming in the snow, was that we were making a heart in our field. I had seen many hearts before, especially on Valentine's Day. I had seen red and pink glittered ones, crayon hearts, scratch and sniff hearts. I had been barraged with hearts that Friday afternoon at school. But making one very large heart out in the snow struck me in a way none of the other hearts had. Together, we had tramped out this massive shape in our very own field.

We returned indoors for a moment to gather up bottles filled with water turned red from food coloring. We poured the red water out into our heart tracks, turning the snow red. We returned inside to refill again and again and then stepped back out into the winter world, despite our noses growing numb and goose bumps beginning to creep down our limbs. And when the heart was a red that matched the tulips from my mother's spring garden, we all packed into the minivan and Dad drove us down to the lower road.

Though it took only minutes to get there, it seemed longer as we rode along, wondering if we'd be able to spot the heart from afar, if our creation was emblazed on our hillside for all those living on the lower road to see. We leaned forward in our seats, yearning to catch a glance of the field. Indeed, there our heart was, not exactly symmetrical, but a heart nonetheless. We cheered from the car and sat for a time looking at what we had made together before driving home.

It's been at least a dozen years since then, and still, I have yet to have a Valentine's Day memory that tops that one. That heart we stomped out in the field that day is not so different from Mom's — large, unique and generous with its presence. Thanks, Mom.

~Rachel Furey

78

Somebody to Turn the Rope

Kids spell love T-I-M-E.
~John Crudele

Growing up with seven brothers and sisters, there was always someone to play with. Sometimes though, when my older brothers were scattered throughout the neighborhood with their friends, there weren't quite enough kids at home to play some of our favorite games. Many times one of my sisters or I would run into the house calling, "Mama, Mama, we need somebody to turn the rope." Mama would put down her broom or turn off her iron and come outside for a game of jump rope.

One evening, my younger sister and I went to Mama, our faces forlorn and our eyes pleading. My sister held our worn jump rope in her hands. I coaxed her to make the plea because she was younger, cuter and harder to ignore.

"Mama, we can't play jump rope by ourselves. It takes two people to turn the rope, and at least one jumper." She gave Mama her most beguiling smile. "Will you play with us, Mama? You can jump, can't you?"

Mama leaned on her mop and gave me a knowing grin. She was on to my ploy. I managed a weak smile and ducked my head guiltily.

"Of course I can jump," Mama said, putting the mop back in the bucket. After that, Mama frequently joined in when we played jump rope. To my chagrin, she was a better jumper than I was.

Games were always more fun when Mama played with us. Neighbors would shake their heads and smile when they saw Mama playing hopscotch, jump rope, leapfrog or softball with us. She was a small woman, so from a distance she looked like just another kid. She always seemed to have as much fun as we did.

Once a neighbor questioned Mama's willingness to drop whatever she was doing and play with us. Mama smiled and said, "I was an only child and I was very shy. I seldom had playmates. I guess I'm making up for what I missed when I was growing up." She looked around at her bevy of kids who were hanging onto her words. "I can't imagine why anybody would rather shine their floors than play with their kids. My house will always need cleaning, but someday all of these kids will be gone."

We were the only kids in the neighborhood who had a mother who came outside to play with us. She joined in our games with as much enthusiasm as we did. When we divided into teams to play ball, we always had to pick a number to decide which side got Mama. Mama would smile as we fought for her since she always got chosen last when she was a girl. I am so grateful that I grew up with a mother who put our childish wishes ahead of her many chores. In her wisdom, she knew that having fun was more important than having a perfectly clean house.

I can honestly say, when looking back, that I can't recall if our kitchen floor was clean or whether there were crumbs in the corners. I don't remember whether our bathroom fixtures gleamed or whether there was a faint ring around the tub. I don't know if our clothes were always starched and ironed or whether we wore them wrinkled to school. But I do recall very vividly how Mama looked as she jumped rope, her ponytail bouncing up and down. I can hear her voice chanting, "Miss Mary Mack, Mack, Mack, all dressed in black, black, black; with silver buttons all down her back, back, back," as she smiled happily. She gave us such wonderful memories that we still talk about them today as middle-aged adults.

Mama is growing old now. Her steps are slow and halting. Her memory is fading. Her shoulders are bent. But when I look into her warm blue eyes, I still see the young mother who thought that happy children were more important than a spotless house.

~Elizabeth Atwater

Spilt Milk

Sing out loud in the car even, or especially, if it embarrasses your children.
~Marilyn Penland

My mother had a knack for embarrassing me, and this was no exception. She was my Girl Scout leader and, when we were working on our skating badges, my mother, the former skater, did the jitterbug on roller skates.

All of my peers thought she was the most beautiful, fascinating thing on wheels. I prayed to my God, and any other god that would listen, that she would fall and break something, an arm at least. It couldn't be anything too serious, of course, because I needed her to take care of me, her precious spoiled child. It just needed to be bad enough to keep her off of the roller skates.

She also sewed all of our short, blue, ruffled skirts to show off our "cute little legs" while skating. Unfortunately, she sewed one for herself. Granted she was young in some eyes, late 30s, but very old in mine. She also had very nice legs. But who wants her mother's legs on display doing none other than the jitterbug on roller skates! I'm pretty sure some of the other mothers were as fond of her that night as I was, and all of the other dads were as envious of my daddy as the girls were of me. She taught us well and we all got our badges and much applause.

As embarrassing as mothers can be at times, they can be lifesavers at others. One summer when all the aunts, uncles and cousins were in town for a family reunion we held a barbecue at our house.

The adults were set up on the patio and the kids had been relegated to a picnic table in the backyard. I was the youngest of all the cousins and one of the few girls. My older brothers teased me mercilessly about everything, and when they had an audience, it was worse. I was trying so hard to fit in with the "big" kids, especially the boys who never wanted me around.

One of my cousins from Oklahoma, Jimmy, was hands-down the funniest person I'd ever known. I laughed at almost everything he said. Well, Jimmy was in fine form that day and we all laughed so much we hardly touched our food. I had to go to the bathroom so badly, but I knew I'd miss something funny so I decided to "hold it," something at which I seldom succeeded.

Then, the worst thing happened. I peed in my pants sitting there at the picnic table with the big kids, the cousins and the teasing big brothers. If I could have died right then, or magically disappeared, I would have. I was the only one who knew. But eventually I would have to get up, and then they all would see my humiliation. So, I just decided to sit there forever in my embarrassment and never leave that table.

Finally, everyone finished eating and laughing at Jimmy and decided to join the grown-ups. I just sat there. There was no way I could let anyone see my wet shorts. None of them encouraged me to go with them because, as I said, I was the youngest and they didn't care if I hung around them or not. Thankfully, my mother noticed I wasn't with the others and came looking for me. There I sat in my shame. I had to tell her what happened and that I could never let the others know.

My mother, the roller-skating, jitterbug queen of embarrassment, picked up my glass of milk and poured it in my lap. I could not have been more shocked if she had slapped me across the face. Then she said in a very loud voice, "Oh, Becky, I'm so sorry, I spilled your milk. Look what a mess I've made. You'll have to go in the house and change clothes." My mother the genius. She saved my life that day as sure as if she'd pulled me drowning from a raging river. I had never been so relieved, happy and proud of my mother.

We walked from the yard to the patio where everyone had gathered, and she made her announcement again and went on and on about how sorry she was. Then she hugged me and said, "Baby, run in the house and change so you can play." I don't think I'd ever loved my mother more than at that moment. I was only eight or nine at the time, and throughout the rest of our lives together, she continued to embarrass me and I started to really embarrass her. But she also came to my rescue more times than I can count in her eighty-two years.

Every time I embarrass one of my own three daughters, and every time I run to their rescue, I think about my mother. I've never thrown a glass of milk on any of them, but I hope they have at least one memory of me that is as wonderful as this one of my mother, "the roller-skating, and jitter-bugging, milk-throwing queen." I do miss her.

~Rebecca Lasley Thomas

Chapter 8

Thanks Mom

Gifts of the Heart

Because You Were There

There's a lot more to being a woman than being a mother,
but there's a hell of a lot more to being a mother than most people suspect.
~Roseanne Barr

I shivered on the sidelines as my freshman high school soccer team played on. Snow began to fall as the playing conditions deteriorated. It was a close game so I knew there was little chance of my entering the action. Across the field I saw a few spectators—including my mom. How I longed to score a goal for her, or for my coach to praise my athletic prowess in her presence, but instead, I never played—that day or many others. She was used to this. I wasn't much of a baseball player either. Thawing out in the car on the drive home and feeling guilty about her coming "for nothing," I told her she shouldn't have bothered. She replied, "I had to." And, when I asked her why, she simply said, "Because you were there." It'd be years before I'd realize the significance of her words, and all it took for this spontaneous epiphany to come to pass was for me to become a father.

With age comes wisdom, and now, after many years as a parent, I've come to recognize and appreciate many of the sacrifices that both of my parents, but especially my mom, suffered for the sake of my siblings and me. To this end, and almost four decades later, I can easily identify with why my mom spent so many autumn afternoons braving the elements to stand on the sidelines during my none-too-stellar high school soccer career. I've also come to understand how her daily existence revolved around the lives and wellbeing of my brothers, sister and me, and how her adult wants and needs took a backseat to the wants and needs of her children. This was an invaluable example I'd come to follow when I became a father.

My friends with kids acted as if they possessed a special knowledge simply because they'd sired offspring. They felt compelled to offer their knowing opinion of how my life would forever change upon my entrance into the world of parenthood. Of course, I simply discarded their warnings; after all, no child could ever have that much influence over the life of an adult—or so I thought.

And then one morning, I became a father. With Michael's birth, as foretold, my life changed. His birth became the catalyst that sparked in me the need to become more keenly aware of all that was happening within my immediate world. Do the cars really travel too fast down our street? How good are the schools? His birth prompted me to focus more on the greater world, too. What was happening in our country and around the world? And how would the totality of all I'd begun to notice impact the life of this precious child for whom I was now responsible? His life mattered more than mine and his wants and needs immediately surpassed my own. I found parenthood to be rewarding, fulfilling, a blessing and sometimes, a scary proposition. The world was a frightening place, and I quickly realized that I could only provide my son with a minimal amount of security, and for a limited amount of time. The birth of my daughter, Tracy, compounded all that I'd been feeling.

Eventually, I became more comfortable in my role as father, protector and provider. And, I also learned that, as my friends with kids had predicted, parenthood had forever changed me. My children came first, and to this end, I gladly surrendered whatever I might've done for what I knew I had to do—echoes of my own childhood and of my mom's devotion. My willingness to participate in various facets of their lives sometimes surprised me, whether it was taking time off to be a "class mother" for the preschool pumpkin picking trip, crafting an edible castle complete with a moat filled with Goldfish crackers for a Cub Scout bake-off, or corralling a herd of out-of-control hormone-raging middle schoolers while chaperoning an overnight class trip.

As time went by, I began to realize that long before I'd even become a father, my education in proactive and participating parenting had already begun—the result of the unconditional love, guidance and example set forever in stone by Mom. So many subtle and yet valuable lessons were being taught during my childhood.

My son was a four-year member of his high school lacrosse team. He'd played in almost every game—mostly as a starter, but during his last year his playing time evaporated. Still, I attended his games, celebrating when he had a few minutes of field time and commiserating with him when he didn't. Sometimes I wondered if he ever felt awkward about my attending, but if he did, he never mentioned it. Regardless, I simply had to be there. It was a dad thing, but it was taught to me a lifetime ago by my mom. I was always proud of him for his dedication to his team and to the game. Maybe one day he'll ask why I came to all of his games, his elementary school plays and field trips, his scouting events and every other thing that he ever did. If he does, I'll respond to his question with the same answer Mom once gave me, "I had to, because you were there."

~Stephen Rusiniak

The Quilt

Our lives are like quilts—
bits and pieces, joy and sorrow, stitched with love.
~Author Unknown

I had heard about it for about a year and a half before I ever saw it. In our cross-country, bi-weekly phone calls, my mom would talk about the progress she had made.

"I have the material picked out.... I finally finished piecing it together.... I've been working on basting it to the batting....," and finally and triumphantly, "I've finished the last stitch!"

Through the whole process, I was enthusiastic and supportive, but, curiously, somewhat disconnected from the actual work that was taking place. My mom had created fabulous quilts for my sister and brother and now it was my turn.

I first saw it on Christmas morning at my parents' home in Whisler, Ohio. I knew it was finished and that it would be making its way into my hands. The thought warmed me and made me feel very much like the little girl that I had been growing up in the country all those years ago. Christmas morning rituals came and went, bringing with them a sense of wholeness that I sometimes felt was missing in California because of the distance that separated us.

The moment had come at last. Mom went to the closet and returned with her treasure. There it was! The culmination of literally hundreds of hours of work that she had repeatedly told me was "a labor of love." As we spread it out before us, the vibrant colors and patterns delighted me. She had captured my love of nature in the cool greens. The maroons and oranges were a reflection of countless sunsets I had witnessed throughout the years. Each large square contained five stitched hearts to represent the timeless bond between a mother and daughter. The pattern was called a Dresden Plate, and it did indeed look like a plate with fans of material radiating from the center.

As my eyes drank in the myriad colors, I was overwhelmed with thoughts and emotions.

"I really don't deserve something as beautiful and special as this!" I reflected on the many occasions on which I felt I had disappointed my mom. But her eyes told me a different story. I saw pride and love, and I know she saw it reflected back from me as she looked into my tear-filled eyes. I really don't know what I had expected to feel, but this was more raw and intense than I had imagined.

As I touched the fabric and ran my hands across the warm, textured surface, I remembered something Mom had said to me during the course of her creation. "I sit, and as the needle moves in and out, I think of you. I remember you as a smiling baby on my lap, your first steps and utterances, sending you off to elementary school in the new dress I made for you, sleepless nights waiting for you to get home on the weekends in high school, helping you pack for college, and watching you drive away with your friends in your rusty old van on your way to California."

It hit me then with such clarity! With every stitch, she was memorializing our memories. To a stranger, this piece of work might have seemed like an attractive but ordinary quilt. But to my mother and me, it was a legacy, something no one else in the whole world could share. It was ours. And now she was giving it away to me. I wondered how she was feeling. Was it difficult for her to let it go? Or was it a relief to pass it on?

I would get a sense of what she might have been feeling eight years later when, in the same room, in the same house, I too gave away something I had worked hard on. I had hand-stitched a baby quilt for a family friend. This was a project I had therapeutically worked on during the month I spent at home helping to take care of Mom as she slowly slipped away from this world from cancer. During that time she, along with my sister and aunt, taught me how to quilt, and Mom was shocked that her un-crafty daughter would take it up and do a terrific job on top of it. She never knew this, but this was a mission, and it kept me sane. I needed her to see that I could and would continue her legacy.

Unfortunately, the passing on of my quilt was somewhat anti-climatic. Our friend expressed gratitude, but it wasn't the big, over-whelming reaction I had expected. I knew what my mom and I had felt eight years before was deeper. My mother had given me the ultimate gift of love, made up of a series of squares, patterns, and colors that would warm and comfort me until we could meet again.

~Hope Justice

82

A Mother's Faith

Fall seven times, stand up eight.
~Japanese Proverb

Christmas with my brother, Ken, was always a magical time. He never got "too cool" to be excited over the holidays the way the rest of us did. Ken was born smack in the middle of my parents' twelve kids. He was born a month early in an era when pediatric intensive care units weren't what they are today. Halfway through the delivery, the doctors realized the umbilical cord was wrapped around Ken's throat cutting off the oxygen to his brain. By the time he was in the doctor's hands, it had been cut off long enough to leave him with cerebral palsy, mild retardation and profound deafness. But God is good and he more than compensated for Ken's disabilities by lavishing on him a sparkling personality, gusto for life, childlike faith and a magnetic smile that drew people to him.

Because my brother, Mark, was born less than a year after Ken, and my sister, Gail, had been born ten months before, babying Ken was not an option. He was part of the gang from day one, and although he didn't walk until he was twelve, he never had trouble keeping up with the rest of us, or the passel of neighborhood kids and cousins who hung around our house.

In the hospital, the doctors had advised my parents not to see Ken, to put him in a "special home" and forget they'd had him. They predicted he'd never walk or talk, never feed himself, and wouldn't live past his tenth birthday. Ken was seven by the time I was born and I'm glad the doctors never told him any of the above. The Ken I knew was lean and taut, feisty and impish and ate anything that didn't eat him first. He loved a party, loved being the center of attention and loved everything to do with Christmas.

One of my favorite Christmas memories was a year when our grandparents sent us a new swing set. From first glance, Ken was fascinated with the slide. He spent the holidays on the ground offering a blow-by-blow commentary as the rest of us slid down. He'd squeal with delight as we started down the slide, throw his head back and laugh when we landed with a splat at his feet, then chase us on all fours trying to grab us and tickle us before we could crawl back up the ladder again. (You did not want to get caught, because when Ken tickled you, he did not know his own strength.) He never tried to traverse the ladder himself. His scrawny, twisted legs just didn't work the way they needed to.

The day the rest of us started back to school, Mama knew what she had to do. She bundled Ken up, took him out to the backyard, pointed him toward the ladder and began to pray.

"Okay, Lord, Ken wants to go down the slide. I'm gonna need all the help I can get to let him try."

Years later, she told me how hard it was watching him climb and fall, climb and fall again and again. He tore both knees out of his pants, which he generally did most days anyway (his patches had patches), cut one elbow, bloodied his forehead and had one particularly bad tumble that left him rocking on the lawn crying and holding a knot on the back of his head while Mama forced herself not to run to his aid.

The neighbor to the back of us came to the fence and yelled at my mama, "What kind of woman are you? Get that baby off that ladder!" Mama told her as nicely as she could that, if it bothered her, she'd have to close her curtains and stop watching. Ken had decided he was going down the slide, and down the slide he would go, no matter how long it took him.

By the time the rest of us got home from school, Ken was black and blue and smiling from ear to ear. Not only could he get up and down the slide with lightning speed, but heaven help any kid who got in his way.

That swing set was a generous gift my grandparents gave us. I'm sure it set them back a bit. But the real gift came from my mom—my mom who loved my brother, Ken, enough to watch him struggle, to pray for the courage not to interfere, knowing how important it was for him to do things on his own.

That was almost fifty years ago. I wish I knew where those doctors are now. They were so ready to tell us all what my brother would never do. Obviously, they didn't know the God we knew. What would they say if they could see Ken now at age fifty-five, living independently and holding down a job? They didn't know back then that God had a much bigger plan for my brother and they didn't know the mama who loved him enough and trusted God enough to give him the best Christmas present he'd ever receive.

~Mimi Greenwood Knight

83

Nobody's Child But Mom's

When someone you love becomes a memory, the memory becomes a treasure.
~Author Unknown

I was six months pregnant, but instead of feeling thrilled and excited, I was devastated. The woman I called "Mom," who'd raised me since infancy, had just passed away. I grieved for my baby, who would never experience the joy of knowing this amazing woman.

After my biological mother left my father and me, he decided there was no room in his life for a child. He signed legal guardianship over to a close friend of his family, a forty-seven-year-old woman who thought she'd remain childless forever.

While my father paid child support, he was never more than a remote and distant figure in my life. It was Mom who helped me with my homework and accompanied my class on field trips. When some of the kids teased me about not having "real" parents, Mom sat me down and gave me advice in her usual no-nonsense manner.

"Forget about them," she said. "Hold your head up, be the best you can be, and always remember to smile. It'll make them wonder what you're up to."

When I graduated from high school, Mom encouraged me to attend college, even though she herself hadn't gone beyond the ninth grade.

The day after I received my bachelor's degree, she threw a huge party.

"Congratulate my daughter, the teacher," she said to one of her cousins. "The first one in our family to graduate from college." It didn't matter to her that, technically, none of these people were related to me. I was her daughter and that was that.

A few months before my wedding, Mom had a heart attack. While the doctors were pessimistic about her being able to attend, Mom was determined. Instead of arguing with the doctor as she usually did, she followed his instructions to the letter, and was able to walk me down the aisle.

When I found out I was pregnant, Mom was the first person we told. As soon as she heard, she grabbed me and danced around the room.

"My baby's having a baby," she sang. She kissed me on one cheek and then the other, before wrapping me in one of her voluminous hugs. Her excitement grew when I told her my plans for being a stay-at-home mother.

"We can take walks to the park together," I said, then joked, "You can even come over any time you want, and change a diaper or two."

"Like I haven't changed enough of those in my lifetime," she laughed.

Mom did everything but hire a skywriter to announce the fact that she was going to be a grandmother. One evening, she rode her bicycle over to our house looking as excited as a kid at Christmas.

"I came across these this afternoon. I'd forgotten I saved them for you," she said, handing me a small box. Removing the cover, I found a tiny ring, bracelet and necklace.

"These were my welcome home gift to you," she said with a look of nostalgia. "If your baby turns out to be a girl, she can wear them."

To celebrate our wedding anniversary, my husband and I made reservations at a resort two hours from home. When I called Mom to say goodbye, her last words to me were, "I love you. Now go have a great time. You may not have a chance to celebrate like this once you have the baby."

That evening the hospital called. Mom had collapsed at a friend's house while playing cards. Her condition was listed as grave. We raced to the hospital, but by the time we arrived, Mom was gone.

In spite of everyone's expressions of sympathy, I was inconsolable. I was carrying a child of my own, yet I felt like an infant myself as I wept for my mother. I turned down invitations from friends who wanted to take me to lunch or go shopping. Instead I continued to grieve, taking solitary walks during the day and long drives in the evening. Even my husband couldn't cheer me up. The only person capable of doing so was gone.

One Sunday, Aunt Annie, Mom's sister, invited me over for the afternoon. When she opened the door, twenty-five of my friends, and Mom's, surprised me with a baby shower.

After the party games and refreshments were over, it was time for me to open my gifts. Soon, the living room floor was covered with tiny clothing, baby toys, and even a stroller. I was almost relieved when I'd opened the last of my presents. I didn't know which hurt worse, my feet or my back. I couldn't wait to get home and flop down on the couch.

"Just one more." Aunt Annie ran back to her bedroom and reappeared with a bulky package. Laughter erupted throughout the room. Never one to waste money on fancy paper and ribbon, Mom had always wrapped her gifts with whatever was handy, securing them with remnants she found in her sewing box. This one was wrapped in the comics' section of the newspaper and tied with a long piece of green silk.

When I removed the silk, and the paper fell to the floor, I was left holding a crib quilt done in shades of red, green and blue. I gazed at the precise stitches and longed more than ever for my mother.

Everyone rushed over to gush over the quilt. I kept a tight grip on it, refusing to let anyone else touch it. There was something so familiar about those colorful squares, but I couldn't pinpoint where I'd seen them before.

Annie, who'd been watching me, came over and bent her head close to mine. "The squares are made from some of the dresses you wore as a little girl," she whispered. "Your mom said she loved them so much she couldn't bear to give them away. When you announced you were pregnant, she was so excited...." She stopped, overcome with emotion.

I held the soft quilt close to my face. I had a vision of Mom, bent over one of her projects, while at the same time trying to help me with my math. More memories washed over me as I stroked the quilt with my fingers.

"She loved you so much," said Annie with shining eyes. "She always said every day she spent with you was a gift."

Through my own tears, I glanced down at the card, attached to a corner of the quilt by a slender thread. It was written in Mom's endearing scribble.

"It's time for you to make your own memories, but never forget that you will always be my baby."

"Thank you," I whispered. "And you will always be my mother."

~Ellen Fink

84

The Blue Dress

Mother's love grows by giving.
~Charles Lamb

I am the eldest of six children and was usually in agreement with my parents on issues of money. Like them, I felt it was foolish to spend needlessly, and I worried about their scarce finances. But, on this one day, I did not want to be frugal. I had been invited to the junior/senior prom, my first formal dance, and I wanted a gown that would make me look like an angelic princess. I had envisioned the gown for weeks—pink fabric with little white bows and a two-boned hoop sewn into the skirt. I would wear pretty little sandals and carry a beaded purse.

As we were shopping for this dress, we walked past a consignment shop which had some of its items on the sidewalk for display. As I recall, I practically leapt, in slow motion, to block my mother's view of this powder blue, used dress of gauze fabric that I just knew would accompany us home should the two meet. The meeting did occur and the bonding took place the minute my mother eyed the price tag—$20!

"Oh, honey, look!" she exclaimed, "It's you, don't you think?"

I would have bent over backwards to make things easier for my parents. I also knew the dress I wanted would cost more than my mother had in her budget. I just couldn't see any choice but to agree with my mother.

I smiled and told my mother that I, too, thought it was a godsend.

Not only was the cost simply unbelievable, but the dress presented my mother with something she just couldn't refuse—a challenge! I could almost hear the thoughts screaming with excitement in my mother's head.

"So, it's not pink. Powder blue will be much prettier against her winter pale skin."

"It's an inch and a half too short. But, I saw the most beautiful lace in the fabric store the other day that should be just wide enough to add the necessary length."

"But, the skirt. It doesn't come with the hoop and (sigh) a double-boned hoop will cost twice as much as this dress."

As she struggled with the challenge the hoop presented, she kept holding the dress up to my face and pointing out all the delicate details this dress had which the other dresses did not. We agreed right then that this was the dress I would wear to my first formal dance. We proceeded into the store, one proudly, one reluctantly, with this dress of fine detail in hand, and paid the clerk our $20.

All the way home, Mom chattered about her ideas for altering the dress. As she talked, I fought with my internal conflicts. I was amazed at my mother's ability to seek out finds, and I took pride in her creative talents and can-do attitude. However, I knew all the girls would be wearing store-bought dresses that didn't need an added inch and a half of lace just to make them fit properly. I was struggling with my immaturity and my selfishness. I didn't want to settle, once again, for what I thought was second best. I didn't want to be reasonable. I didn't want to have five siblings at home who also needed things. I just wanted the perfect dress that would transform me from my plain self to a sophisticated young lady.

But my tantrums were always internal and never manifested themselves outwardly. I didn't know at the time that my mother could see the contents of my heart by looking at my face. She never let on that she knew I was secretly disappointed. She just did her best to change my disappointment into the excitement she was feeling.

So, as I climbed the stairs to my room that night, I looked at the dress hanging on the door next to my mother's sewing machine and told myself it wasn't such an ugly dress, really, and that the gauze-type fabric was as soft to the touch as rose petals. A little sigh and that was the end of my internal tantrum.

The next morning, as I awoke, I heard the zig-zig-zig of my mother's sewing machine. When I gently placed my hand on her back to ask her what she was working on, she jubilantly exclaimed that she knew what to do about the hoop issue. She then, to my astonishment, held up two heavy white sheets that she explained would be sewn together, gathered at the waist with elastic and inserted at just the right levels with the boning to turn me and my dress into a proper Southern Belle. I could muster up only one question. "What about these little bleach holes that are all over the sheets?"

Voila! She was holding up a little powder blue cloud shaped piece of fabric. "We'll sew these little clouds over the holes with a tiny blue satin bow in the middle of each cloud," she told me. "Okay, Mom," I said, "If you really think it'll work."

What was I talking about? Of course she thought it would work! She was as stubborn as she was talented. After several trips to the fabric store, the day of the prom arrived. As I held my arms straight up into the air, Mom slipped the hoop over my head and pulled it down to my waist. Although it was tilted just a tiny bit to the left, I had to admit she had exceeded all expectations. While all the other girls wore hoops purchased from the same local store in our small town, I could look down and discreetly admire the hand stitching around each cloud that only my mother and I knew covered a tiny hole underneath. The small satin bow in the middle of each cloud was daintier than anything I had envisioned.

When Mom slipped the dress over my head next, it gracefully fell into place and gently brushed the tops of my toes. The lace was beautiful and looked as if it had been part of the original design. Mom fashioned a perfect bow in the middle of my back and I was ready to go.

When my date arrived, beautiful white and baby blue wrist corsage in hand, his eyes sent the message I had heard in my dreams. I waved goodbye to my family and left with my date for the dance.

It's funny how only time teaches us to truly appreciate the special gifts of the people we love. My mother told me not long ago that she knew how much I did not want the $20 dress. She knew what a sacrifice it was for me, despite my insistence that it was nothing.

What she doesn't know is that the $20 she spent that day paid for much more than a prom dress. It paid for a deepened love of a child for a parent. It paid for lessons in economics and creativity. It paid for lessons in heartbreak as well as for lessons in appreciation and maturity. The $20 allowed my mother to give me, in addition to a dress and slip, the gift of herself, of her mother's love.

~Jennifer Gilkison

85

The Best Coloring Book Ever

Simply having children does not make mothers.
~John A. Shedd

"**M**om, I need a new coloring book." I was sure my mother would understand. Anyone looking at my old coloring books could see that I couldn't continue to use them. Using each crayon in my sixty-four-count box, I had sampled every page.

With barely a glance she said, "They're fine, Becky. Go on and play." My neighborhood friend, Denise, and I slowly made our way back to my bedroom. I knew I was meant to be an artist. I loved to color. I was just never able to translate the beauty I saw in my mind through the crayons onto the page. What I really wanted was a sketchpad, a true artist's pallet. Not the scratch paper Dad brought home from work, with writing on one side. I wanted a blank slate.

I slowly flipped through the pages, hoping to find a fresh place to start. I wanted to create perfection, just the right combination of colors, blended and shaded. My dream was to create the kind of picture with which people could identify. Until then, I would settle for just being able to stay inside the lines of a pre-printed picture.

I was still flipping through the pages with the blind hope of a child, when I glanced up to see my mother in the doorway to my room. "Hey, I found a coloring book for you," she said. Denise and I grabbed all the crayons we could carry and ran after my mother. We followed her down the hall and all the way to the family room at the other end of the house. We were so excited we were giggling like, well, like little girls. So, where was it? It had to be super special for us to have to use it in the family room!

"See this wall? That is your coloring book. But only this wall, understand?" We froze. This had to be a trap. I may not have figured out all of life's rules at that young age, but there were a few I had down pat. Don't draw on the walls was one of the biggies. I couldn't move. I just stared at my mother and wondered why she was trying to trick me. She gave me a little shove toward the wall. I looked at my crayons. If this was really going to happen, this would be my masterpiece—a blank wall, all for me. I slowly drew a line then quickly looked to see if my mother had changed her mind. She just smiled and went back into the kitchen. I became engrossed. For hours I colored, drew, created.

Being the fourth of five children in a neighborhood full of children, word quickly spread. Soon the room was full of kids of all ages, vying for space to leave their own mark on the wall. Being allowed to draw on a wall was so unheard of it was like being allowed to eat ice cream for breakfast. My mother quickly blocked off a small space for my older sister to draw on when she came home. I wasn't worried about losing the space. I was sure a teenager would think that this was baby stuff and walk away. But age made no difference that day. Even my older brothers, who were normally "too cool" for such things, were eagerly grabbing crayons to scribble and draw. The room was filled with laughter and shouts of "look at this!" and "give me some room." All too soon, there were no empty spaces left to fill.

Thanks to my mother, my dream of drawing on a blank canvas was realized. She gave me this unique opportunity to draw outside the confines of a coloring book and to experience the magic that is possible when we are not restricted by boundaries. I learned later that my parents were remodeling the house and that my canvas was the wall destined to be knocked out. After the demolition crew came and went, most of us combed through the debris of plaster and drywall trying to find our pictures, remembering, and perhaps, reliving the joy.

~Rebecca Olker

86

Chicken Soup for the Soul

Fan Appreciation

Don't wait to make your son a great man — make him a great boy.
~Author Unknown

I remember when I was sixteen years old and sitting in the kitchen with you at our house in Miami, Florida. I was feeling frustrated and confused after having some girlfriend issues that day. I looked right at you and said, "Women! Mom, I sure am glad you are not one of them!"

Ten years later, I asked you to stand to be the "Best Man" at my wedding. While I suppose that is an unconventional concept (having a woman stand to be the groom's best man), it seemed so natural and obvious to me. From my perspective, I believed that the person who should stand next to you on the most important day of your life, the day you get married, should be the person you feel is the most important to you up until that moment in time. That person was you, Mom.

You earned it.

I did not grow up in a broken home or one without warmth, love or resources. It seems like a lot of stories of successful people start with some difficult personal beginning. I was not cut from that cloth. What I had was a mom who loved me, unconditionally. You really went above and beyond when it came to giving to me and cementing in me every bit of good that you knew how to give.

When I was nine years old, you broke your finger playing catch with me. Did you complain or even stop? Nope. You made me feel that getting my fastball over the inside corner of the plate was much more important than your finger. Which I guess made sense at the time because, after all, you had ten fingers but I only had one fastball.

Then you fed the batting machine with an endless bucket of baseballs so I could practice my hitting, and you drove me to practices and games, sitting through all of them. Rain or shine, it did not matter. You were there, watching every pitch and cheering for every swing, throw and catch. And making me feel like it was your first choice of things to do each and every time. Now that I am a parent of three incredible children, I fully understand, appreciate and admire the sacrifices you made for me.

Probably the most amazing part was that you did it effortlessly, or at least that is how it seemed to me. We are all human, and have our limits to patience. And even with the ones we love most, sometimes we don't feel like doing something with them or for them. But if you ever felt that way about me, I never knew it. Whenever I asked for help or just your attention — it did not matter how big or small — you responded as if nothing else in your world mattered. That is unconditional attention. And that is what you always gave me.

Remember the time I was a junior in high school and came home from baseball practice? I was upset, as it was the first time in my life I had been told by a coach that I was not good enough to start on the team. I was ready to quit. It didn't matter to me that I had played ball and been the best player on the team for twelve of the seventeen years of my life. In my mind, the coach was a jerk and I was done with baseball.

We were standing next to the washing machine. You listened to me as I vented through frustration, disappointment and tears. I know you felt every moment of the pain I was experiencing, but you were the voice of reason when I needed it most.

You told me that I could quit, that it was my choice; but that I should think about it more carefully and not rush to decide while I was so upset. "Just take the weekend to think it through some more," you encouraged. You also reminded me that there were eight other positions on the field and that I could learn how to play one of those.

You reminded me that failure is a critical part of achieving success later and that dealing with and overcoming setbacks and defeats are what define a person's character.

I ended up working hard to learn the outfield position. I started that year as an outfielder and then went on to play at Colgate University, becoming the captain of the team my senior year in college. When I graduated, they retired my baseball jersey, which is framed and hanging on my wall next to me as I type this. It serves as a constant reminder to me of the life lesson you taught me over twenty years ago standing next to that washing machine; which is that in life, what happens to a person is not as important as what a person does with what happens to him.

This timeless life lesson, the one that you taught me, has become the core philosophy that I have built my peak-performance coaching career around as I help people find their own inner greatness.

We just celebrated your sixty-fifth birthday. I stood up and said some words to a room full of friends and family you have collected over the years. Every word I said was from my heart. Holding back tears of joy, love and admiration as I spoke each sentence. You are a remarkable person, Mom. I know I don't tell you often enough.

When I look back now that I am a parent of three children, I realize that you really did the four greatest things I think any parent can do for their children:

1) Make them feel loved, unconditionally
2) Make them feel safe at all times
3) Show them their wings
4) Give them the confidence to use those wings

To this day, I am not sure if you were ever a fan of baseball. But if baseball was what I was playing, then baseball was what you were sitting in the stands watching. I remember you once telling me that your friends would say to you that they didn't realize you were such a big fan of baseball. You would tell them, "I am not a big fan of baseball, I am a big fan of Doug!"

Well, thank you, Mom for being my first and biggest fan, for making me feel loved, for making me feel safe and most of all for showing me my wings.

~Doug Hirschhorn

Silent Reassurance

All that I am or ever hope to be, I owe to my angel Mother.
~Abraham Lincoln

Nine years after Mom suffered her stroke, we remained optimistic that she would make a full recovery. Her therapy showed signs of progress, but after a couple of years passed, our optimism was slapped with a challenging reality. Frequent visits to the doctor resulted in a prognosis of progressive dementia and her diabetes was getting worse. We were faced with finding the best possible health care for her. Most of us lived out of town and were not financially able to quit our jobs to provide the care she needed. After exhausting all of our options, we had to make the agonizing decision to admit her to a nearby nursing facility. During our visits, we made a concerted effort to remain positive and upbeat. The mere thought of the atmosphere in the nursing home left us depressed and resulted in endless long distance phone calls to comfort each other.

Another hurdle came when her doctor notified us that gangrene had set in to her left leg and foot. Amputation was the only solution to keep her alive. Knowing that she was not capable of making any coherent decisions, we had to decide what to do. We prayed desperately for a miracle, but realized that her operation was inevitable. My mother always had beautiful legs. Her calves shouted for a pair of stiletto pumps. Seeing the outline of the remaining portion of her leg under the bedspread left me weak, sad and mentally drained. Three months after her operation we had to revisit the same scenario, but this time it was for her right leg. The second amputation was done quickly, but the painful, emotional side effect was no easier to bear.

How did Mom really feel? Was she depressed, bitter or angry? There were so many questions we would never get answers to because she had become nonverbal a couple of years earlier. It will always be a mystery to us what caused her to stop speaking. She managed to display looks when we visited, but we could not decipher them. Was she in pain, lonely, content, disappointed? Was she resentful that we had placed her in a home? That they had taken her legs? We could only manage encouraging smiles, conversations to let her know that she was going to be okay, along with our prayers.

Two months later on the eve of Easter, my sister phoned to tell me that the nursing home was transporting Mom to the hospital. Her blood pressure was becoming dangerously low. Around mid-afternoon on Easter Sunday, my sister updated me on Mom's condition. Her blood pressure was still dropping. The doctors were trying a different procedure to see if it would help, but it was to no avail. Mom's breathing became laborious. I went to my bedroom, cried and prayed, asking God not to take her right now. This was probably selfish on my part, but we always called her the comeback kid. Just when things began looking bleak, she would pull through with flying colors. Always! Now, I had to quickly get a grip on myself. This time my spirit felt different. I prayed to God that if the time had arrived for him to take her, I would reluctantly accept it. I did not want my mother to suffer anymore. It was evident that the hour was approaching for Mom to make her transition to another place. I had to let go, and I did.

Mom passed away on the night of Easter. This holiday has now become even more divinely significant for us. As expected, the week of her funeral was challenging, not only for her family, but for everyone who loved her. We were flooded with wonderful memories and reminders of the indelible marks she left behind. Never knowing her thoughts or feelings in her final days will always haunt us. For quite some time we longed to hear her simply say, "I love you" again. As we all sat under the funeral home canopy at the cemetery, with rain pouring down around us, those words we wanted to hear were buried with her body.

A few weeks later while rummaging through my night stand, I came across a couple of letters Mom had written eleven years earlier. One was addressed to me, and the other to my sister and me. Ironically, the letter addressed to my sister and me was a thank you note from her for the Easter cards and gifts we had given her that year. The Easter notation prompted me to sit down on the floor of my bedroom and continue reading. Tears filled my eyes as I finished. She ended it by writing, "I love you all so much, Mom." I couldn't believe the words I was actually seeing. After putting that letter down, I couldn't resist reading the second one addressed to me alone. She wrote how much she appreciated what I had done for her that summer. She ended it with, "Please know that I love you very much, Mom."

I was overwhelmed by finding these letters. I could tell from the postage stamps that I had read both of them eleven years earlier. After drying my tears, I called my sister and read both letters to her. She was just as stunned as I was. The sweet, comforting words we had wanted to hear our mother speak before she died were communicated to us at the right moment we needed to hear them. It was then that my sister and I found peace. Mom had wrapped her reassuring, heavenly arms around us.

~Kym Gordon Moore

New Dresses

Your children need your presence more than your presents.
~Jesse Jackson

Although I knew we were not wealthy as a child, I didn't know we were "poor." I always had everything I needed and wanted, including fancy dresses. But according to my mother, I did not have enough dresses. I can still remember so vividly going to KMart to look at them—the beautiful dresses. When my mother said that we would be doing this, I knew it meant that I would soon be performing as a model, trying on new dresses for an eager audience of one—Mom.

I also knew that I would be going home with a new outfit. I always held my mother's hand in the parking lot and through the store. She would lead me to the fitting rooms in the rear, and as I marveled at all the lights and displays of items available for purchase, she would scour the store for anything and everything she wanted me to try on. She could examine sizes, styles and prices and still know exactly what I was doing. It amazed me how she seemed to know when I was about to be tempted to dive under the clothes racks or wander away.

Once her load of dresses was ready for me to model, the dressing room lady would set me up in my own room to begin the show. After each fitting, my mom would rush up with a new dress and maybe a coordinating hat. The look in her eyes is still etched in my memory—an eager, loving look that said, "Yes, this one may be better than the last." She'd say, "Baby, try on just one more," and then, when I walked out of the dressing room, she would put her hand over her mouth in awe, and smile.

Sometimes, during this process, I would look up at her and see a sort of yearning. It was a painful look. It was almost like she'd give up any of her things just to buy me one more pretty dress. But even more than that, she had a look of pure love and joy. She wanted so much to give to her little girl everything she needed and wanted, but what she didn't know was that her little girl already had everything she needed and wanted—her mom.

~Stacia Marie Erckenbrack

89

A Ride Down Memory Lane

Life is like riding a bicycle—
in order to keep your balance, you must keep moving.
~Albert Einstein

t was a bright sunny day. I was enjoying a nice cold Coca-Cola and lying in my backyard hammock when I heard children shouting and quarrelling in the back alley. I turned my attention to the conversation between two little girls for only a second before I figured out what they were arguing about.

"Quick, get back on the bike, you almost had it that time," said the older girl.

"I can't do it, let me put the training wheels back on," said the younger of the two, whose legs were covered with scrapes and Band-Aids.

"No, this is my bike, and I don't want to drive around with training wheels all the time because you think you can't ride without them."

I chuckled at the innocence of the two girls, sisters who lived across the alley from me. I readjusted my ball cap over my face and continued to rest my eyes. I tried to get back to the state of total relaxation I was in before it was interrupted, but their conversation took me back to the memories I had the day I learned how to ride a bike. I was about four years old.

"Christopher," my mother called from the family room doorway, leaning against it with a tea towel thrown over her shoulder. She had snuck up on me as I was playing with my toy cars on the carpet. Pushing the cars around, I drove to and from the imaginary neighbors, stopping over in the field to say hello to my father. I had been playing all morning with my little brother but he had tuckered himself out and was napping on his back, arms stretched away from his body, his head to the side with drool coming from his little face, his fat little belly protruded from underneath his shirt.

"Yah," I said when I briefly turned my head toward my mother then back toward the car that was exiting the imaginary field.

"Come, let's go outside," she said. "It's a nice day out today and I'm finished with my work."

At that moment, I really wasn't interested, thinking she would want me to help her in the garden or something like that, so I continued playing and asked, "What are we going to do?"

"Oh, I don't know," she paused. I looked up at her and a smile came over her face. "I thought you could learn how to ride that bike today."

I jumped up in joy as a rush of excitement spread through my body. I ran through the house as fast as I could, out the door and onto the deck. I grabbed my muddy rubber boots from beside the door and dove out into the sun, grabbing my sister's little purple bike with white tires. My mother came out of the house behind me, "Take the bike over to the garage."

I was wound up, so I ran the bike toward the garage. The driveway in the farmyard was slanted slightly; we were going to use it for a starting hill. I jumped on the bike and waited for my mother's instruction.

"Okay, Christopher, when we start, I'm going to hold on to the bike and you pedal as fast as you can and don't stop."

"Don't let go," I warned.

She placed a hand on the handlebars and the other on the back of my seat, "I won't," she assured. "Okay. Ready?"

I nodded and stared straight ahead; ready to take off like a gust of wind.

"Go!" she shouted. I started pedaling fast as the bike started to move down the small hill, picking up speed. My mom was running alongside me with both hands on the bike like she promised; I had all the faith in the world when I was with her that nothing bad would happen. She started to tire. Out of breath, she hollered, "Good job, but stop the bike and we'll try again."

We did the exact same thing four or five more times. Each time we both gained more confidence in my abilities. The next couple of times, Mom took her hand off the handlebars, giving me more of a taste to explore balance on my own. When it looked as if the bike was wobbling too much, she guided me back to safety.

"Okay, now this time, I'm going to let go of the bike," she warned.

"No! Don't let go!" I pleaded. "I'm not ready yet."

"Okay, I won't let go this time."

I started out again just like the times before. I was pedaling furiously as Mom sprinted to keep up, holding the seat in one hand, pumping her other arm in sync with her legs, her voice always making its way to my ear, constantly reassuring and encouraging, "Good job, keep going. Good job. I'm letting go now."

"Don't let go!" I shouted in fear. "I'm not ready, don't let go. Don't let go!"

"Fine. I won't," she lied. "Keep going, faster, faster, you're doing so well."

Her voice became quieter and quieter. Then I realized what she had done and became angry. "You let go!"

"Keep going; you're doing it all by yourself. Good job!" she shouted. My anger suddenly turned to joy at the realization that I was riding a bike for the first time.

I flew down the driveway toward the gravel road. My old tired dog woke from his afternoon nap on the deck and came up to run beside me, barking as though he was applauding me as the wind blew through my hair. The smile on my face was a mile wide as I slowly turned the wheel and made a large turn back toward my mom. I rode the shiny purple bike up beside her and came to a wobbly stop and was greeted with hugs and kisses, and a good lick on the cheek from my loyal dog.

A car in the alley woke me from my daydream. I had a feeling I had only reflected for a matter of seconds. I smiled; I hadn't thought about that for a really long time. Mom passed away later that winter, and my few memories of her had faded away like footsteps in the sand. I try as hard as I can to never forget our times together. My brothers and sister and I gather during the holidays and share our memories of her to help us to never forget. The stories have been getting old and repetitive lately but this one is a new one; I have never told this memory. I have never remembered it before now. It is a memory as simple as learning how to ride a bike, yet cherished more than words can describe.

I rose from the hammock, reached down into my cooler, and pulled out a couple of cans of pop. I walked across the lawn toward the back alley where I could still hear the girls arguing over the training wheels. I offered them a drink to quench their thirst in the hot summer sun. Their eyes lit up as they gladly accepted my offer. I turned back to go into the house when I heard from behind me, simultaneously, "Thank you!"

The two words hit me in an unusual way as if I didn't deserve their thanks. I turned back and waved. I was in debt to them for rescuing the memory. Softly I muttered back to the girls, "No. Thank you!"

~Christopher Hartman

90

The World's Best Care Packages

What a wonderful thing is the mail,
capable of conveying across continents a warm human hand-clasp.
~Author Unknown

Recently, I found out that a friend of mine from England now teaches in upstate Connecticut. Through the time machine of Facebook, we realized that we were near each other, so Simon drove down to Greenwich for a visit.

Twenty-two years before, I was an English-Speaking Union Fellow, and the only American, at King's College, a boarding school in Taunton, Somerset, in England. Simon was on my hall in Meynell house just across the way from me. We also played on the basketball team together. During his recent Connecticut visit, though, our biggest laugh ended up being over the number and size of care packages my mother had mailed me while I was at King's for that year. It was my first time away from home, and I was eighteen.

Mom's famous cardboard boxes alone attracted quite a bit of attention, given that they were absolutely massive. Almost every three weeks, I would receive a huge parcel filled with Kool-Aid, Pop-Tarts and candy bars, which attracted the entire school to my room. When the gift arrived, I received a small slip in my mailbox. Then I would retrieve the box in one building and schlep it quite a ways to my dormitory. Consequently, everyone—masters and students—could see me hobbling along with my back-crippling care package. I happily disseminated the international goodies to my friends. Butterfingers, Milky Ways, Snickers.

As Simon and I reminisced recently, we laughed about how her gifts ended up being his introduction to Pop-Tarts, an item he was thrilled to buy once he was in the States as a teacher.

However, to me, those packages became Mom's way of showing affection when I was not home. She also handwrote many lovely letters, which I still have saved in a box in my closet. One particular package contained a tiny stuffed animal called a Pound Puppy. The guys on my hall, including Simon, used to kidnap Pound Puppy and hold him captive.

If you have ever been away from home for a long time and have ached to return, you know that *any* mail from your family is beautiful. Little mail is wonderful. Big mail is a dream!

Times have changed. I'm forty-one. I don't eat Pop-Tarts that much anymore, but when I had one of the worst years of my life in 2008 (as many did), the packages continued to come. Sometimes they would have a nice herringbone wool jacket from the thrift store. Or used J. Crew dress shoes. Or a cutout cartoon from the paper.

Mom even came up to Connecticut from Virginia on the train and bought me the silver trumpet I now play, purchased for ten dollars at a yard sale. It is handmade and vintage silver. She also sends me music books. Most of these things she buys in thrift shops, places we enjoy visiting when we're together.

I can picture her finding the stuff, gathering it on her dining room table, making the trip to the post office and, finally, taping it up so well that a machete couldn't even rip it. I always need a knife to slice through the inches of tape. Once the top is open, I pull out all the balled newspaper stuffed in there for insulation. Then the fun begins. What has she thought to send me this time? A book she knows I will like? Some comfortable clothes? A St. Joseph statue?

On my visits home to Virginia, there is usually a little surprise waiting. Last time, it was a ceramic Elvis with a blue shirt and black hair. Of course, I always score a free haircut and leave with all the dirty laundry I brought cleaned and folded.

Her most recent package contained a small wooden carved typewriter that had been painted black and white. It's an intricate paperweight that she bought for maybe fifty cents. And it looks like a miniature old Underwood. I even cut out a small piece of paper that says, "Type something" to put on the little typewriter. It resides here on my desk, an ongoing reminder that Mom is thinking of me.

The surprise boxes are still coming after twenty-three years. They seem to arrive when I need them, possessing a sweet maternal timing that lets me know she loves me. I look around my apartment at my ceramic Elvis, my miniature typewriter and, yes, my Pound Puppy on my bed, and I'm quite sure that my mother's care packages are the best in the world. My friend Simon will certainly back me up on this. I have international proof.

~Mark Damon Puckett

Chapter 9

Thanks Mom

My Mother's Legacy

91

A Thousand and One Stories, A Million and One Words

That best academy, a mother's knee.
~James Russell Lowell

My mother didn't leave me much. She didn't give me very much. She didn't have time—either on Earth or in her life.

At the end of the 60s, when I was a child and my mother was a beautiful woman in the prime of her life, she and my father were caught up in what seems a staple feature of that era: They were relentlessly social.

At the height of her partying and her beauty, my mother died, very quickly, of the same kind of brain cancer that killed Senator Ted Kennedy.

I was not yet twenty and thought I felt—I still feel—that I hardly knew her.

On the night she died, I remember thinking, who will I try to impress now? Who will be proud of me? A high-school dropout with a fierce intelligence, my mother insisted that my brother and I be strivers—the best, the brightest and the most beautiful. So I guess you could say my mother gave me the gift of never quite being satisfied with myself—which was no gift at all and has, in fact, been the source of most of the grief in my life.

The other gift she gave me, however, balanced that vague and familiar sense of not being quite good enough.

My mother gave me words. I suppose you could say that, in the truest sense, she inspired words in me. She breathed them into me.

In what seems now a quaintly tender gesture, she never left me without a story. In her stiletto heels and black, off-the-shoulder cocktail dress, she would stop before going out to read something to my brother and me. And that something was never garbage.

When I was a young woman and *The Jungle Book* was made into an animated movie, I remember my disappointment at how jolly Disney made an essentially heartbreaking tale. I remember the tears in my mother's eyes as she read of the wolf mother releasing her son Mowgli to go back to the human world, telling him that she and Mowgli's father were growing old. I remembered how the wolves greeted the other animals in the Indian jungle: "We be of one blood, ye and I."

I remember the story of a young girl called Velvet who got a horse for a shilling in a lottery and won the Grand National Steeplechase. I don't remember a time that I didn't realize that I was Jo in *Little Women*, and Laura in *Little House in the Big Woods*. My mother read me the story of the Firebird, and the ancient Norse tale of Baldur, slain with an arrow made of holly, and all of the Greek and Roman myths—until the names of the gods and goddesses were as familiar to me as friends.

She read me poems. We had an old set of *Childcraft Encyclopedia*, bound in fake red stuff that looked like leather, and, over and over, until I could repeat every word, my mother read to me of Bess, the landlord's black-eyed daughter, of the moon that was a Griffon's egg, of The Raven that spoke only one word (but what a word!), of the phantom deer arising when Daniel Boone went by at night, of Paul Revere and the rude bridge that arched the flood. So passionate a reader was she that, though I've been to the rude bridge that arched the flood in Concord, MA, a hundred times, I still can't repeat the words to that poem without choking up. My mother never explained to me what anything was about in the stories and poems she read to me. The way that she read them made the meaning self-evident. She could barely get through the end of the Robert Burns poem "Jon Anderson, my Jo!" or "Gunga Din" (why was she reading those things to a kid, anyhow?) because those poems were so noble and so sad.

And she wasn't just stuck on reading, but on words.

She didn't encourage me to play sports. She didn't come to the plays I was in and it wouldn't have occurred to me to ask her to participate in the bake sale at school or be a Brownie leader.

Maybe all she really cared about was reading words. The fact that words had an almost alchemic power, she didn't have to tell me. It was evident from her inflection. It was evident in the power words had over us, her children.

I suppose that my brother and I were the same sort of bickering, bouncing, bellowing kids that my own kids are. But our mother could bring us to our seats with a sentence. "There was a gypsy woman who had one son...." She could send us flying into our beds by picking up a book. Even seated at her dressing table, applying kohl in elaborate strokes over her fabulous eyes, she would create characters from her tubes, pencils and brushes and put them in the stories she told us, from the story of Diane the Hunter to the story of Gypsy Rose Lee. We could tell that Juliet wasn't pining but really frustrated when she snapped, "Wherefore art thou Romeo?" (But how did my mother, who wouldn't have, by the age of fifteen, gotten far enough in school to know Shakespeare from Rod McKuen, put that over to an eleven-year-old person using a jar of Noxzema as the balcony?)

Maybe my mother could have been the writer I'm probably never going to be.

Not only did she have a flair for the dramatic in life and art, she never settled for anything but the best—in our selves (to our despair), but also in what we read (to our exaltation).

Now, it occurs to me that my mother probably was bored by reading to kids and would have considered reading contemporary kid things a waste of her time. So she read us things that moved her and excited her. Perhaps, indeed, she was reading them for the first time when she read them to us.

To a greater or lesser degree, with some success, I've done the same thing with my children.

They don't dare bring me bedtime books based on Scooby-Doo or Transformers or even *A Christmas Carol* in any form but the original Dickens. For this, they all sort of hate me. But most of them could recite any number of Emily Dickinson poems by second grade because they heard them so often. At the end of the day, that's probably a better gift to them than all the soccer games and school plays and Saturday nights at home I've put in. They all know a good word or a good tale when they hear it.

When my mother died, my father asked me if I wanted to choose a line for the stone on her grave. I did want to, and I did it. I chose "She walks in beauty, like the night..." And I know my mother would have gotten it, and would have approved.

~Jacquelyn Mitchard

92

Hand-Me-Downs

What the daughter does, the mother did.
~Jewish Proverb

My mom had four daughters. There must've been something in the water, because my aunt had four girls, too. Our ages were stair-stepped. Her youngest was just a bit older than I was. When spring greens emerged or autumn gilded summer leaves, I awaited the arrival of a brown cardboard box—hand-me-downs passed from the hands of one mom to the hands of another.

The doorbell rang, and I jumped up from my coloring book like a jack-in-the-box. My ten-year-old legs were gangly but strong. I rushed to the door, pulled it open, and gulped down a blast of cold air.

"You're here! Come in," I said.

My aunt stepped through the doorway and shook her boots on the old braid rug. She smiled above the hefty box that was anchored in her arms.

"We're in the back," called Mom from around the corner. "The girls have been waiting." Then I heard her pick up the rhythm of the song she'd been singing without missing a beat.

I followed my aunt to the kitchen. She pushed Mom's fruit bowl aside and plunked the box on the table. My sisters and I clustered our chairs and sat on our hands to keep from ripping the cardboard open. Anticipation giddied our tummies and widened our eyes.

I admired the box's bulging sides. Then I glanced at my mom. She nodded and started to hum.

Our hands flew over the smooth, tucked flaps. We pulled the contents free. There were shoes and skirts and jeans and shirts. I tugged a nubby wool sweater over my head and smiled.

I was filled with happiness. I thought I'd experienced hand-me-downs to the fullest.

Years passed and I grew up to have just the opposite of my mom—plus one. I had five boys. Hand-me-downs remained a natural way of life, and I was glad Mom had taught me their value.

"Let's go to the attic and see what we can find," I said one day. Summer had delivered a blast of warmth, and the boys were excited to use our backyard pool. We trudged the skinny attic stairs together. I hummed as we climbed.

The afternoon dissolved into Rubbermaid totes while we rummaged for last year's swim trunks. We peeked under the lids of the heavy plastic containers. We tugged the deep blue boxes across the dusty attic floor. At last we found the tote that was filled to the brim with swim trunks.

I thought we'd found the treasure as we bolted for the pool.

The water was crisp, cool and refreshing after the attic's swelter. We bobbed and splashed and tossed beach balls. It was natural for me to sing as we played—a simple, silly song that my boys caught easily. We belted the words *a cappella*, though our tune was broken by bouts of laughter.

Any deficit of talent was covered by an abundance of joy.

"Mom, you sound just like Nana," called my son, Grant. "Singing all the time." Then he dolphin-dove past me.

At the time, I didn't think too much about what he'd said. I just carried my babes into the next verse.

But later that evening, when the house was quiet, Grant's words came drifting back. The boys had worn out early, and my husband and I were nestled side-by-side on the couch. As I considered what Grant had said, my mind wandered from the living room and into my childhood.

My mom must've been born with a song in her heart. She sang endlessly. Her voice drifted through our home, over her flower beds, and traveled with us when we all piled in the car. She sang while she rocked us at night, when we blazed with fever, while she toasted bread, packed Dad's lunch, braided hair and pushed the swing. Mom's song was natural to our home. Her voice faithfully covered our family with joy and love.

I sat for a while and thought about Mom. I was thrilled that my boys recognized her in my song. I delighted to know that something so simple had touched their lives and their hearts.

Mom's song had become mine.

As I sat in the growing darkness, I understood that the best treasures are not held in boxes or bins. They do not grow threadbare with time. And they aren't passed from the hands of one mother to the hands of another.

They're passed from heart to heart.

They are the timeless treasures of love and joy, held in the rhythm of my mother's song.

"A hand-me-down," I whispered. "The best kind. Thank you, Mom."

I closed my eyes and smiled.

Then I hummed into the quiet of the night.

~Shawnelle Eliasen

93

A Poem in Her Pocket

Poetry is a packsack of invisible keepsakes.
~Carl Sandburg

My mother always had a poem in her pocket. Instead of memorizing lines to the most recent Michael Jackson song, my mother and I would recite the harmonious words of Poe's "Annabel Lee," Frost's "Stopping By Woods on a Snowy Evening" or of some unknown poet whom we had just heard at a local college. Poetry was not reserved only for the classroom or the poetry reading. Her poetry tapped me on the shoulder at unexpected times—when we were sitting in a tub full of bubbles or riding in the car on the way to school. She collected words. Not just in her memory, but on her bookshelf as well. Living close to New York, we would often pop into that bustling city to catch a poetry reading and top off the adventure with a frozen hot chocolate at Serendipity. Before leaving the reading, we would ask the author to sign her collection. My mother's bookshelf slowly filled up with a magnificent and eclectic assortment of texts that included Gwendolyn Brooks, Sharon Olds, Mark Doty and a number of other poets who were not as famous, but were equally talented. I never realized how important those texts were to me until I lost them.

During my senior year at Princeton, my mother passed away from ovarian cancer, but the tangible memories of our sojourns into the world of poetry stayed on our shelves. A few years later, I helped my father clean out their house. The books on the shelves had grown dusty and so had my memories of those poetry trips. We held a garage sale to rid the house of clutter, and along with it, I lost this fortune. I watched a woman at the sale pick up every book from my mother's side of the bookshelf and open up to the first page. She then decided to either keep it or put it back. I knew exactly what she was doing. She was searching for buried treasure. Those signatures, those memories, were like little gold nuggets found while shifting through a dirty stream. And I watched her. Just watched her. After a while she came up to the desk where I had sorted my quarters and nickels and she plunked down her change to carry off those precious moments with my mother. I did not say a word. For some reason, I was too shy or embarrassed to tell her that the signed books were not for sale.

For many years, I did not look back at the shelf to see which books she had taken with her. I was too angry with myself for letting this stranger walk away with my heritage for pocket change. After a number of nomadic years, I returned to my childhood home to collect all of the things that I had left behind during my travels. I wanted to settle and build a little nest of my own. I clenched my eyes, then opened them and searched through the bookcase to see what remained of my mother's collection—if anything.

To my surprise, many of them were still there. The stranger had not taken them all! I gathered up what was left and brought them to my new home. Regardless of the lost books, the poetry encircling my childhood is still fixed in my head thanks to my mother's love of words. When my little ones get older, I will take them on new poetic adventures to fill up their pockets with poems as my mother did with me many years ago. Our little shelf of literary journeys will grow along with my children and their love for these musical words.

~Michelle Dette Gannon

94

Ode to Old Yeller

No cord nor cable can so forcibly draw, or hold so fast,
as love can do with a twined thread.
~Robert Burton

Sometimes it's the simplest things that give us joy, but it's often these very things that are the hardest to give up. We love them so much because they connect us to each other in special ways, making us grateful for our lives and the people in them. It was just such a special connection that I experienced with my youngest son, Chris, many years ago when he was forced to confront giving up something simple that he loved.

When Chris was small, he toted around a worn yellow blanket that our family took to calling Old Yeller. Made of fuzzy, thermal-weave cotton, the blanket had actually been given to my mom as a baby gift for me, but for some reason Mom hadn't used it and she passed it down to me in prime condition. I didn't remember it, of course, but that situation would soon change. I was grateful for any help Mom could give me in those early years as I struggled with being a new mom myself, but little did I know that an old yellow blanket could thread so meaningfully through three generations. Mom had folded it up neatly in its original gift box, and though the box had crinkled with age, the blanket itself looked soft and new.

That was before Chris claimed it, however. Before he dragged it across beaches and through mud puddles, before he knotted it around tree branches and wore it as his hero's cape, before he (yikes!)

dropped it in the toilet or commissioned it to make his tricycle tires spit-and-polish clean. Yes, Old Yeller became something of a legend in our house, Chris's ever-pliable companion. He and that blanket were all but inseparable.

Even the separation during laundering seemed too much for him. "But Mommy," he would protest in his most forlorn voice when I'd take the blanket to wash. "What if something happens to Old Yeller while he's gone? What if you lose him and I never get him back?"

"He needs a bath, Critter," I would say, using the apt nickname I'd given my boy. "Nothing's going to happen to Old Yeller, I promise."

But over time, something did happen to Old Yeller.

Old Yeller got really, really old. His color started to fade, from smile-at-me yellow to my-throat-is-parched white. His threads started to unravel, leaving gaping, ragged strands. The blanket unraveled so much that I began to worry about my son sleeping with it at night. What if one of those strands got caught around Chris's neck and choked him? I knew the time had come to think about letting Old Yeller go—and I knew that this feat wouldn't be easy.

"But Mommy," said Chris, a soft sheen of tears coming into his big brown eyes at the mere hint of the suggestion. "Just because something's old doesn't mean you have to throw it away."

I swallowed back my own tears. I had to admit that I couldn't bear to throw Old Yeller away either.

So, together, we decided to retire Old Yeller and replace him with something new. We came up with a plan and went shopping.

The plan went without a hitch... initially. At the store, Chris picked out a new yellow blanket, as downy as a fresh-ripened peach. We called the blanket New Yeller, and packed Old Yeller away in a shiny plastic bag at the top of my son's closet, where the poor old thing could finally get some rest. Chris appeared happy with New Yeller, his new faithful friend, and I felt relieved.

Problem solved. Until the next morning when I went to awaken Chris for school. He was a big second-grader that year, and though I knew there would come a time when we'd have to address letting go of New Yeller too, at least we were one step closer. We had just moved to a new city, a new home, my children were going to new schools and Chris was having a bit of trouble adjusting. I hadn't wanted to take away yet another familiar thing, and I believed New Yeller was our short-term answer. But there was my Critter, fast asleep, Old Yeller curled up by his side, New Yeller tossed in a heap on the floor.

I sat down on the edge of his bed. "Honey," I said when he awoke. "How did Old Yeller get here? I thought we had a deal."

Again, his eyes brimmed. "I can't do it, Mommy. I can't let Old Yeller go."

He described how, in the middle of the night, he had dragged a chair into his room, climbed to the top of his closet and retrieved his ever-pliable companion. The thought of that climb worried me, too, so I knew our plan needed some refinement.

We decided, in the end, that maybe the two yellers could live in Chris's room side by side—with one tiny caveat. He would have to promise to keep Old Yeller folded up at the foot of his bed, while he slept with New Yeller in his arms. When I went to awaken him the next day, he and his yellers were just where they should be, as promised. I bent down to kiss his forehead, just as he wrapped an arm around my neck. "Thanks, Mommy," he whispered.

"You're welcome, sweetie," was all I could manage as, again, my eyes blurred with tears.

Sometimes outcomes can seem like failures when they're really successes in disguise. So it was for Chris and those blankets—both of which we still have, by the way. Often, in my office while I write, I rub my cheek against New Yeller, which is draped across my desk chair, and I'm transported back to those innocent, long-ago days. Chris keeps Old Yeller with him, in that now stiff-with-age plastic bag, and my daughter-in-law, Nicole, tells me that he's quite protective of his old childhood friend.

As I look back now, I know that Old Yeller served us well. For he taught us that there are some things so comfortably worn, so important in our lives, that they can never truly be set aside or forgotten. They are the threads that bind us, that clean our skinned knees when we fall, that love us in all our faded and torn glory.

Thanks, Mom, I find myself thinking, for giving me that old yellow blanket in the first place, that I might give it to my son. Thanks, Son, for the privilege of being your mom, and the memory of your sweet little voice that reaches out to me still when I awaken in the dead of night, frightened by how swiftly life is passing: "Just because something's old, Mommy, doesn't mean you have to throw it away."

Could we have asked for anything more from a ragged yellow blanket?

~Theresa Sanders

But Wait, There's More

Motherhood has a very humanizing effect.
Everything gets reduced to essentials.
~Meryl Streep

When my mother phoned with the news that my sister Cathy had delivered her second child, a boy we'd come to call Tommy, she said, "Sheila, I don't know how she does it!"

At the time, I didn't think to remind Mom that she'd given birth herself. If you're doing the math, you're thinking "Right! At least twice."

The truth is stranger still. My mother had ten labors. Yes. Even back in the Sixties when many Catholics followed the Church's ban on birth control, I remember friends' parents reacting to the news I had so many siblings. They'd gasp, "But your mother doesn't look like she's had ten children!"

And she didn't. She was, and is, a beauty. Tall, slender, Grace Kelly features, and a sense of fashion that was both classic and cosmopolitan, she presented an aura of calm tolerance, both to the world at large, and more importantly, at home with us.

How did she do it? Ten pregnancies in twenty years. Morning sickness night and day, month after month. I figure Mom spent nine years of her life seasick, simultaneously having to contain the crew, swab the decks *and* steer the ship.

Moreover, my father was an Air Force fighter pilot, which meant she never stopped worrying. Even after the war, when no one was trying to shoot him down, crashes were common. Friends of theirs died, including a member of Dad's acrobatic flying team at an air show our family was watching.

Like all military families, we got transferred every other year. They say the stress of moving is second only to losing a spouse. For Mom, I imagine the two were strangely linked. Would the ringing phone bring the worst news of all, or, if she was lucky, would it be my father telling her it was time to start packing? Again.

Narrating her story is like one of those late night infomercials. *But wait! There's more!*

For starters, there's the time before I was born, when my mom was diagnosed with tuberculosis. In those days, the disease was a death sentence, and highly contagious. One minute my mother was at the doctor with her newborn, the next she was whisked away to a hospital room, under a quarantine that lasted a full year. Picture this: *Anchorage, Alaska, 1949, Christmas morning.* Dad stands outside the hospital with my four eldest siblings, aged six weeks to six years. They're bundled in snowsuits, all waving up at Mommy, who's trying to smile convincingly from an impossible distance.

Decades later, when my younger brother Tom, then twenty-eight, was diagnosed with stage four cancer, it would be this story we repeated. Mom had a terminal illness, but because of a new experimental drug, she *survived.* Not only that, three years later, she'd start what we call the "second half" of the family, six more children, including Tom. There was hope. Miracles happened.

This was a story we all clung to, even when the doctors suspended Tom's treatment. It was March of 1992, the same month, coincidentally, that my sister Cathy needed surgery during the aforementioned pregnancy, to remove a cyst that hadn't "resolved."

You get used to this medical terminology, to words like "resolved" and "encapsulated," when they're used by doctors who are trying to help you understand the unimaginable.

That surgery saved my sister's life. Her right ovary was removed, its germinal carcinoma contained by a sturdy wall of normal cells.

Two months later, she'd deliver her healthy son, Tommy, into the arms of my dying brother, who would live two months and two days past that miraculous event.

Miraculous Event. His words, not mine. Tom wasn't prone to sentimental language. If he described the birth that way, who was I—who'd never witnessed the process—to disagree?

Our family doctor gave my brother's eulogy. He said that though he'd never believed in an afterlife, he found it impossible to accept that someone of such magnificent energy wouldn't carry on, in some form. The laws of nature wouldn't allow it.

You had to know Tom to understand: he was funny, dangerously handsome and so vital, even in his final days, it *was* impossible to believe he could disappear without a trace.

Until that time of sadness, I'd always claimed I didn't have a "spiritual bone in my body." Strangely, at the worst moment in my life, when Tom stopped breathing, I saw something—or felt it—that changed me forever. Some presence visited me during that moment that I can only describe as overwhelming goodness. I wonder if it's the same sensation people describe when they see a child come into the world.

Scientists might say that after going through so much pain, my brain was rescued by endorphins. Maybe that's how my parents have managed to live on after losing their son. Maybe that's how my mother continues to call with such exuberance, as she did today when my niece got into the college of her choice.

Or maybe it's as simple as this. Having lived through the worst, Mom understands that life is not connected to her remote control. She might as well enjoy it when she can, for the clouds will come back, and so will rain.

As of this writing, six of her children have been diagnosed with cancer. All of us but Tom have survived. We all expect to live a long and happy life, buoyed by the example of my parents, who have shown such valiance and grace, even into their nineties.

My mom is a pretty hard act to follow. Still, why not throw up my hands and give it a try? Why not go out and exult, as my sister Dede did the evening Tom died?

"Hey, you've got to come outside and see this rainbow!"

I know. Hallmark is going to sue, and the literary gods are wailing, "She *didn't*." But even if the truth doesn't comport with Tommy's irreverent streak, I can't say it didn't happen, even if it is the stuff of My Little Pony and the Keebler elves.

Dede took my parents by the hand. The rest of us followed. There in the distance, over the mountains, was the most astonishing Technicolor rainbow this side of those postcards depicting God wearing a nightgown.

Later that night, when my friend from Chicago called, I told her about the rainbow. "That's really weird," she murmured. "I saw one too, about seven o'clock."

But wait. There's more.

My brother John saw one in Florida on his way to the airport, as did two Atlanta relatives, and a friend in Maine, all at roughly the same time on the same day.

Is such a thing even possible? Were these people just trying to make us feel better? Or maybe rainbows are like that, stretching farther than you thought.

And that infomercial hook? *"But wait! There's more!"* Maybe it is a con. Maybe, though, as my mother must know better than I, every package you get will come with a little surprise. Some will be pleasant, others will knock you flat, but the odd thing is, the story's never really over, even when you're quite certain you've come to the end.

~Sheila Curran

96

A Simple, Lasting Legacy

The worth of a book is to be measured by what you can carry away from it.
~James Bryce

ometimes, I think my mother and I are still connected by way of a highlighter pen. As her way of reminding me to embrace the written word, the highlighter was one of the things she left me when she died. All these years later, I feel like she is with me whenever I read and highlight something that surges into my heart and mind.

She was a timid highlighter—a dot at the beginning of an idea and a dot at the end of the phrase. I highlight boldly!

My mother loved to read, and she taught me to look for words that demanded my attention and words that required careful thought. My earliest recollection of written words came from a large collection of the *Oz* books written by L. Frank Baum. I must have been a toddler when my mother began reading chapters to my sister and me every day. Through those early books, she gently led us into a world of imagination and wonder. While my mother's joy of reading and her curiosity about the world led her in many literary directions, it also helped to instill in her children the need and necessity of following our interests and appreciating the variety of books available to us.

She read wherever she could and whenever she could. I do too. I read for the friendship. I read for the mental conversation. I read for that invisible, intangible connection to a kindred spirit. Along the way, I have found that the reading becomes a safe place where both new and familiar thoughts can circle my mind and keep me company. I read because I love to, but I highlight because I have to.

Recently, when I was going through a box of my mother's papers, I found a cartoon she cut out of the newspaper years ago. It shows a man and woman sitting in bed reading books. The man says, "You've been staring at that book every night for a year and a half!" She replies, "If I read the next page it will be the end of the best book I've ever read, and I just can't bear to say goodbye." The cartoon makes me smile. I've read books like that. It is one of the reasons I highlight. I finish the book, but my highlighting helps the characters shine through and gives me easy access to the words I love.

If I could highlight an entire character, sometimes I think I would. There have been some so memorable that every now and then the circumstances in my life call them to mind. I have lived with them through confrontation, shared their joy and heartache, and, hopefully, learned a thing or two along the way.

Like my mother, my passion to highlight along with my inability to "deface" a book that does not belong to me, however, make me a stranger to the public library, a preferred customer at bookstores, and a recognizable face at rummage sales. Some of my highlighted books eventually find their way to second-hand bookstores. Their phrases have found their place, the track from mind to heart complete. They are now part of me, and although years later I may not be able to quote them verbatim, I know their message. So, I will not apologize to the person who ultimately receives my used books. At issue is not that the book has been defaced, but that it has been appreciated.

Perhaps it is the simple things that shape us. The original *Oz* books from my childhood remain on my bookshelves today, and although the highlighter pen my mother gave me was used up long ago, I will always be thankful that the simple legacy of her joy of reading and her reverence for the written word remains.

~Pamela Underhill Altendorf

97

Retaining Memories

Son, you outgrew my lap, but never my heart.
~Author Unknown

"Yes, Mom, I am in Utah with Robin and Steve, our friends from Philly. We're visiting Alex, who's working at a mountain and will be starting graduate school in New York in the fall. We'll be home Wednesday morning."

With that, I get off the phone and shake my head. This is at least the 500th time in the past six months that I have had the same conversation with my mom about her granddaughter. My mom is ninety years old and her short-term memory is long gone.

It is hard watching a parent grow old. If we are lucky, we have a fixed image in our minds of our parents in the prime of their lives. My dad passed away almost thirty years ago. I try to remember all the things that made my dad who he was to me. Every once in a while, this offensive image of how he looked the last time I saw him, ravaged by the effects of his cancer, creeps into my mind. I try to disgorge this image from my brain and replace it with the images of him that I treasure.

I grew up in a *Leave it to Beaver* household. My mom adored my father, and made my sister and I feel like we walked on water. My dad was the man who graduated first in his class from NYU Law at twenty-one years of age, was an all-American fencer, a successful attorney, and an utterly devoted father and husband. My sister, from the time she was little until this day, attempted to protect me and make sure my life was filled only with good thoughts.

I want to make my mom whole again. I want her to wake up this morning with clarity of mind and purpose. I want her to be able to pick up the phone and discuss new matters of import and interest. I want her to be able to drive her car again, like she loved to do. I want her to be able to live independent and strong. I want the mom I remember and still see in my dreams.

But reality does not deal in sentiment. It can be a cruel and unforgiving foe. It does not let us rewind, or cherry pick the moments we retain. It takes us where it wants to take us. If we don't like it, that is of no concern.

My calls with my sister now always begin with, "I just spoke to Mom and she is okay, but..." I never wanted to have a conversation like this with her again. Acceptance of what is, rather than what should be, is not an easy task.

My son has a wonderful capacity for being able to look past the images he sees and hears of his grandmother and interact with her in a gentle, effective manner. While he sometimes has to deal with five or more calls in an hour on the same topic, he never seems to lose his patience. We learn much about others and ourselves in times like this.

I know my mom struggles to cope with what is happening to her. She wants to say she is fine, and always asks what she can do for us. But she comprehends that her difficulties are our difficulties. She knows she can no longer remain thirty-nine, as she tried to do for almost fifty years. She knows that her role as matriarch of the family has been replaced by a new and unintended position. She can recall the glory days, but she has a hard time remembering what she ate for lunch.

I start every morning by picking up the phone to tell her we are all doing well, and asking her how she is feeling. I know she will try to do the best she can to be positive so that I can begin my day without having to call my sister and start the cycle of concern again. I know she wants us to retain the images of her as vibrant and independent, and carry those around with us each and every day.

It is now almost 9 AM in New Jersey. I am sitting in Utah, at the computer, knowing that when I finish my thoughts, I must pick up the phone. I hope it will be a good day for her. I hope she will be my mother again. I hope that there will one day be a cure for dementia so that the next person sitting at the computer does not have to remember the good times past, but can live in the moment. I hope today is the day that the present comes back into focus for my mom. I hope.

~Robert S. Nussbaum

98

China

*People who don't cherish their elderly
have forgotten whence they came and whither they go.*
~Ramsey Clark

The rain grew heavier, and I listened to the hypnotic sweep of the cab's windshield wipers as my mom and I traveled to her parents' gravesite in Tai Shan. Pockets of pine trees emerged against a mountainous backdrop, and wild brush and grass thickened the terrain. Ahead of us, a man wearing a straw hat pedaled a bicycle at the side of the road. His pant legs were turned up to the knees and his work clothes drenched.

We picked up our guide at a gray brick house in an open field near a section of fishponds. The man, sporting a clear rain slicker, pointed ahead and spoke Chinese to my mother in short, clipped sentences as if talking posed a hardship. For one of the few times in my life, I regretted that I couldn't understand my own language.

After we endured a stretch of pothole-ravaged roads, the guide directed our driver to stop on a narrow shoulder and headed out. My mother reached for her umbrella and opened the cab to pelting rain. I slid across the seat and readied my umbrella to follow.

The driver popped the trunk, and my mom and I retrieved the supply bags. The guide waded through knee-high grass to a tight trail, and my mother and I tracked him up the steep and muddy path through rocks and jagged brush.

We trudged forward, the wind and rain whipping against us. In time, we came to a four-foot-wide ravine of rushing water. The man spoke to my mother then walked into a river that completely covered his work boots and soaked his pants to the knees.

My mom marched across, seemingly oblivious to the current spilling over her tennis shoes and pants. I trekked behind her, my lower legs fully immersed. At the other side, I could feel the squishing of cold, wet socks inside my sneakers and the bottoms of my jeans clinging to my skin. Another twenty minutes and we came to a clearing overlooking a valley of pine trees.

Then I saw it — a small cement slab on the sloping bank of the bluff ahead. We made our way to a headstone in the earth inundated with grass and weeds.

My mom dropped her bag, hurried to the foot of the headstone and began pulling at the plant growth with her bare hands. I set my bag and umbrella down to help. We cleared the entire area around the gravesite as if our very lives hinged upon it. My mother was soaked, her hair sopping moisture onto her face.

She wiped the sleeve of her blouse against her forehead and went to get her bag. She carried it to the headstone and removed a container of roast duck. The guide brought the remaining bags while I gathered my umbrella to shield my mom from the rain. She opened a pastry box, put it on an empty sack and rotated it toward the headstone as if positioning a dinner setting for an honored guest. She placed apples, mangoes and plums on another bag.

After arranging the food, she took out the incense sticks and planted them in the ground by the headstone. She dug out a box of matches and struck one against the side of the box. It didn't light, so I bent lower to shield her from the gusting rain. Three attempts were needed to produce a flame, and she held her free hand around it the way a child might cup a butterfly.

Carefully, my mom brought the match to the incense sticks, and the sweet smell of jasmine weaved into the air on thin smoke trails.

Rain swept over us. Drops ran down her neck as she knelt at the headstone, put her hands together, and bowed three times in respect.

She closed her eyes and spoke Chinese in a quiet, solemn voice as if conveying something from the depths of her soul. She continued for a time, and I watched, transfixed.

My mom repeated the bows before opening her eyes. They were red and moist, and I knew the drops trailing down her cheeks were tears. Then she turned and walked slowly toward the edge of the clearing.

I went to where my mom had been, knelt, and propped the umbrella to protect the incense and food. I closed my eyes and bowed three times. As I began to pray, images appeared: My mom as a peach-faced, pony-tailed little girl playing in front of a spacious brick house; her mother, wearing the traditional black tunic top and pants, the long, loose sleeves rolled up to the elbow as she scrubbed clothes by hand in a basin; her father, slender like me, and with silvering hair, working the fields with a hoe, raking and tilling the soil. I could see them clearly.

I started to speak in a soft voice, "My name is Raymond, and I'm your grandson. I'm sorry it's taken me this long to come see you.

"I live in America, and it's important that you know I have a college education. My mom worked hard to give me that chance.

"Sometimes, I don't realize how lucky I am for the opportunities I've been given. I take things for granted—my schooling, my job, my family.

"But on this trip, I've seen the way people live, how hard they work. It's helped me to appreciate my life in America, and that's something I'll never take for granted again."

I paused, drew a deep breath. "There's something else I want you to know. It's about my mom. She brought me here today to be with you. It was important to her.

"She's had a hard life; I didn't know how hard until this trip. That was my fault. For so many years, I didn't want to be Chinese. I didn't want to be different, so I never asked about you. I never wanted to know.

"I'm sorry. It was wrong, and I ask your forgiveness.

"Your daughter has cared for a deeply wounded man, a man who couldn't love her. But she stayed with him and tried to help him. She raised two sons, often by herself. Michael and I are very different. He's practical and business-minded like she is. Someday, he's going to run his own marketing firm, and he'll be successful. He learned from my mom.

"Me, I'm stubborn. Mom would call it hardheaded, and she'd be right. But if there's one thing I know, it's that I'm going to make a difference in this world. Maybe with my work. Or my writing. Or by being the kind of person I am.

"My mom raised me to be a man of integrity and honesty—a person who cares about others. She taught me courage by the way she's lived her life.

"I want you to know these things about your daughter, and I hope that you're as proud of her as I am."

I knew my grandparents had heard me, and they were smiling. I bowed three times and opened my eyes. Then I stood, turned, and joined my mom.

~Ray M. Wong

99

Things My Mother Taught Me

If you want children to keep their feet on the ground,
put some responsibility on their shoulders.
~Abigail Van Buren

At thirty-three years old, I can cook a full-course meal, clean an entire house, do laundry, pay bills, and conduct business professionally—and I am not afraid to speak my mind. While this may not seem unusual for an adult, I was doing all of this by the time I was ten years old.

When I was seven, my mother and I were leaving a friend's house. My mother lost her balance and fell down a flight of stairs. I was so scared for her and cried all the way to the hospital. That night, I fell asleep alone in my mother's bed awaiting her return. She arrived early the next morning with a broken arm that was wrapped in a cast held in a blue sling. After the fall, I noticed she was not quite herself. She also seemed to have an endless number of doctors' appointments. I knew something was wrong but did not know what.

My mother was forty-seven years old when she was diagnosed with muscular sclerosis (MS). That diagnosis changed our lives forever. I am the youngest of seven children, and as the "baby girl," my responsibilities were far and few between. As my mother faced her mortality, she began to reflect on her children's lives and wondered if we would be prepared for the world once she was gone.

With this new diagnosis, my mother became driven to prepare me for the world and make sure that I had all the tools I would need to thrive. She wanted me to be independent. My family knew very little about her life expectancy, or how her body would respond to the disease. As the youngest, I had always spent the most time with my mom. I soon became her "helper." I went with her to the bank, doctors' appointments and grocery store. I helped her do the laundry and various other chores and errands. My life lessons had begun.

One summer day when I was eight, my mom asked me to gather up all her bank statements, bills, checkbook and the phone. While we sat on her bed, she dialed a number and handed me the receiver. She told me, "I need you to find out how much money is in my account."

I was terrified, realizing I was about to be on the phone with a real live adult who was not a relative. As the phone rang, I looked at her and said, "I'm only eight. I don't think I should be doing this."

She just looked at me and said, "I will tell you what to say."

I got all the necessary information, and after that we continued to make numerous phone calls. We called the gas company, the light company and a few more places. She guided me through each conversation. By the time I was ten years old, I was well known at the bank and could balance a checkbook without help. I was eventually able to monitor and manage my own savings account. Each month we paid the bills together, and when she could no longer write, I filled out all the checks, addressed the envelopes, purchased stamps and mailed off the rent along with all the other bills.

My mom was an amazing cook and to this day nobody (not even I) makes better cornbread stuffing. Thanksgiving was always a huge feast at our house. With a large family, my mom always wanted to make sure that she had enough food for everyone to eat and enough leftovers to seemingly last us a lifetime. Two days before Thanksgiving, my mom bought all the groceries that she would need to make dinner. The night before, she stuffed the turkey and put it in the oven to cook. The next morning, I found her very upset and crying because she was not feeling well. She did not think she was going to be able to finish Thanksgiving dinner. For the best cook in town and the mother of seven children, this was more than she could bear. I told her I would cook; all she had to do was tell me what to do. I started cooking at seven in the morning and cooked all day. She sat at the kitchen table instructing me at every step. That was the first time that I cooked a full-course meal for my entire family including my brothers' wives, friends and our regular strays. It was the first of many cooking lessons.

By the time I was fourteen, I was cooking dinner on a regular basis. I was able to cook for our family during the holidays, and I could do a lot of it without instruction. However, there were still dishes that I had not mastered. Consequently, my mom had to taste-test everything before it made it to the table. I loved being able to cook, and I enjoyed the time with my mom.

As her MS progressed, she became bedridden. One day she just got in the bed and never got out. I continued the work of helping my mother to manage our lives. When I was seventeen, we lived in a "bad" area. I remember thinking to myself, "We're moving!" I walked into my mother's room and said, "I don't want to live here anymore." The next day, I started making phone calls and looking for a new place to live. In the process, I met the woman who would become our new landlord. She told me that she could not believe that I was only seventeen and insisted on meeting my mother. She was so impressed with the way my mother had raised me that she gave us the house, and we moved two weeks later. I made the necessary calls to get the utilities turned on, have our address changed on our checks, and have the mail forwarded. During the move, there was not one skill that my mother taught me that I did not utilize.

My mother was the single greatest influence in my life. Through every challenge she faced, she led our family with grace and awe-inspiring strength. She made sure that we would be self-sufficient and capable. Ten years after her passing, I still miss her very much. Nonetheless, when she died, I never felt scared or wondered about my future. And the year my mother died, my family and I celebrated her birthday with all her best dishes. I was able to make each one for my family in remembrance of her.

With the blessing of hindsight, I realize how scared my mother must have been, having a young daughter and not knowing how long she would have to teach her all she would need to know. Even though I had different responsibilities than many of my friends, I understood why. My mother did her very best to make sure that I would have the tools I needed to be a responsible, independent and capable adult. And for that, I am grateful.

~Kris Hale

The Note

I remember my mother's prayers and they have always followed me.
They have clung to me all my life.
~Abraham Lincoln

The small note is always with me. I carried it in my billfold through the Vietnam era, a terrorist episode in Italy, Desert Storm, Sarajevo, and the Balkan Conflict—every day of my thirty-six years in the military. It remains there still, folded in the same pattern as when I first placed it in my wallet many years ago.

I found the note on the desk in my room the night before I left to enter the military. My mother wrote the note on the reverse side of a sheet of accounting paper left over from the course I had disliked so much. I suspect she scribbled it quickly to make sure it was there when I returned home from one final night out with high school friends.

My mother was a wonderful writer, but possibly because she was hurried or distraught, the note is not particularly elegant or well written. It is, however, just right. At least for me, there was something about it—the obvious caring, the pride, the assured feeling that remained after reading it that, although I would be away from home, part of home would always be with me—that touched my soul from the first time I saw it.

The note reads:

I'm such a "cry baby," but I want you to know even though we will miss you so much, we're proud of you (no mother was ever prouder and more in love with their kids than I am of you all). I want you to be happy and I know you will like the Air Force and do a good job no matter where you are. No matter where you are the same God watches over you and cares for you.

It is always the going away that is the worst.

You will make friends though and with your work—that always helps.

We love you.

Mom

The note was twenty-five years old when my daughters left for college. I made copies of it and sent it to them. I hope it evoked the same feelings in them that it did in me.

Over the years, I have taped the note together several times where age and wear have otherwise separated it along the folded creases. I take it out and re-read it on April 28th of each year, a small memento of things worth remembering. On the most recent "anniversary," I taped it together again and placed it back in my billfold, where it will always remain.

~Tom Phillips

Why I Play

I'm a great believer in luck, and I find the harder I work the more I have of it.
~Thomas Jefferson

In the mid-Seventies, in the rather conservative and religious city of Bogotá, Colombia, my mother decided to go against the social rules of her time and become a single mother. At that time, this was a substantial undertaking—personally and financially.

My grandparents were musicians. My grandfather owned a concert band and played the trombone, and my grandmother played the guitar. The family was centered around music. My mother grew up with that love for music, but at the same time she had observed the dark side of the musical entourage through my uncles and the difficult life they had been living in New York. When I was born, my mother hoped to have a child with a different profession, someone with a "real" career.

My childhood was beautiful—a dream. My grandparents' and my mother's love amply filled the void of my father's absence. We breathed music; we danced and we sang every single day. Unfortunately, I lost both of my grandparents to cancer, and when I was seven, my mother and I were left all alone. Financially difficult times followed; we would eat beans and rice, or lentils and rice, or chickpeas and rice, from paycheck to paycheck. My mother worked very hard and sometimes weeks would go by where we wouldn't see each other because of her work schedule and my school. Still, the strength I saw in her, and our circumstances, compelled me to be responsible.

As adolescence hit, so did the search for my identity. I longed for my childhood, my grandparents, the music they used to listen to (New York Salsa and Latin Jazz). I started to dig up the records at home, to listen to—over and over—and fall in love with the music of Tito Puente, Eddie Palmieri, Miles Davis, but mostly, Ray Barreto and his congas. On one occasion, I told Mom that I was fascinated with music, but because of her familiarity with that environment, she always avoided the issue, or said I was too old to become a musician. She suggested it would be better for me to be a sound engineer, or an artist manager, or anything other than a musician.

My passion for music continued to grow, to the point it became evident to Mom's friends that I wanted to be a musician and follow in my uncles' footsteps in New York. One evening, the issue came up in conversation, so Mom asked, "Samuel, do you really want to be a musician? Do you know how difficult it is?"

I replied, "Is what you do easy?"

From that moment on, she supported me with all she had. The following term, she signed me up for the youth musical program at Javeriana University in Bogotá. "If you're going to be a musician, you're going to be a good musician, and you'll have to study a lot!"

At the onset of my musical education, I experienced tough days. Every morning, I woke up at six and went to school. After school, I went to my music classes at the university and got home around eight to finish my schoolwork. I also went out two or three nights a week to play at nightclubs or to see other musicians, which meant I would not get to bed before 2 AM. It was difficult, but I could not complain; my mother had taught me that the only way to make it was through hard work and persistence.

My passion was the congas, so every weekend when I was fifteen, my mother and I would go out to dance to salsa or Cuban music. When bars were closing, music connoisseurs would gather to discuss the latest in Cuban music, jazz or classical music. My mother and I would stay and participate, and it was during those gatherings that I was able to come in contact with much of the music that influenced my professional development.

We were well known by bar owners and DJs. We were regular clients, though not very profitable ones, as we only drank water. They took care of me (I was still a teenager), and guarded me, especially from alcohol and drugs—constants in the music environment. The day came when my mother could no longer come out with me, so I had to be wary of those around me and to figure out whom to trust and whom not to. I had seen firsthand how drugs had destroyed entire lives. It was no wonder my mother did not want me to be a musician.

I am now a musician, and my musical career continues to evolve. Through it all, my mother has been there to support me. Now some time has passed, and I see how much I owe to the example my mother set for me, and her willingness to go forth and overcome strong personal challenges. She showed me that life is a constant struggle filled with rewarding moments.

At times, when I feel frightened or insecure, I think of everything my mother has achieved and I feel inspired to carry on. Thank you, Mom, for you have taught me to establish goals and to reach them, you have taught me to question the rules of society and not follow them blindly.

Thank you, Mom, for all the love you have given me. I am grateful because being your son is the greatest gift that life could have given me.

~Samuel Torres (translated by Becky Ortiz)

Thanks Mom

Meet Our Contributors
Meet Our Authors
About Joan Lunden
Thank You!
About Chicken Soup
Bonus Story

Meet Our Contributors

Pamela Underhill Altendorf lives in Wisconsin with her husband. She studied writing at the University of Wisconsin-Stevens Point. Her stories have appeared in *Christian Science Monitor*, *The Chicago Tribune*, *Chicken Soup for the Father's Soul*, and several other magazines and newspapers. Pam is also a volunteer tutor in English as a Second Language, and enjoys traveling.

Desiree Diana Amadeo is the proud daughter of Diana Marie Amadeo and Leonard Ray Amadeo. Desiree is truly appreciative and thankful for her family and for their continuous love and support. Desiree is currently studying Chemical Engineering at the Massachusetts Institute of Technology in preparation for a career in alternative energy.

Michelle Anglin received her Bachelor of Arts, with high honors, from Salem State College, where she is currently pursuing a Master's Degree in Middle School Education. Michelle enjoys writing non-fiction pieces, and plans to write children's books someday.

Joyce A. Anthony is a writer, mother and animal advocate with a strong Psychology background. She is currently working toward a Criminal Justice degree in Forensic Psychology. Her "motto" is

"Writing Rainbows of Hope" Contact Joyce via e-mail at rainbow@ velocity.net.

Ronda Armstrong and her husband enjoy ballroom dancing. They also chase after their two beloved cats and connect with family and friends. Ronda's essays and stories have appeared in *Chicken Soup for the Soul*, *The Des Moines Register*, and a Midwest anthology — *Knee High by the Fourth of July*. E-mail her at ronda.armstrong@gmail.com.

Aditi Ashok is currently a high school student living in the Bay Area. She enjoys writing, photography, lacrosse, and spending time with friends and family.

Elizabeth Atwater is a small town Southerner who has loved writing ever since she was old enough to grasp a pencil in her hand. Life is sweet and contentment abounds on the nine acres she shares with her husband Joe, where they raise race horses.

Christy Barge was born and raised in Papillion, NE. She is currently a sophomore at Nebraska Christian College.

Sandra R. Bishop graduated from Purdue University, and is a Registered Nurse and an Elementary Science teacher. She lives with her wonderful husband of thirty-one years and enjoys writing and photography. Sandy's role as Mom and Nana has been her true vocation, an honor inspired by her mother, Marian.

Julie Bradford Brand received her BS from Susquehanna University and went on to attend NYU toward her MBA. She worked in Human Resources before deciding to stay home with her three children. Julie enjoys running and spending time with her family. Her mom continues to be a source of inspiration to her.

John P. Buentello is a writer who has published fiction, nonfiction, and poetry. He is the co-author of the novel *Reproduction Rights* and the story anthology *Binary Tales*. He is currently at work on a collection of nonfiction and a new novel. He can be reached at jakkhakk@yahoo.com.

Steve Chapman received his B.A. in 1996 and his Master's in 2006. He teaches English at Crowder College in Neosho, Missouri and is the author of *The Miller's Wife*. Steve currently lives in Monett, Missouri with his wife Sabina. Contact him at schapman711@hotmail.com.

Harriet Cooper is a freelance writer, editor and language instructor. She specializes in writing creative nonfiction, humor and articles, and often writes about health, exercise, diet, cats, family and the environment. A frequent contributor to *Chicken Soup for the Soul*, her work has also appeared in newspapers, magazines, newsletters, anthologies, websites and radio.

Maryanne Curran is a freelance writer based in Lexington, Mass. This is her first contribution to *Chicken Soup for the Soul*. Maryanne enjoys traveling and reading. Please e-mail her at maryannecurran@verizon.net.

Sheila Curran is the author of *Everyone She Loved*, about a woman's efforts to protect her own family even after her own expiration date has come and gone. Her first book, *Diana Lively is Falling Down*, a romantic comedy Jodi Picoult called warm, funny, inventive and original and *Booklist* called a gem. Visit www.sheilacurran.com for more information.

Jim Dow lives in the Northeast with his wife and two children. He enjoys reading, watching sports, and spending time with his family. He is pursuing a college degree in night school.

Aviva Drescher lives in New York City with her husband Reid and three children. She attended The Fieldston School, Vassar College where she received her BA, New York University to receive her MA in

French and Cardozo Law School. She spends her free time counseling amputees.

Megan Dupree received her Bachelor of Arts from Texas State University-San Marcos where she currently works in the Housing Department. Megan enjoys reading, traveling, writing and spending time with her family which includes her husband Geoff and daughter Lilah. Megan can be e-mailed at mgdupree@msn.com.

Shawnelle Eliasen and her husband Lonny raise their five boys in an old Victorian on the Mississippi River. She home teaches her youngest sons. Her work has been published in a number of magazines. She writes about life, family, friendship, and God's grace.

Stacia Erckenbrack, born and raised in California, graduated with an Associates Degree in Liberal Arts from San Diego Mesa College. She has always enjoyed writing, hiking and water sports. Her favorite activity is spending time with her loving family. Stacia can be contacted at myboyz2000@yahoo.com or (707)655-3303.

Joanne Faries, originally from the Philadelphia area, lives in Texas with her husband Ray. Published in *Doorknobs & Bodypaint*, she has stories and poems in *Shine Magazine* and *Freckles to Wrinkles*. Joanne is the film critic for the *Little Paper of San Saba*. Check out her blog: http://wordsplash-joannefaries.blogspot.com.

Norma Favor currently lives in British Columbia with her daughter and family. She comes from a long line of story tellers. Norma loves to put those stories on paper. She has had a number of stories printed in *Chicken Soup for the Soul* books and some have been used by Adams Media.

Aaron Felder is the Executive Director of the Brooklyn Queens Conservatory of Music, a community music school in New York City. He lives in Windsor Terrace, Brooklyn with his wife Michelle and their daughter Lucy. He can be reached via e-mail at aaron_felder@ hotmail.com.

Ellen Fink lives in Woodstock, Georgia. She is married and has three children. When she's not writing, she spends her time gardening, walking her dog, reading mysteries and doing volunteer work.

Christina Flaaen currently resides with her parents, sister, six cats, and two dogs. She enjoys reading, traveling, and collecting Lucille Ball memorabilia. Christina is presently pursuing a Bachelor of Science in Accounting at Arizona State University. Following graduation, she hopes to study Entertainment Law and someday become a television executive.

Carol Fleischman has been a regular contributor to the *Buffalo News*. Her articles cover a wide range of everyday events, from yard sales to wedding showers. Carol's recurring theme is life as a blind person, especially the joys and challenges of working with guide dogs.

Carolyn Mott Ford enjoys spending time with her family at the Jersey Shore and writing poetry, essays and children's stories. Her work has appeared in a number of publications including several *Chicken Soup for the Soul* books and her picture book, *Ten Hats, A Counting Book*, has just been published.

Betsy Franz is a freelance writer and photographer specializing in nature, wildlife, the environment and human relationships. Her articles and photos reflecting the exquisite wonders of life have been published in numerous books and magazines. She lives in Florida with her husband Tom. Visit Betsy on the web at: www. naturesdetails.net.

Originally from Upstate New York, **Rachel Furey** is a current PhD student at Texas Tech. She is a previous winner of Sycamore Review's Wabash Prize for fiction. Her work has also appeared in *Women's*

Basketball Magazine, *Chicken Soup for the Soul: Twins and More*, *Freight Stories*, *Squid Quarterly*, and *Waccamaw*.

Michelle Gannon graduated from Princeton with a degree in art and archeology. After building up her frequent flier miles as a consultant, she returned to her true passion, the arts. Following graduation with a master's from Columbia, Michelle began teaching Humanities, literature and film. Michelle just finished teaching at Temple University in Japan to move back to the US.

Diane Gardner received her Bachelor of Arts in Journalism and Master of Arts in Mass Communications from California State University, Fresno. She and her husband live in beautiful Colorado, where she works from home as a freelance editor. She enjoys oil painting, reading, attending the theater, and working with children.

Jessica Gauthier received her B.S. in art education from Millersville University of PA in 2002. She works as an art educator at the Allentown Art Museum in Pennsylvania. Jessica is the mother of one daughter, Camden Isabelle and is currently working on a series of children's books.

Jenny R. George lives on a five acre hobby farm north of Coeur d'Alene, Idaho with her husband and two children. She grew up in Alabama but calls the Northwest home, relocating soon after graduating from Arizona State University. Jenny's parents moved nearby to watch the grandkids grow up.

Jennifer Gilkison received her Bachelor of Arts in English and American Literature from the University of South Florida in 1995. She resides and works in Lutz, FL. Jennifer enjoys horseback riding, women's ministries and writing about the simple pleasures in life. Please e-mail her at brad933@aol.com.

H.M. Gruendler-Schierloh has a BA in journalism and advanced credits in linguistics. Working as a language instructor and translator, she also has been writing for years. Some of her shorter pieces have been published. She is currently seeking a publisher for two novels while working on a third one.

Stephanie Haefner is a wife, mother and novelist of Women's Fiction and Contemporary Romance. Her first book, *A Bitch Named Karma*, will soon be available from Lyrical Press. Visit her blog at www.thewriterscocoon.blogspot.com or her website at www.stephaniehaefnerthewriter.com.

Kris Hale is currently working on her degree in English. She plans on becoming an English teacher at her former high school and following in the foot steps of her favorite teacher Shiela Dunn. She has worked with children for more than twenty years. She enjoys reading, movies, traveling, and spending time with friends. Please e-mail her at mskris253@aol.com.

Gemma Halliday is the author of several romance and mystery novels, including the *High Heels* romantic mystery series, and the *Hollywood Headlines* series. She currently makes her home in the San Francisco Bay Area, but you can visit her cyber home at: www.gemmahalliday.com.

Kathy Harris graduated with a B.S. in Communications from Southern Illinois University and works full-time in the entertainment industry. She recently completed the second book in her Christian fiction trilogy, the *A New Song Series*. Visit her website at www.kateshiloh.com.

Christopher Hartman received his Bachelor of English Education, with honors, from Minot State University in 2008. He teaches at Athol Murray College of Notre Dame in Wilcox, Saskatchewan. Chris enjoys coaching hockey, tennis, and traveling.

Rebecca Hill is aware that the relationship between mothers and daughters can be complex. Recently, she's longed for situations as simple as the one described in "You'll Always Be 'Mom'." Through good times and bad, Rebecca is grateful for the love her mom, dad and brother have shown her. E-mail her at bohoembassy@verizon.net.

Dr. Doug Hirschhorn has a PhD in Psychology with a Specialization in Sport Psychology. He is the author of *8 Ways to Great* (Penguin/G.P Putnam's Son). His clients include elite athletes as well as many of the largest financial institutions in the world. You can reach him at www.DrDoug.com.

Teresa Hoy lives in rural Missouri with her husband and a large family of rescued cats and dogs. Her work has appeared in the *Chicken Soup for the Soul* series, *The Ultimate* series, and other anthologies. In addition to writing, she creates art from recycled paper. Visit her at www.teresahoy.com.

Elizabeth M. Hunt is a stay-at-home mother of two. In her free time she enjoys reading, writing, arts & crafts, and spending quality time with her family.

Janelle In't Veldt, of Ontario, Canada, wrote this story at the age of sixteen, and owes this success to everyone who cheered her on. In her spare time, Janelle loves to edit videos and perform in musical theatre. She would like to thank her mom for being such an amazing role model.

Jennie Ivey lives in Tennessee. She is a librarian, a newspaper columnist, and the author of three books. She has published numerous fiction and non-fiction pieces, including stories in several *Chicken Soup for the Soul* books.

Hope Justice graduated from the Ohio State University with a Bachelor of Science in Education. She is currently teaching 5th grade in Northern California. Hope enjoys spending time with family, friends, and the many animals on her mini ranch that she shares with her long time partner, Robyn.

Kiran Kaur has been writing stories since grade four. Her hobbies include reading, writing stories and screenplays, travel, and her dog. She has always found escape in good books.

Mimi Greenwood Knight is a freelance writer living in South Louisiana with her husband, David, four kids and way too many dogs. She has over four hundred articles and essays in magazine, anthologies and on websites. Mimi enjoys butterfly gardening, baking artisan breads, Bible study and the lost art of letter writing. http://blog.nola.com/faith/mimi_greenwood_knight/.

Karen Kullgren is a freelance writer/editor with a particular interest in exploring women's lives, spiritual journeys, diverse cultures, and the universality of human experience. For twelve years she's been Contributing Editor for *Washington Parent* and *Washington Woman*, where her "Grace in the Gray Areas" column appears monthly. Learn more at www.graceinthegrayareas.com or via e-mail at graceinthegrayareas@gmail.com.

Terri Lacher is a freelance author and columnist, and mother of a blended family of six, grandmother of fourteen. Her love of storytelling was encouraged by her family, providing her an endless supply of humor and wit. She lives in Texas with her husband and Lab. Contact her via e-mail at btlacher@sbcglobal.net.

Tom LaPointe is a loving husband and stay-at-home dad for a special-needs adopted son. A compelling motivational speaker and trainer, he runs an automotive marketing company from their Florida home. He's a longtime freelance magazine writer and author of *Modern Sports Cars*. Contact him at www.tomlapointe.com, tom.lapointe@yahoo.com or 727-638-0195.

Mary Laufer is the fifth child of Betty Jane Smithley Penfold, an extraordinary mother who inspired her daughters to write stories and poems. Laufer's work appears in several anthologies, including *Chicken Soup for the Girl's Soul* and *A Cup of Comfort for Military Families*. She lives in Forest Grove, Oregon.

Corrina Lawson, a mother of four, is currently a core contributor to the Geek Dad blog on Wired.com and also writes romantic fiction. Her first book, *Dinah of Seneca*, an alternate history romance, is due out in 2010. You can find her at http://corrinalaw.livejournal.com.

Kiashaye Leonard, age 12, is on the Student Council for Figure Skating in Harlem and a New York State representative for the Congressional Youth Leadership Council. She is a High Expectations Scholar at the Harlem Educational Activities Fund, and enjoys writing, crocheting, collecting unique Barbie dolls, ballroom dancing and singing.

Linda Burks Lohman retired from the State of California and has been published in *Reader's Digest*, *Solidarity*, and *The Sacramento Bee*. She contributed to the *Red Hat Society Travel Guide* and spends time "playing" with Red Hat friends. She enjoys beading, writing and four grandchildren. E-mail her at laborelations@yahoo.com.

Gary Luerding is a retired army NCO and resides in southern Oregon with Lynne, his wife of forty-six years. They have three children, eight grandchildren, and one great granddaughter.

Jeannie Mai is the host of Style Networks' popular makeover show *How Do I Look?* and a correspondent for *Extra*. Influenced by her mother to always stand out in a crowd, Jeannie enjoys transforming lives one makeover at a time by helping people feel beautiful from the outside in.

Kathy Marotta lives in Atlanta, GA with her husband Mike and son

Zachary. She received a BS in Interior Design, with honors, from Florida International University's College of Engineering and Design. She enjoys writing, blogging, photography and cooking. She is currently marketing her first devotional book. Please e-mail her at kzmarotta@ aol.com, or visit www.blessedbybosnia.blogspot.com.

Barbara Mayer is a Benedictine sister of Mount St. Scholastica, a monastery in Atchison, KS. She received her Master's degree in English from the University of Kansas. Barbara is a freelance writer in Kansas City, KS, who has had poetry published in several literary and religious magazines. She enjoys traveling, reading, cooking and helping students with writing.

Kate E. Meadows is completing a personal essay collection recounting her experience as an only child growing up in rural Wyoming. She is pursuing an M.F.A. degree in Professional and Creative Writing from Western Connecticut State University. She lives in Omaha, NE, with her husband and baby boy. E-mail her at scribbler_kate@ yahoo.com.

Brad Meltzer is the #1 *New York Times* bestselling author of *The Book of Fate* as well as six other thrillers. His first non-fiction book, *Heroes For My Son*, was just published, and his newest thriller, *The Inner Circle*, will be released in January 2010. But to see what's far more important, please go to: www.BradMeltzer.com. P.S. He still loves Marshall's.

Judy M. Miller lives in the Midwest with her husband and four children. She holds degrees in anthropology and forensic science. When not writing she enjoys time with friends and family, traveling and hitting the tennis ball around the court. Please e-mail her at Judy@ JudyMMiller.com.

Jacquelyn Mitchard is the *New York Times* bestselling author of eighteen books for adults, teens and children—including the first selection of the Oprah Winfrey Book Club, *The Deep End of the Ocean*. Mitchard lives with her husband and nine children. Visit Jacquelyn on the web at www.jackiemitchard.com.

Tasha Mitchell resides in Northwest Georgia with her husband Heath and son Parker. She is a full time student pursuing a nursing degree. She enjoys traveling, writing, and spending time with her family. Please e-mail her at tashakmitchell@yahoo.com.

Kym Gordon Moore, author of *Diversities of Gifts: Same Spirit*, is an award winning poet, syndicated freelance writer and transformational speaker. She is co-founder of the mission, "Favorite Things for a CAUSE" and is completing work on her next book scheduled to be released in 2010.Visit her at www.kymgmoore.com.

Robert S. Nussbaum lives in New Jersey in the same town as his mother, who is now ninety-two. They spend several days every week reminiscing of past good times. Robert's writing also appears in *Chicken Soup for the Soul: The Golf Book*, and he frequently posts essays to his blog, www.tooearlytocall.com.

Ann O'Farrell is an MA graduate of Trinity College, Dublin. She is the author of two Irish historical novels, *Norah's Children*, the sequel, *Michael*, and several short pieces published in newspapers, magazines and anthologies. Ann is presently working on the third novel in her Irish family saga. Learn more at www.annofarrell.net.

Rebecca Olker received her Bachelor of Arts from UC Riverside and her master's degree in Taxation from Golden Gate University. She is an accountant in the heart of Silicon Valley. When she is not writing, she enjoys reading, knitting and spending time with loved ones. Contact her via e-mail at Rebecca_Olker@comcast.net.

Penny Orloff was a working LA actor when a Juilliard scholarship took her to NY. Currently an arts journalist and holistic life counselor, the former NY City Opera principal soprano and Broadway featured actress lampoons her showbiz misadventures in her novel, *Jewish Thighs on Broadway*. E-mail her at malibran@aol.com.

Emily Osburne is the author of *Everyday Experts on Marriage*, and she leads marriage workshops for newlyweds in the Greater Atlanta Area. She and her husband Clay have been married for nine years and are the proud parents of a lazy Golden Retriever. Learn more through her website at www.emilyosburne.com or e-mail her at emily@emilyosburne.com.

Saralee Perel is an award-winning nationally syndicated columnist and novelist. She is honored to be a multiple contributor to *Chicken Soup for the Soul*. Saralee welcomes e-mails at sperel@saraleeperel. com or via her website: www.saraleeperel.com.

Tom Phillips served thirty-six years in the Armed Forces. He led a unit through a terrorist incident, served as Director of the Air Force Personnel Readiness Center during Operation Desert Storm, and commanded troops in Bosnia. He plays softball at every opportunity and is the author of the books *A Pilgrim in Unholy Places* and *Battlefields of Nebraska*.

Janine Pickett is a freelance writer living in Anderson, Indiana. She is currently working on the biography of George R. Durgan, a popular mayor of Lafayette, Indiana. Janine loves spending time outdoors with her family. Please e-mail her at jpatterson@wildblue.net.

Mark Damon Puckett received his M.F.A. in Creative Writing from University of Houston, as well as his M.A. in English and M.Litt. in African-American Studies from the Bread Loaf School of English at Middlebury College. He admires and loves his intelligent mother. Visit him at www.markdamonpuckett.com.

Jennifer Quasha is a freelance editor and writer. Check out her website at www.jenniferquasha.com.

Over five hundred of **Stephen D. Rogers'** essays, stories, and poems have appeared in over two hundred publications. His website, www.stephendrogers.com, lists these and other timely information.

Stephen Rusiniak is a husband and father of two. Stephen is a former police detective who specialized and lectured on juvenile and family matters, he now shares his thoughts through his writings and has appeared in various publications, including the anthology *Chicken Soup for the Father and Son Soul*. Contact him via e-mail at stephenrusiniak@yahoo.com.

Theresa Sanders considers it an honor to be a frequent *Chicken Soup for the Soul* contributor. An award-winning technical writer and consultant, she lives with her husband in suburban St. Louis and is blessed with four beloved children, two beautiful daughters-in-law, and one sweet soon-to-be son-in-law.

Shannon Scott is a mother of two children: ages three and five. She is blessed with a large, loving extended family that has always supported her dreams. She works in Atlanta, Georgia as an administrative assistant and spends her free time writing and being with her family.

Michael Jordan Segal, who defied all odds after being shot in the head, is a husband, father, social worker, freelance author (including a CD/Download of twelve stories entitled *POSSIBLE*), and inspirational speaker. He's had many stories published in *Chicken Soup for the Soul* books. To contact Mike or to order his CD, please visit www.InspirationByMike.com.

A recovering public relations executive, **Al Serradell** currently resides in Oklahoma City, OK, and works as a Compliance Officer for Federal grants. Although born in Los Angeles, CA, Al has completed the Sooner transformation and considers himself an "Okie."

Keith Smith, retired park ranger, received his Bachelor of Science in Recreation and Leisure Services from the University of Maine at Maine in Presque Isle in 1982. He's currently Manager of Minocqua Winter Park & Nordic Center in Wisconsin. Keith enjoys bicycling, hiking, skiing, and good coffee. E-mail him at keithsmithbsp64@ hotmail.com.

Sandy Smith received her degree in Childhood Education and is currently teaching private school. She LOVES being a wife and mother and believes that writing is one of the most important forms of expressing the emotions of the soul. She plans to continue mentoring young writers who also dream of discovering the joys of writing short stories.

Kathy Smith Solarino feels blessed to be able to share her thoughts, feelings and ideas through words. She lives in NJ and works for a non-profit arts in education organization. Kathy wrote feature stories and articles for local publications. She hopes to devote more time to her writing in the future.

Joyce Stark lives in Northeast Scotland and since retiring from local government splits her time between touring in the USA and writing for journals in the UK and US. She has also written a children's series under review for TV rights.

Wayne Summers has a Diploma of Teaching (Primary), Certificate in English Language Teaching to Adults (CELTA) and a Diploma of Counseling. He works as a teacher and counselor in Perth, Western Australia. He enjoys writing horror stories and has been published many times in both the US and the UK. He also enjoys movies and the beach.

Annmarie B. Tait lives in Conshohocken, PA with her husband Joe and Sammy the "Wonder Yorkie". Annmarie has contributed to the *Chicken Soup for the Soul* series, *Reminisce Magazine* and *Patchwork Path*. When not writing, Annmarie enjoys cooking along with singing and recording American and Irish folk songs. E-mail address: irishbloom@aol.com.

Rebecca Lasley Thomas dreams of living by the ocean, but currently resides in Albuquerque with her husband and special needs daughter. Rebecca and her husband share six daughters and seven delightful grandchildren. She loves writing, reading, gardening, traveling and Bible studies. This is her first published work. Please e-mail her at nodexn@yahoo.com.

Born in Bogotá, Colombia, **Samuel Torres** traveled to the United States in 1998, where he was played with Arturo Sandoval, Richard Bona, Tito Puente, Lila Downs, Boston Pops, LA Phillarmonic, amongst others. Samuel won the Second Place at the 2000 Thelonious Monk International Jazz Competition for Hand Percussion. His second CD "YAOUNDE" is coming out in 2010. More info at: www.samueltorres. com & www.myspace.com/samueltorresgroup.

Kara Townsend received her Bachelor of Arts at Texas A&M — Corpus Christi in 2006. She is currently an actor in New York City. She enjoys reading, writing, and walking through the city.

Terrilynne Walker holds a Masters Degree in Education Leadership and is currently an educator in Southwest Florida. All of her adult life, Ms. Walker has been an active volunteer in a political party, holding office and running political campaign headquarters. Her family and country are her most vital interests.

Jane Dunn Wiatrek, a retired educator, and husband Ben, live in Poth, Texas. Her sons are Grayson, Jared and Cory and she has one daughter-in-law, Cory Rene. Jane is active in her community and church. She enjoys reading, writing and working on her small farm. E-mail her at janedw3@yahoo.com.

Brandy Widner is a freelance medical content writer. She received her degree in nursing in 2002 but after the birth of her son, she decided to follow in her mother's footsteps and stay at home and devote herself completely to him. For questions or inquiries about this wonderful story please contact her via e-mail at kbwidner@windstream.net.

Gail Wilkinson lives in Illinois where she works as a human resource director for a software company. Gail loves traveling and writing, and is interested in stories that preserve and honor family histories. Her middle grade novel about her grandparents' lives, *Alice and Frosty: An American Journey* was recently published by Iowan Books. E-mail her at wilkinson.gail@yahoo.com.

Ferida Wolff is author of seventeen children's books and three essay books. Her work appears in anthologies, newspapers and magazines. She is a columnist for www.seniorwomen.com and recently started a nature blog http://feridasbackyard.blogspot.com. Her latest book is *Missed Perceptions: Challenge Your Thoughts Change Your Thinking*. Visit her at www.feridawolff.com.

Ray M. Wong is a devoted husband and father. He's also a freelance writer and contributes the column "Family Matters" to newspapers in the United States. He has completed a memoir called *Chinese-American: A Mother and Son's Journey Home*. Visit his website at www.raywong.info or e-mail him at Ray@raywong.info.

Dallas Woodburn is the author of two collections of short stories, a forthcoming novel, and eighty articles in publications including *Family Circle*, GradtoGreat.com, *The Los Angeles Times*, and seven *Chicken Soup for the Soul* books. Learn more about her nonprofit literacy foundation and youth publishing company at her website, www.writeonbooks.org.

Lucas Youmans is a grade 9 student in Calgary, Alberta and enjoys all forms of art and entertainment media. Lucas enjoys writing poetry and short stories, drawing, digital photography and basket-ball. He regularly publishes his work on Facebook. Please e-mail him at youmans12@hotmail.com.

Meet Our Authors

Jack Canfield is the co-creator of the *Chicken Soup for the Soul* series, which *Time* magazine has called "the publishing phenomenon of the decade." Jack is also the co-author of many other bestselling books.

Jack is the CEO of the Canfield Training Group in Santa Barbara, California, and founder of the Foundation for Self-Esteem in Culver City, California. He has conducted intensive personal and professional development seminars on the principles of success for more than a million people in twenty-three countries, has spoken to hundreds of thousands of people at more than 1,000 corporations, universities, professional conferences and conventions, and has been seen by millions more on national television shows.

Jack has received many awards and honors, including three honorary doctorates and a Guinness World Records Certificate for having seven books from the *Chicken Soup for the Soul* series appearing on the New York Times bestseller list on May 24, 1998.

You can reach Jack at www.jackcanfield.com.

Mark Victor Hansen is the co-founder of Chicken Soup for the Soul, along with Jack Canfield. He is a sought-after keynote speaker, bestselling author, and marketing maven. Mark's powerful messages of possibility, opportunity, and action have created powerful change in thousands of organizations and millions of individuals worldwide.

Mark is a prolific writer with many bestselling books in addition to the *Chicken Soup for the Soul* series. Mark has had a profound influence in the field of human potential through his library of audios, videos, and articles in the areas of big thinking, sales achievement, wealth building, publishing success, and personal and professional development. He is also the founder of the MEGA Seminar Series.

Mark has received numerous awards that honor his entrepreneurial spirit, philanthropic heart, and business acumen. He is a lifetime member of the Horatio Alger Association of Distinguished Americans.

You can reach Mark at www.markvictorhansen.com.

Wendy Walker began writing and editing several years ago while staying home to raise her children, and is now the author of two novels, *Four Wives* and *Social Lives*, both published by St. Martin's Press. She recently edited *Chicken Soup for the Soul: Power Moms* (2008) and *Chicken Soup for the Soul: Thanks Dad* (2009).

Before becoming a mother, Wendy worked as an attorney in private practice both in New York and Connecticut, and served as a *pro bono* lawyer at the ACLU. While attending law school at Georgetown University, she spent a summer in the Special Prosecutions Division of the U.S. Attorney's Office for the Eastern District of New York.

Wendy obtained her undergraduate degree from Brown University with a double major in economics and political science. Her junior year was spent at the London School of Economics. Upon graduating, she worked as a financial analyst in the Mergers and Acquisitions department of Goldman, Sachs & Co. in New York.

As a young girl, Wendy trained for competitive figure skating at facilities in Colorado and New York. She now serves on the board of Figure Skating in Harlem, an organization committed to the development of underprivileged girls, which she has supported since 1997.

Wendy lives in suburban Connecticut and is busy raising her three sons and writing her third novel.

About Joan Lunden

Joan Lunden is one of the most visible moms in America. As co-host of *Good Morning America* for almost two decades, a best-selling author, an international speaker, and a mother of seven, Joan has been a vocal woman's and parenting advocate throughout her career. Joan created an online community with her website **JoanLunden.com** where she provides information to help make women's lives and the lives of their families easier, happier, and healthier. From healthcare to skincare, safety to style, **JoanLunden.com** has quickly become a go-to site for women across the country.

Featured on JoanLunden.com:

Joan created her home décor line, **Joan Lunden Home** to help today's modern multitasking woman find easy solutions to keep her home beautiful and stylish. With a passion for home decorating and having travelled the world experiencing locales from African villages to Royal palaces, Joan shares her love of design while making achieving style in any home easy. Joan Lunden Home represents comfort, luxury, and style at affordable prices.

Joan created **Camp Reveille** as a haven where women of all ages can take a break from their busy lives to take care of themselves, relax, renew their sense of play, and be re-energized. These getaways are designed for the modern woman and offer a myriad of options such as traditional camp activities, health and fitness classes, and most importantly much-needed time with other women like themselves.

Joan admirably balances her career with motherhood and does so relaying a consistent message that other women can do the same. She speaks all over the country and authors books about how to maintain balance, how to remain healthy, and how to take time to be the best wife, friend, career woman, and of course her priority—mother—that you can be.

Thank You!

Once again, I have been astounded by the emotional depth and honesty embedded within the stories from our contributors. Not every story could be used, but every story added to the richness with which we were able to explore the relationship between mother and child in this book. I offer my deepest gratitude to the thousands of people who submitted their personal, heartfelt stories. By sharing your experiences and insights, you help create the special bond that exists among the vast Chicken Soup for the Soul readership.

Chicken Soup for the Soul: Thanks Mom was truly a collaborative effort! Editor Barbara LoMonaco read thousands of submissions and did the impossible job of selecting among them. Assistant Publisher D'ette Corona worked with all the contributors to make sure that everyone's story was edited properly. Publisher Amy Newmark guided the manuscript with a sharp eye, trained opinion, and exceptional diligence that kept us all on schedule. Editor Kristiana Glavin perfected every line with meticulous editing. And a big thanks to Brian Taylor at Pneuma Books for the gorgeous cover design and layout.

Under the leadership of CEO Bill Rouhana and President Bob Jacobs, Chicken Soup for the Soul continues to connect millions of people every year through the most human, relevant topics. It is truly a privilege to be a part of this team.

~Wendy Walker

Chicken Soup for the Soul

Improving Your Life Every Day

Real people sharing real stories—for fifteen years. Now, Chicken Soup for the Soul has gone beyond the bookstore to become a world leader in life improvement. Through books, movies, DVDs, online resources and other partnerships, we bring hope, courage, inspiration and love to hundreds of millions of people around the world. Chicken Soup for the Soul's writers and readers belong to a one-of-a-kind global community, sharing advice, support, guidance, comfort, and knowledge.

Chicken Soup for the Soul stories have been translated into more than forty languages and can be found in more than one hundred countries. Every day, millions of people experience a Chicken Soup for the Soul story in a book, magazine, newspaper or online. As we share our life experiences through these stories, we offer hope, comfort and inspiration to one another. The stories travel from person to person, and from country to country, helping to improve lives everywhere.

Chicken Soup for the Soul.

Share with Us

We all have had Chicken Soup for the Soul moments in our lives. If you would like to share your story or poem with millions of people around the world, go to chickensoup.com and click on "Submit Your Story." You may be able to help another reader, and become a published author at the same time. Some of our past contributors have launched writing and speaking careers from the publication of their stories in our books!

Our submission volume has been increasing steadily—the quality and quantity of your submissions has been fabulous. We only accept story submissions via our website. They are no longer accepted via mail or fax.

To contact us regarding other matters, please send us an e-mail through webmaster@chickensoupforthesoul.com, or fax or write us at:

Chicken Soup for the Soul
P.O. Box 700
Cos Cob, CT 06807-0700
Fax: 203-861-7194

One more note from your friends at Chicken Soup for the Soul: Occasionally, we receive an unsolicited book manuscript from one of our readers, and we would like to respectfully inform you that we do not accept unsolicited manuscripts and we must discard the ones that appear.

Chicken Soup for the Soul.

Presents its new line of
Quality Movies
for the Whole Family!

Chicken Soup for the Soul®

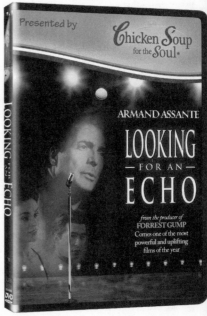

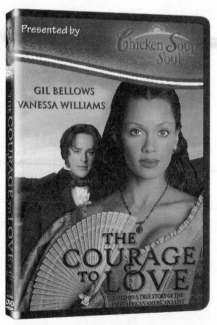

A bonus story for our readers from *Chicken Soup for the Soul: Power Moms,* a great read for all you multi-tasking moms who juggle a million things every day. Whether you work inside the home or outside, you are all Power Moms.

How I Became an Author in the Back of My Minivan

I can't tell my children to reach for the sun. All I can do is reach for it myself.
~Joyce Maynard

One day not too long ago, I was at my son's preschool to help out with a class party. As I waited with the other moms for the party to start, one of them looked at me strangely and then pulled something from my hair. It was a Goldfish cracker. She asked me how I managed to get a Goldfish stuck in my hair and I drew a long breath. Then I told her. I'm a mom. I am also an author. I do most of my writing from the back seat of my minivan, and on this particular morning while I was waiting for party duty, I got a little tired and had a nap. In the car. On the back seat. Where the Goldfish live. This all sounded absurd, of course, and I suppose it is. But it came about through a series of events that are entirely sane.

The story begins over a decade ago when I became a mom in the suburbs of Connecticut. In spite of my four years at an Ivy League school, two years working on Wall Street, and three years of law school, I jumped at the chance to "opt out" of my career as a lawyer and raise my kids. For me, it was a simple decision. I could use whatever talents I had helping corporate clients, or I could use them to nurture my own offspring. There were millions of lawyers, but only one mother for my son. It didn't occur to me that by leaving the life I had worked years to create I was also leaving a piece of myself behind.

As it turned out, I had joined masses of former-professional-women-turned-moms whose talents were now being directed at their children. My job was my child; my child was my life. My schedule became a maze of baby groups, mommy-and-me classes, nap schedules and brain stimulation exercises. There were baby birthday parties, massage classes, post-partum Pilates, and, of course, a vast array of discussion groups. At every turn, my small accomplishments were replaced by new worries. Why isn't my baby sleeping through the night? Why isn't he crawling yet? Is his baby food really organic? Should I make it myself? Yes! Suddenly I had a freezer full of kale and broccoli ice cubes. The piece of me I had abandoned became fully embedded in this new job of mothering, and the drive for perfection began to overshadow the small moments of joy that all of this was for.

By the time my baby was a year old, I was deeply unsettled. I had become a case study from Betty Friedan's epic work *The Feminine Mystique*, and I knew that it had to stop; I needed an outlet that transcended fabric samples and lunch dates. I had never thought of being a writer. But this was the dream I discovered when I reached inside myself for something to save me from the trap of perfecting motherhood. For the next two years, I wrote a little bit here and there, stopping and starting with morning sickness and again when my second child was born. I wrote during every babysitter hour that I had, during naptime and the other stolen minutes in a mother's life. And as I became more committed to this dream, I also became a more efficient time scavenger. When my three-year-old started nursery school, I decided to skip the long drive home and instead work somewhere in town.

On the first day of this new plan, I swallowed my guilt, left my baby with the sitter, dropped my older son at school and went to Starbucks—suburban mommy Mecca and home to my favorite dark roast. I got a coffee and a table in the back, then pulled out my laptop and some notes. Taking a sip of the coffee, I instructed my brain to focus. *Focus.* An alternative rock band I had never heard of was playing in the background. *Focus.* A woman I'd met at a playgroup came over to chat. *Focus.* The two *baristas* were discussing their body piercings. This was NOT working and time was slipping away, precious time I was paying for with mother guilt and cold hard cash. I packed up my things in frustration and went to my car. But instead of getting in the driver's seat, I slid open the side door and ducked into the back. I moved the boosters, sat down and started to type. It was brilliant! No one could see in through the tinted glass. It was quiet. And there was nothing to do after I swept the Goldfish crumbs to the floor—nothing to do but write.

This became my new office. I stocked it with blankets when the weather turned cold. I bought an extra battery for my laptop and a coffee reheating device. I wrote and wrote, telling no one for fear that the slightest discouragement would break my resolve. When I was overcome with morning sickness again, I stopped writing. When it passed, I dusted off my laptop. Then came the third baby and another interruption. But the need persisted, and so I started again. Through these years, I began to make small concessions to buy myself more time. I gave up the gym and ran with the kids in a jogger. I turned down any social invitation where I couldn't bring them along. Every minute of school or sitter time was devoted to writing in the back of my minivan outside the nursery school, YMCA, or back at the Starbucks. My life had taken on a frenetic pace. But I was happy.

I finished my first novel, *Four Wives*, when my youngest son was nearly two. It is a story about women, about the choices we make and the lives we forge as we muddle through the inherently conflicted worlds of work, marriage, and motherhood. I wrote it because these were the issues that had been living inside me and so many women I had come to know. And, ironically, writing about this conflict gave me my own personal resolution.

Four Wives was published in the spring of 2008, marking the beginning of a new career that actually fits in with my life as a stay-home mom. My days have become jigsaw puzzles—baking muffins at 6:00 A.M., driving the boys here and there, cleaning up toys, making dinner, and writing in between. I am settling into a reality that was once a crazy dream, born of inner conflict and executed in the back of my car.

Just this year, I have set up shop at a desk in my home. All of my boys are in school now, giving me time to work in the mornings. It is an odd luxury to no longer worry about battery power, warmth, or finding a bathroom. But there are times when I get stuck, when the house is calling out to me or my thoughts are frozen, and I find myself parked outside that Starbucks, nestled in among the Goldfish. Sometimes the best part of a dream is the journey that makes it come true.

~Wendy Walker

Chicken Soup for the Soul

for the Soul

Power MOMS

101 Stories Celebrating the Power of Choice for Stay-at-Home and Work-from-Home Moms

With stories by:
Jane Green
Melora Hardin
Liz Lange
Jodi Picoult
Lynne Spears

Jack Canfield,
Mark Victor Hansen
& Wendy Walker

with a foreword by *The New York Times*' Lisa Belkin

This book is for all those moms who juggle and multi-task and do it all well, with 101 great stories from mothers who raise their kids, care for their husbands, run their households, and do a million other things. Well-known mothers such as Jodi Picoult, Lynne Spears, Liz Lange, and Melora Hardin share their stories, as do grateful husbands and children. Perfect for mothers book groups, it contains a reader guide.

978-1-935096-31-3

More great stories

Chicken Soup for the Soul®

Like Mother, Like Daughter

Our 101 BEST STORIES

Stories about the Special Bond between Mothers and Daughters

Jack Canfield & Mark Victor Hansen

edited by Amy Newmark

How often have you seen a teenage girl pretend to be perturbed, but secretly smile, when she is told that she acts or looks just like her mother? Fathers, brothers, and friends shake their head in wonder as girls "turn into their mothers." This book contains the 101 best stories from Chicken Soup for the Soul's library on the mother-daughter bond. Mothers and daughters will laugh, cry, and find inspiration in these stories that remind them of their mutual appreciation.

978-1-935096-07-8

for moms and grandmothers!

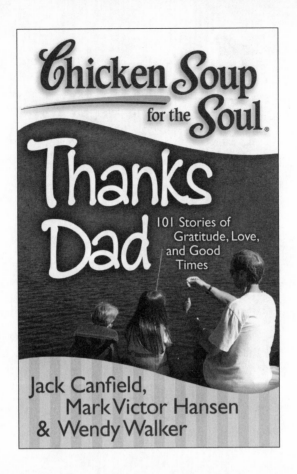

Chicken Soup for the Soul®

Thanks Dad

101 Stories of Gratitude, Love, and Good Times

Jack Canfield,
Mark Victor Hansen
& Wendy Walker

This book gives fathers the pat on the back they deserve. Children of all ages share their heartfelt words of thanks and loving memories in this collection of 101 stories. Personal accounts of learning from Dad's example and lasting lessons, special moments and memorable outings, encouragement and expectations will bring any father joy, inspiration, and laughs. Whether the reader is a new dad, a father of teens, a father of grown children, or a grandfather, these heartwarming and humorous stories will resonate with him. He may even find that his kids did pay attention after all!

978-1-935096-46-7

...And great stories